Women and Sport: From Myth to Reality

CAROLE A. OGLESBY, Ph.D.

*Associate Professor of Sport Psychology,
College of Health, Physical Education
and Recreation, Temple University,
Philadelphia, Pennsylvania*

WITH 12 CONTRIBUTORS

Lea & Febiger · 1978 · Philadelphia

Library of Congress Cataloging in Publication Data

Main entry under title:

Women and sport.

Bibliography.
Includes index.
1. Sports for women—Addresses, essays, lectures. 2. Feminism—Addresses, essays, lectures. 3. Sports—Social aspects—Addresses, essays, lectures. I. Oglesby, Carole A.
GV709.W57 1978   796'.019'4   77–19255
ISBN 0–8121–0618–0.

Published in Great Britain by Henry Kimpton Publishers, London

Print Number: 3 2 1

PRINTED IN THE UNITED STATES OF AMERICA

To Sojourner Truth and all my other black sisters whose consciousness had not entered my own when this book was conceived.

PREFACE

This book is a tale, never told before. Its premise is that a group of women, competent in various fields, can theorize about sport in a unique and insightful way. Its premise is that such a group can effectively describe woman's experiencing of present-day sport and propose alternatives which promise a better sporting future for women and men.

The subject matter of this book concerns women, sport, and society, including various permutations of those elements. Because of the complex and complementary nature of woman/man roles, I suspect the book has a good deal to say about men, sport, and society as well.

The contributors accomplish their goals in three different ways. They review the literature in their area of expertise from feminist viewpoints. Familiar findings are presented in a new light and interpretations are questioned. In many instances, a re-interpretation seems imperative. Some of the contributors present new and original data on women's sport problems, while others offer feminist definitions and descriptions of sport and what it can be.

Sports feminism, then, is what the book is about. From a pre-feminist vantage point, the label sport feminism is a contradiction: Feminism—a philosophy of the equality of women; Sport—a human endeavor wherein males historically have excelled. In this book, the apparent contradiction is treated as an artifact of our society.

We have lived in a world where sport is symbolized and verbalized as a male domain. For example, East Overshoe High School has a basketball team. The local newspaper runs headlines which read, "East Overshoe Varsity Goes Undefeated." No one ever thought it an aberration that "The East Overshoe Varsity" only had male players. No one ever thought it an aberration that *if* any "girls" at East Overshoe played basketball, they were the "girls team," not to be confused with the "East Overshoe Team." Certainly the term *sport feminism* is a contradiction in the world in which we have lived. But that world is changing. Feminism is changing the face of the world around us. Women, through asserting their rights within the sport environment, are strengthening and speeding the impact of feminism in our society.

In the hands of readers, the book may perform several functions. For those interested in changing sport, information is provided which can become helpful tools. Source material may also be utilized by students of sport pursuing research interests. The book may also provide a psychological slap (thanks . . . I needed that) to individuals who have failed to see the changes demanded in sport as we have known it.

Philadelphia, Pennsylvania   CAROLE A. OGLESBY

CONTRIBUTORS

Susan Birrell

Lecturer, Sociology of Sport
School of Physical Education
McMaster University
Hamilton, Ontario, Canada

Patricia Del Rey

Associate Professor
Coordinator of Graduate Studies
Department of Health, Physical Educa-
tion and Recreation
Cleveland State University
Cleveland, Ohio

Mary E. Duquin

Assistant Professor of Health, Physical
and Recreation Education
University of Pittsburgh
Pittsburgh, Pennsylvania

Elizabeth R. East

Instructor, Women's Gymnastics
Coach and Assistant Athletic Director
Cortland State College
Cortland, New York

Irene Hanson Frieze

Assistant Professor of Psychology and
Women's Studies
Department of Psychology
University of Pittsburgh
Pittsburgh, Pennsylvania

Susan L. Greendorfer

Assistant Professor
Department of Physical Education
University of Illinois
Urbana, Illinois

Wilma Scott Heide

Registered Nurse
Visiting Professor
University of Massachusetts
Amherst, Massachusetts

Jackie Hudson

Instructor of Physical Education
Temple University
Philadelphia, Pennsylvania

Maureen C. McHugh

Teaching Fellow in Psychology
Department of Psychology
University of Pittsburgh
Pittsburgh, Pennsylvania

Sharon Mathes

Associate Professor of Physical Educa-
tion
Iowa State University
Ames, Iowa

Carol L. Rose

Attorney
Mitchell, Silberberg & Knupp
Los Angeles, California

Betty Spears

Professor of Sport Studies
University of Massachusetts
Amherst, Massachusetts

CONTENTS

Chapter 1
PROLOGUE: THE MYTH

Betty Spears

In chapter 1, "Prologue: The Myth," Professor Spears performs a remarkable service for the reader and the rest of the contributors. With a combination of broad pen strokes and dramatic understatement, an historical context is supplied for women's participation in sport from the time of the ancient Greeks to the present.

In the chapter, three elements are discernible. The essential thesis is advanced that, over the centuries, social norms have permitted sport for a few women but discouraged or completely denied the experience for the masses of women. Proof of this thesis is then offered through tracing the history of selected significant periods which highlight the paradox of woman and sport. Finally, the chapter closes with an important caution. While feminism and the women's rights movement have recently expanded the role of women in sport, further progress is a potential, not an outcome to be automatically achieved.

The great body of material in the chapter deals with women and sport in various historical periods: (1) Ancients—Crete and Greece; (2) Medieval Europe; (3) 1600-1850—Europe and the United States; (4) 1900-present—the United States. The consistent theme of these historical accounts is the intrusion of a male-dominated social order on the existential sphere of individual women. Such a theme does not make pleasurable reading. I must confess to one honest-to-goodness smile, however, as I noted the similarities when historical explanations of the Amazons are compared with explanations of "super bright medical student Anne" which are found in Matina Horner's original fear of success study. Truly the more some things change, the more they stay the same.

In determining how the chapter contributes most to the overall goal of establishing sport feminism, it is clear that it enables us to continue the process of knowing our roots. Much that has been identified as "sport history" has not concerned itself with women's experiencing of the phenomenon of sport. Spears makes a significant contribution to the identification of HER-STORY of Sport.

C. A. O.

Chapter 1
PROLOGUE: THE MYTH

Betty Spears

Sport for women has been more a myth than a reality because the western world has both accepted and rejected women in sport. Society has always been enthralled by the athletic skill and prowess of a few women and, for these women, sport is real. But for most women society has created a role which excludes them from sport and, for these women, sport has been a myth. While accepting the idea of sport for a few women, society has created many myths and folk tales which reinforce the rejection of sport for most women. Certain significant periods in the history of women's sport in the western world highlight the paradox of acceptance of the few and rejection of the many. An examination of these periods provides an understanding of the present, when, for the first time, sport may become a reality for all women.

Over 3500 years ago vigorous sport for women was accepted on the Mediterranean island of Crete. The small, slender, wiry Cretans were highly civilized with a system of writing, weights and measures, and indoor plumbing. The major deity was the Mother Goddess, demonstrating the prominent position women held in Cretan society. Not only did women spin, weave, grind corn, and make pottery, but they also drove chariots, hunted, and engaged in bull-grappling or bull-dancing. This vigorous sport is portrayed in frescoes found in the Palace of Knossos, illustrating young women and young men vaulting over a large, low-slung bull.

Although Cretan civilization had some influence, still largely unknown, upon the developing Greek culture, the Greek attitudes toward women in sport differed markedly from those in Crete. In Greece, sporting activities were interwoven in the lives of goddesses and supernatural women, thus expressing the approval of physical prowess, at least for immortal women. Greek mythology tells of women horseback riders, hunters, swimmers, and sprinters. Artemis, goddess of nature, was portrayed as a huntress, but it was Atalanta who epitomized the athletic female. According to mythology, Atalanta could marry only a youth who could outrun her in a foot-race. This appeared impossible, for she was very swift, but one young man rolled a golden apple in front of her during a race. She stooped to pick it up. Twice more he rolled apples in front of Atalanta and twice more she picked up the apples, allowing the youth to move ahead of her. He won the race and married the fleet-footed goddess.

Supernatural women included mermaids such as the Naiads, or water-nymphs, and the Nereids, Neptune's fifty beautiful daughters. The most athletic of the supernatural women were the Amazons, described as "shining young women in shining armor, living with a horse between their legs and arrogantly scrawling the supremacy of their sex on the unending scroll of the wind."[7] They conquered men warriors, lived apart from men, except for a certain period when they conceived their children, and developed a completely matriarchal society. Several theories are advanced to explain the Amazons. Many authorities insist that the Amazons are only a myth, while some theorize that the Amazons were young men in costumes and others that they were simply young women who enjoyed the skill and prowess resulting from horsemanship. Recent investigations suggest that such tribes of women may, in fact, have lived in Libya and parts of Greece.

The role of sportswomen in mythology is subject to fruitful speculation. Have these highly skilled women been accorded a place in mythology *because* of their prowess? Does man need to dominate woman, as illustrated in Atalanta's race? Or do men secretly wish to be dominated by women and, therefore, admire the powerful woman? Do the Amazons represent women's need for physical prowess and sport experiences? These mythical sportswomen suggest inquiries relevant to today's society. Do women require the same sport experiences as men? And, is sport a function of sex or the human condition? These questions, for which we do not have ready answers, can help us probe the study of women in sport.

While the immortal women who swam, raced, and rode were admired, mortal sportswomen in Greece were viewed differently. The contrast of women in Sparta and in Athens represents two very diverse approaches to women's sport; in Sparta, an early city-state with a highly organized dictatorship, the girls as well as the boys were educated and trained physically. Spartan girls practiced the same sports as the boys, but instead of preparing for military service they were preparing for motherhood. According to Spartan philosophy, a strong, healthy woman would produce strong healthy babies for the state. Everything in Sparta was directed toward developing citizens who would serve the state. Athens also believed in service to the state, but emphasized an education which was a harmony of mental, physical, aesthetic and moral development, for men only. According to most authorities, Athenian women were confined to special quarters where they supervised the house, the slaves, the education of the young children, and spent long hours making themselves attractive. Such a life did not include sport.

There is, however, evidence that other women in Greece were accepted in athletic festivals. Predating the Olympic Games were the Herean Games, honoring the goddess Hera. The hill of Cronus at Olympia was the site of a temple to the Great Earth Mother and it is suggested that the Herean festival originated in an ancient fertility race offering thanks for a good harvest. The only event in the festival was the foot-race, run over a course about five-sixths the length of the stadium. While women were not permitted to enter the Olympic Games, they did enter their horses in the chariot races. Also, by the 1st century A.D. girls were competing in athletic festivals in various parts of Greece. Archaeological findings prove that girls won races at Corinth, Nemea, Delphi, and other cities. Thus the Greek culture demonstrates the paradox of both acceptance and rejection of women in sport. Over a period of 1000 years, girls' sport was accepted in Sparta for eugenic purposes, and rejected in Athens, but by the end of the period accepted for a few girls who raced in Greek athletic festivals.

The next significant period in the history of women in sport occurred in western Europe and England in medieval times. By the 13th century this section of the world had blended into a racial and cultural unit whose major influences were the Roman Catholic Church and the feudal system. Each of these institutions played a role in the history of women in sport. Woman's place in society varied according to her social group, but women "were not all quiet Griseldas passively watching the exploits of pure-hearted knights."[1] Family life was rough and boisterous. Many women worked alongside their husbands on small farms, in home industries, and guilds. Women managed complex households in castles and frequently administered the affairs of large abbeys and convents.

Sport for the noble women appears to have been accepted as part of their lives. Numerous illustrations in illuminated manuscripts and references in literature indicate that the women hunted with hawks and also with bows and arrows. We have evidence that by the end of the 14th century noble women skated on ice, jousted, and played games such as jeu-de-paume. Strutt reports, "A French writer speaks of a damsel named Margot, who resided in Paris in 1424, and played at hand-tennis with the palm, and also with the back of her hand, better than any man; and what is more surprising, . . . at that time the game was played with the naked hand, or at best with a double glove."[9] Dame Juliana Berners, a prioress in England, wrote the first book on sport, a treatise on hunting and hawking. The daughter of a nobleman, she was described as ". . . a second Minerva in her studies, and another Diana in her diversions."2 In sharp contrast to the sporting activities of the noble women, the women of the lower social groups had little time for anything other than the tasks required for daily living. However, the women did take part in contests at fairs and in holy day festivities, and women acrobats called gleemaidens were part of the wandering troupes of minstrels and tumblers who entertained in the castles and at fairs.

In the later medieval period, physical, social, and religious restraints on women developed. The ideals of chivalry and courtly love placed women high on pedestals conferring their favors on knights. At the medieval tournaments women were the spectators, awarding the prizes of the day and accepting tributes from the knights. In the course of the period the long, loose garments of the early middle ages were replaced by apparel which made the upper part of the body appear small and hid the lower part of the body in voluminous skirts. The corset, "one of the most sinister phenomena in her history,"5 became part of the woman's wardrobe. While such clothing and attitudes did much to prevent physical activity, there are some paintings and wood-cuts which portray women playing shuttle cock, riding, hunting, and dancing. The emerging higher social group, not born into nobility, but moneyed through banking and commerce, sought to emulate the lives of the aristocracy. Since the tournaments of the period excluded all but the nobility, they pursued other means to demonstrate their success. The bankers and merchants bought elaborate articles for their households for show, and heavy, rich clothing for their wives as if they, too, were for show. The husband's ability to provide a life of idleness for his wife became a mark of status, and since most of the merchants lived in towns, country sports of hunting and hawking were inaccessible to them. Thus, for most of these women, physical prowess was neither available nor deemed desirable.

Further restrictions in physical activity resulted from the codes of behavior designed for the developing Protestant sects, in which activities not pertaining to salvation were regarded as sinful. Some psychologists suggest that Puritans disapproved of sport because it provided means for spontaneous expression of undisciplined impulses, while others hypothesize that the Puritan attitude to sport and recreation was an over-reaction to powerful emotions unloosed by them. Generally speaking, by the end of the 16th century, women's sport was accepted only by nobility. For women in the emerging higher social groups, as well as those in the Protestant groups, sport for women was rejected.

The next 250 years, until about 1860, can be considered a transitional period, significant not because of sport for women, but because of changes in the lives of some women. During this time the concept of the frail, fragile female representing true womanhood was reinforced by most sectors of society; but a few women began to speak out against this mold, challenging ideas on the education of women, revolting against the clothing fashions imposed on them, and demanding their legal and political rights. In the first part of this transitional period, the 17th and 18th centuries, educational reformers such as Pestalozzi, Froebel, DeGenlis, and Rousseau proposed radical ideas such as universal education for both boys and girls, daily exercise, and play. DeGenlis believed that girls, no less than boys, should run and jump. She designed gymnastic exercises especially for girls. Rousseau, the most influential of these educators, espoused such enlightened ideas as finding projects which would interest children, encouraging sport and exercise; but, at the same time, he proposed unequal education for boys and girls. He believed "Woman was made especially to please man; . . . If woman is formed to please and to live in subjection, she must render herself agreeable to man instead of provoking his wrath; her strength lies in her charms."[6] In her book, A Vindication of the Rights of Women, Mary Wollstonecraft answered Rousseau, "The woman who has only been taught to please will soon find that her charms are oblique sunbeams . . ."[12] For Wollstonecraft, the education of women should foster independence and equality. As the first modern woman to speak out against the problems which had been created for women by the highly restricted and idealized mold into which they had been placed, she is important in the history of women in sport. Although Wollstonecraft lived and wrote in London and Paris, it was in the United States of America that many women were in agreement with her ideas. Even before the Vindication was published, an American woman, Judith Sargent Murray, decried the unequal education for boys and girls.

In the early years of the newly established colonies, women were few in number and a certain amount of physical prowess was valued. Women were not infrequently treated as equals because they were needed to maintain the new settlements. However, as communities became established and life assumed a pattern more nearly like that in Europe, the role of the woman tended toward the European model. Because the nobility of Europe did not come to the colonies in large numbers, it was the Puritans and other religious groups, the new merchants, and adventurers who developed life styles in colonial America. In the Puritan colonies little if any recreation was permitted. It is probably safe to assume that the one story of Massachusetts women on an 18th century swimming party did not refer to Puritan women. We do know that in the South women were spectators at horse races and occasionally rode horseback themselves. Little research has been done on women in the colonial period and, with additional information, a different picture might be drawn.

The first recognized attempts at dress reform for women occurred in this transitional period. At the Oneida, New York, commune the women found their long, full dresses difficult for many of their tasks and by midsummer 1848, they had cut off their skirts to about knee length and made pantalettes to cover the lower leg. But it was Amelia Bloomer in the 1850's who provided the term "bloomer" for the costumes which paved the way for active sportswear in later decades.

Early in the 19th century a few women pioneered in the education of girls and young women. Emma Willard established the Troy Female Seminary in New York State, Catherine Beecher opened a female seminary in Hartford, Connecticut, and Mary Lyon founded Mount Holyoke Seminary in western Massachusetts. The generally poor health of women was becoming a major concern and the founders of these institutions recognized the need to improve the health of their students through physical activities such as light gymnastic exercises, dancing, horseback riding, and walking.

Further evidence of change in the lives of women is reflected in a meeting convened in Seneca Falls, New York in 1848 by five Quaker women who set forth a Bill of Rights based on the Constitution of the United States, and prepared resolutions which were debated by the three hundred people who attended. This meeting was the beginning of the 19th century women's movement, in which thousands of women's groups grappled with the educational, legal, and political rights of women. While the Seneca Falls meeting did not deal with sport, it did help create a climate in which women could become involved in a variety of social issues. As O'Neill stated, "The more women did, the more they wished to do, the more they pressed against the barriers that prevented them from exercising their full powers, and the more eager they became to equip themselves for the tasks ahead."[4] By the middle of the 19th century, the ideas of reform for women in education, dress, and their basic rights had been initiated. These seeds of change, as well as the impact of urbanization, industrialization, technology, and immigration in the last half of the 19th century created the next significant period in the history of women in sport.

The hope of an improved life attracted thousands of immigrants to the United States in the last half of the 19th century, where they settled in the sprawling tenements of the growing cities. Many saw their dreams of a better life fade before the daily struggle of living and working in a strange land. The lower and middle class women aspired to the ideals of "true womanhood" displayed by the upperclass women whose homes demonstrated their inability to perform useful tasks or engage in physical activity beyond an occasional game of croquet.

Many of the inventions of the period improved the lot of these women. More and more homes boasted inside plumbing and modernized kitchens with coal stoves and running water. The sewing machines and gadgets such as ruffling irons saved hours of the women's time. Newspapers, books, magazines, and the new-fangled phonograph brought literature and music into the home. In spite of increased time and the opportunities for more knowledge, the fragile female remained the epitome of womanhood. Piety, purity, submissiveness, and domesticity were the desired characteristics of the mythic woman. Delicacy was desired and ill health accepted as her fate. These ideals, the fashions of the period, and the social role created for women led to the acceptance of the idea that women were not suited to higher education. Women were considered mentally inferior to men and physically too weak to attend class regularly.

Opponents of women's education argued that 45 per cent of women suffered from menstrual cramps and another 20 per cent suffered from assorted ills. Thus, for physiological reasons alone, 65 per cent of the women would require the college program to be adjusted for them. Also, it was reported that overstudy would give the girls brain fever. They would be weak and unable to have children.[8]

Two men undertook the task of disproving these ideas. Matthew Vassar, who established Vassar College in 1865, and Henry Fowle Durant, who founded Wellesley College 10 years later, wished to show that young women could engage in college work equal to that of young men. Both Vassar and Durant used sport as part of their plans. Vassar's first gymnasium, the Calisthenium, included a gymnasium, bowling alleys, and a riding school. Also available at Vassar were boating, swimming, flower gardening, and ice skating in the winter. At Wellesley College, in addition to required exercise classes, Durant provided boats for rowing, tennis, and ice skating in the winter.

These experiments in higher education for women proved successful and other colleges followed. Most of them required gymnastic exercises to improve and maintain the health of the students. However, gymnastics did not hold the attention of the students and, as early as 1876, sports began to be part of the required physical education program. At Vassar College, after spring vacation of that year, students were permitted to elect a game or sport in place of gymnastics. And in 1893 Lucille Eaton Hill at Wellesley College conducted a 5-month experiment which demonstrated that sport could produce the same physical results as gymnastics. In the last decade of the 19th century, the advent of team sports established the acceptance of sport in the physical education curriculum. Basketball, introduced to Smith College students in 1892, just 1 year after its invention, was immediately popular. Later in the decade the new game of volleyball and English field hockey added to the interest and excitement of sport in the colleges. The women enjoyed the new sports and their interest in gymnastics declined. Sport became the dominant component of college physical education programs and, as such, was an accepted part of the college woman's experience.

Sports for women were more readily accepted not only in educational institutions, but also in philanthropic agencies, private clubs, and community programs. After centuries of constraints there appeared to be a frenzy of sport activities among women. From a social perspective the bicycle gained the widest attention. It had both adversaries and advocates. A patent-medicine company hinted that riding was harmful to the weaker sex, while other opponents denounced the road-houses and resorts visited by bicycle riders of *both* sexes. For women cyclers, however, emancipation was the theme. Some rode in exhibitions, and, for a brief time, there were lady professional cycling teams, but for the average American woman, the bicycle meant mobility and increased freedom.

In 1885 a national golf championship for women was held and in 1887 a tennis championship. Increasingly women fenced, bowled, swam, ice-skated, roller-skated, and engaged in team sports. There were private women's sport clubs, one of which, the Staten Island Ladies Athletic Club, included dart games, archery, and tennis in its program. Associations and organizations which both promoted and controlled women's sports were established. As early as 1899 the American Association for the Advancement of Physical Education appointed a Woman's Basketball Committee to determine *one* set of rules.

From the elite city athletic clubs to the neighborhood bowling alley and skating rink it appeared that sport would mirror society's acceptance of women outside the home in education, business, professions, and the voting booth. Perhaps scholars studying women's sport in the distant future will speak of the period of great restraints, 1600 to 1875, and will treat this past century, 1875-1975, as the century of emancipation of women in sport. But for our purposes, the period from 1920 to 1975 will be examined as the last significant period in the history of women in sport. Fashions, depression, war and individual personalities affected women's sport, but interwoven among these components were two major influences—the controversy over the philosophy of women's sport and the 20th century women's movement.

The twenties, characterized by prosperity and increased leisure, made sport possible for many women. Short bloomers for active sports and one-piece brief bathing suits for swimming became fashionable. Individual athletes excelled in a variety of sports and drew international attention. Helen Wills ruled the tennis courts of the United States and England. Annette Kellerman, a frail young woman from Australia, who started swimming for health reasons, starred in aquatic extravaganzas. In 1926, Gertrude Ederle swam the English Channel, bettering the men's record by 2 hours. It appeared that society was ready to accept the 20th century sportswoman. However, acceptance was accompanied by publicity, notoriety, and exploitation. Newspapers, real estate firms, and advertising agencies sold their products by using women in sport as an inducement to read the advertisements. Paul Gallico, sportswriter of the period, wrote that "Newspaper publishers discovered that, whereas reproductions of nightclub cuties in leotards or tights might bar them from the mails, . . . photographs of an octet of naiads, lined up at the end of the pool in their wet, clinging, one-piece garments were legit, even though more revealing" and that "An appreciable part of the great Florida real estate boom was built upon photographs of girl swimmers used in advertising, and certainly no newspaper suffered a drop in circulation when it was able to publish this kind of cheese-cake."[3] Men coaches, unchaperoned travel arrangements, and questionable uniforms, as well as the inappropriate use of women in sport advertising, drew criticism from many women physical educators who had worked for consistently high standards of conduct and sportsmanship for women. Further, men's intercollegiate athletic programs were accused of being too professional and many women did not wish to follow the men's pattern of athletics. Early in the 20th century Hill had expressed concern over the evils in men's athletics and formulated a "new" athletic philosophy for women based on securing "the greatest good to the greatest number," thus articulating the philosophy which has influenced women's athletic programs in educational institutions throughout this century. In 1920 the Association of Directors of Physical Education for College Women denounced intercollegiate athletics as leading to commercialization and professionalization, and reaffirmed Hill's basic principle of a broad program of activities.

The women physical educators' stand was reinforced as a result of a controversy in 1922 over an international track meet in Paris to which the Amateur Athletic Union (AAU) was invited to send a women's team. The AAU had consistently refused to conduct women's sport, but in 1916 had finally undertaken a swimming meet for women. Although in the process of studying the desirability of organizing women's track and field, and in spite of the fact that it had not yet reached a decision, the AAU agreed to sponsor a team for the Paris meet and appointed a man, Dr. Harry Stewart, as coach. The women

physical educators considered the male coach another form of exploitation, and through their Committee on Women's Athletics, protested
sending the track team to Paris. Regardless of the women's protest,
the United States women participated in the meet. Following the
meet, the AAU voted to include track and field in the women's sports
under their control.

At about that time the newly formed National Amateur Athletic
Federation, which concerned itself with sport at the national level
in a social, scholastic, and ethical context, requested Mrs. Herbert
Hoover to convene a conference on Athletics and Physical Education
for Girls and Women, in order to consider organizing a woman's
division of the federation. In 1923 a Woman's Division of the Federation was formed, which reaffirmed the basic tenets of the women
physical educators. Their platform stressed sport opportunities for all
girls, protection from exploitation, enjoyment of sports, female leadership, medical examinations, and the necessity for international competition to be approved by the federation.

The newly adopted platform, virtually the same position adopted by
the Association of Directors of Physical Education for College Women
just a few years earlier, further curtailed women's intercollegiate and
interschool athletics. In a search for alternatives to inter-institution
competition which would not lead to commercialization and professionalization, playdays and sportsdays were devised. Playday teams
were picked at random from the schools participating. If six schools
participated in a playday, each team would include a player from
each school. Many times the program for the day consisted of novelty
events rather than sports events. At a sportsday, the institution played
as a team, but usually in a modified form of competition such as a
round robin tournament. Both the Committee on Women's Athletics
and the Women's Division of the National Amateur Athletic Federation continued to support such events and to oppose programs such
as the Olympic Games which they considered improper for women.
They approved of athletics ". . . motivated by joy and love of play,
not play for the purpose of making a record or beating an opponent."[11]
Both of these committees joined the growing opposition to sending a
United States Olympic women's team to Antwerp in 1928, and again,
in 1932, but to no avail. By that time women had gained unquestioned
participation in a number of Olympic events.

The thirties reflected sharp contrasts in sport for women. The enforced leisure resulting from unemployment gave women time to
participate in sport, and the public works programs provided more
facilities for participation. City leagues and town industries sponsored
inexpensive sports teams such as bowling, softball, and swimming.
Stars such as Babe Didrikson emerged from industry-sponsored sports

to national prominence and Olympic fame. While sport helped occupy unemployed women, it also led to inventions of sport forms such as synchronized swimming which was introduced for the 1934 Chicago World's Fair. On the other hand physical educators continued to reject women in inter-institution competition and promoted playdays and sportsdays.

During World War II women in service and industry engaged in work formerly reserved for men, and the All-American Girls Baseball League gallantly responded to the call for sport entertainment. After the war, in the affluent fifties, many women had time to play and money for equipment and instruction. Thousands of women finished high school and entered college seeking more and more sport opportunities. However, the opportunities were not always there. Sports for women had been tacitly identified as "ladylike" or "unladylike." Swimming, gymnastics, riding, skiing, and tennis were among the accepted sports. These required both time and money; in this period of affluence, more women took part in these sports giving them an appearance of greater acceptability. On the other hand, the softball and basketball players of the period, as well as the track stars, whose sports were thought of as "unladylike," might be questioned as to their femininity, and be discouraged from sport.

During the sixties the controversy over high level competition for women erupted in the colleges and universities and eventually led to a change in educational athletics. The Committee on Women's Athletics of the twenties had absorbed the Woman's Division of the National Amateur Athletic Federation and had been reorganized as the Division of Girls and Women's Sports (DGWS). DGWS sports committees continued to determine rules, develop official's ratings, prepare teaching materials, and formulate standards. By 1950 "the greatest good to the greatest number" slogan was revised to "a sport for every girl and every girl in a sport" and resulted in the virtual exclusion of the highly skilled woman athlete. She had to go outside the educational institutions for competition. Sport organizations, youth agencies, private clubs, coaches, and families supported the serious woman athlete. Finally, DGWS began to recognize the needs of the skilled women athletes as legitimate and began to modify its position. At about the same time the United States Olympic Development Committee also expressed an interest in women athletes and organized a Women's Board. To increase the opportunities for women and girls in athletics the Women's Board invited DGWS to co-sponsor a series of institutes in several Olympic sports for women. For the first time, the women physical educators officially indicated an interest in Olympic competition. Additional impetus to increased sport programs came in response to overtures by the National Collegiate

Athletic Association (NCAA) to provide women's intercollegiate competition. DGWS promptly formed a Commission on Intercollegiate Athletics for Women in 1967 for the purpose of providing a framework for appropriate intercollegiate athletic opportunities for women, including national championships. In 1971 the Commission's functions were assumed by the newly created Association for Intercollegiate Athletics for Women (AIAW) which functioned under the American Association for Health, Physical Education and Recreation. Educators and educational institutions appeared to accept women's sport not only as a healthful recreation, but also as intense, high-level competition.

The general prosperity since World War II, accompanied by time and money for sport, the growing concern for Olympic athletes, and the approval of championships by the most influential organization in educational athletics contributed to the impression that society was in reality beginning to accept women's sports. While the Olympic program included the "ladylike" sports, the new AIAW championships covered the "unladylike" sports of basketball, volleyball, and softball.

Still more backing for women's sports has been provided by the twentieth century woman's movement and the civil rights movement of the sixties. Not only did women's political and legal rights come under scrutiny, but a broad range of social rights were questioned. Among these were women's right to the sport experience, both as amateurs and professionals. From the women jockeys who established themselves as capable competitors to Billie Jean King who became an advocate for women pros, women made great strides in professional sport. As part of the civil rights movement, federal legislation in 1964 barred racial discrimination and provided the framework for legislation to bar sex discrimination. The United States Congress passed Title IX of the Educational Amendments of 1972, "No person in the United States shall on the basis of sex be excluded from participation in, be denied the benefits of, or be subjected to discrimination under any education program or activity receiving Federal financial assistance. . . ."[10] Deceptively simple, it became amazingly complex as the Federal Guidelines for Title IX were debated. On July 21, 1975 these guidelines became law. For the first time institutions which receive federal aid, and that includes the majority in the country, must provide equal opportunity for women's and men's sport. This legal guarantee, however, cannot insure society's acceptance of sport as a living reality for the average American girl or woman.

For at least 3000 years sport has been identified mainly with the youthful male. While sport for a few women, whether goddesses, aristocrats, circus performers, or Olympic athletes, has always been accepted, sport for the average girl or woman comparable to sport for the average boy or man has not been accepted. Neither approved championships nor federal laws, nor national Olympic teams can assure society's acceptance of women's sport.

In the United States, society appears to be moving toward a healthy population with time and money for sport, toward an acceptance of a broadening spectrum of life styles, including approval of physical prowess of women, and toward a climate of civil and social rights enforced through legislation. But the myths and traditions of centuries die hard. The coming decades will be critical in the interpretation of women's sport and the education of the general public to the acceptance of sport for women. Especially challenging will be the opportunity to design and carry out appropriate sport programs. New traditions are built slowly and will be accompanied by new myths, but for the first time, social, economic, and technological forces are opening the possibility of sport for women as a reality instead of a myth.

REFERENCES

1. Beard, M.: Woman as a Force in History. New York, The Macmillan Co., 1946.
2. Berners, J.: The Book of St. Albans. Ann Arbor, University Microfilms, 1946.
3. Gallico, P.: The Golden People. Garden City, Doubleday & Co., Inc., 1964.
4. O'Neill, W.: The Woman Movement. Chicago, Quadrangle, 1971.
5. Putnam, E.: The Lady. Chicago, University of Chicago, 1970.
6. Rousseau, J. J.: Emile, Julie, and Other Writings. Edited by Archer. New York, Barron's Educational Series, 1964.
7. Sobol, D.: The Amazons of Greek Mythology. New York, A. S. Barnes & Co., 1972.
8. Spears, B.: The emergence of sport as physical education. In Coping with Controversy. Washington, D.C., The American Alliance for Health, Physical Education and Recreation, 1973.
9. Strutt, J.: The Sports and Pastimes of the People of England. London, Chatto & Windus, 1898.
10. U. S. Department of Health, Education, and Welfare, Office for Civil Rights. Final Title IX Regulations, June, 1975.
11. Wayman, A. R.: Education through Physical Education. Philadelphia, Lea & Febiger, 1928.
12. Wollstonecraft, M. M.: A Vindication of the Rights of Woman. New York, W. W. Norton & Co., 1967.

Part 1
Women's Sport: Society and Ourselves

Section 1

SOCIETY AND THE FEMALE BODY

In 1976, Jackie Hudson became involved as a consultant in a legal challenge of an administrative policy excluding all women from beat patrol in Philadelphia. This police ruling and its rationale are good examples of the use of insufficient empirical data to undergird arbitrary decisions which are (in legal understatement) overbroad in their applications. Hudson's contention is that this kind of overgeneralization in administrative regulations prevails in the sport and athletic environment. Two postulates are presented to buttress this contention. Hudson illustrates that in instances where female performance is poorer, in general, than male performance, environmental and social factors should be thoroughly investigated before genetic causation is accepted. Hudson then presents data which suggest the jury is still out in the matter of the theoretical limits of female performance. This chapter focuses on the capacities of females vis a vis males and between-sex competition. Hudson does not propose that this is the only legitimate avenue for women in sport, but simply that the opportunity should exist for women who choose it.

It seems incumbent upon sport feminists to work to modify the rigid prohibitions against between-sex competition. Records seem to indicate that, at present, females generally are a different class of competitors than males. Hudson suggests that an unknown amount of the difference in performance is socially induced. For the present we support female-oriented programs for the majority with allowance for the exceptional female to find her own level of competition by open selection. Males, no matter what their size, strength, or endurance, have the freedom to choose whether to risk life and limb to try out for the varsity. It is not healthy to build in an automatic restriction of freedom for females.

Hudson points out that the East German female Olympic swimmers are performing up to 97 percent of the performance times of East German male Olympians. Assuming that male Olympic medalists are the *creme de la creme* of swimmers all over the world, the Wundermädchens seem to be competitive with anyone, anywhere. If one of them came to the United States to live, we would want her to swim in any program she wished, wouldn't we?

C.A.O.

Chapter 2

PHYSICAL PARAMETERS USED FOR FEMALE EXCLUSION FROM LAW ENFORCEMENT AND ATHLETICS

Jackie Hudson

The unquestioned presumption of the absolute physical inferiority of girls and women relative to boys and men has been used as a method of restricting female participation in many sports. Several myths and ill-founded arguments proposed for limiting athletic activity are also being used with respect to occupational activity.

As an example in the realm of sports, Torg and Torg[93] have described the misconceptions proposed by Little League, Inc., as rationale for preventing girls from participating in their private piece of Americana. According to Dr. Creighton J. Hale, executive vice-president of research for Little League, there are "incontrovertible facts" substantiating the physiological and anatomical differences between girls and boys which make it unsafe for girls to play baseball with boys. His main contentions of female inferiority were the susceptibility of female bones to fracture and the slower reaction time in females.

To prove that the bony skeleton of the 8- to 12-year-old female was structurally different and inherently weaker than the 8- to 12-year-old male, Dr. Hale cited studies appearing in the Japanese literature which measured various strength characteristics of adult cadaver bones. Comparing the results from the dead bone of postmenopausal, osteoporotic cadavers to living immature skeletal systems is totally invalid. The only recognized difference between female and male bone structure in the Little League age group is that the female skeleton is from 18 to 36 months more mature than the male.[93]

To establish that females have a slower reaction time than males, Dr. Hale presented data from a small study which demonstrated that a group of boys whose average age was 7.3 years had faster reaction times than a group of girls whose average age was 5.4 years.[9] Besides a difference of 2 years between the groups, neither were of Little League age. There is no evidence to support the contention that girls of Little League age have slower reaction times than boys of the same age.

Besides his "incontrovertible facts" Dr. Hale also argued that girls should be denied the experience of Little League baseball because cancerous lesions could be produced by traumatic impact upon female breast tissue, an hypothesis for which there is no actual medical fact. His argument that females would suffer a higher incidence of dental injuries and thereby have cosmetic problems of greater consequence was regarded by the hearing officer as "gratuitous."[34]

The fact that situations such as girls playing Little League baseball have to be *litigated* demonstrates how bias in the area of female athletics continues to be justified on misconceptions and perpetuated by ignorance.

Misconceptions and ignorance with regard to the abilities of the female are not limited to the field of athletics. The same variety of myths and pervasive illogic are also preventing women from entering many occupations.

The exclusion of women from sector patrol (beat patrol) by the Philadelphia Police Department because of the physical inferiority of women has caused Penelope Brace to file a suit of discrimination against the City of Philadelphia. Less than 1 per cent of the police officers in Philadelphia are women and they are mainly confined to working in the Juvenile Aid and Community Relations divisions. Ms. Brace has filed suit because no women are allowed on sector patrol and serving on sector patrol is a necessary requisite for promotion to the ranks of sergeant, lieutenant, and detective.[82]

WOMEN ARE "DIFFERENT"

The City of Philadelphia assumes that discrimination is justifiable in this case because women are physically inferior, or as Police Commissioner Joseph F. O'Neill has said in a sworn statement—"because God, in His wisdom, made them different." Commissioner O'Neill's reasoning, by which the exclusion of women from beat patrol is justified, parallels much of the mythology underlying exclusion rules against women in sport.

One argument given by O'Neill is that the bone structure of the female is not as strong. This is supported by the anatomist Edwards[25] as he lists some of the anatomic-physiologic features which distinguish between males and females, such as size, weight, muscular and bony structure, and mental attitude. He says that males have a more powerfully built skeleton. According to Klafs and Lyon,[48] the male skeleton is more rugged with the bones being more massive and of greater density.

There are several factors which influence bone structure including heredity, nutrition, disease, hormones, and function. As an example of what function alone can do to a bone, noticeable atrophy occurs when muscular and functional forces are retarded by a few weeks in a plaster cast. Another way to examine the effect of function on bone structure is to look at test-tube bone. It has been found that bone which is growing in culture will adapt to artificial forces present and grow stronger.[76] Intermittent stresses of normal muscular activity generally seem to favor bone growth. We could say bone strength develops with use. According to Klafs and Lyon, the well-conditioned female athlete will have strong, healthy bones which can withstand stress, torque, and shock. It may be that the amount and variety of activity has as much influence as gender on the strength and density of bone. Certainly intra-sex differences make questionable the practice of disqualifying all women on the basis of bone strength.

Specific differences between females and males are frequently given in relation to bone length, width, and angle of inclination. Ulrich[95] stated that the knee of the female is wider and therefore more stable for its size than the male knee. This finding has not been corroborated by other researchers. In using the data of Wilmore[99] on knee diameter and height, the ratio of knee width to height in the females is 0.0504 and for the males 0.0505. A difference of 100th of 1 per cent hardly seems conclusive but perhaps other data will support the theory of Ulrich.

According to a statement made in 1974 by Rasch and Burke:

> The inward inclination of the female arm accounts for women's difficulty in handling screwdrivers and other equipment requiring rotary motion. The fact that women's thighs incline in toward the knees makes it more difficult for them to maintain their balance. Due to the relatively greater average width of her pelvis, her acetabula are farther apart. Consequently a greater lateral shift of the center of gravity is necessary to bring the body weight over the hip joint at each stride and she is likely to show a marked lateral sway of the pelvis during running.[76]

Adrian[1] takes exception to the statement that there are genetic structural differences between the sexes with regard to the arm. She notes than an eminent anatomist[55] does not describe any differences in the shoulder and elbow joints and the muscular structure about them. Adrian suggests that if these differences were to be observed, functional development would have to be considered as a causative factor. With respect to the conclusion that lateral sway is prominent in the running style of the female, Rose [78] and Oyster and Wooten[69] have found that lateral imbalance has no relationship to the velocity of the run.

Several myths regarding genetic differences between females and males have originated with the observance of a difference without attention being paid to the underlying causes. An example of this in relation to the strength of bone is found in the statistics compiled from automobile accidents. It has been observed that men sustain femoral fractures, but women are more likely to dislocate their hips. Rather than a structural difference which seems plausible, this phenomenon seems to be caused by social conditioning which dictates that women sit with their knees or legs crossed and men sit with their legs spread apart. At impact a person with crossed legs has the head of the femur driven out of the acetabulum and a person with legs apart has the head of the femur driven further back into the acetabulum until the femur buckles and breaks.[77]

Another reason cited by Commissioner O'Neill to prohibit women from sector patrol is that "there are periods in their life when they are psychologically unbalanced because of physical problems that are occurring within them."[82] Presumably Mr. O'Neill is referring to the menstrual cycle and its associated incapacitating elements. Historically women have been advised to withdraw from active participation during menses because of concern about the ill effects of exercise on the menstrual cycle and pregnancy. Participation was also feared because of the risk of injury to the reproductive organs and the breasts.[92] Klafs and Lyon[48] state that it is the consensus of doctors that women should avoid extremely strenuous activity, particularly that which produces excessive torque or strain on the pelvic floor, during the first 2 days of the menstrual period. Rarick[74] points out that some authorities are concerned about the possibilities of damaging the female organs by excessive jumping and jarring. But he also says there is little evidence in support of this. With respect to the injuries which might result to the female organs McCloy[62] quoted Paramore as follows:

> Dr. R. H. Paramore, who has experimented extensively in this field has called attention to the additional fact that the uterus is surrounded with structures of practically the same specific gravity as itself, and that it normally has no air spaces around it. Thus it floats free in a miniature pool of pelvic viscera, just as it might, if detached, float in a jar filled to the brim with water. Such a body suffers only such shock as occurs within itself and does not fly violently through the fluid when shaken. This can easily be proven by placing a raw egg in a liter jar filled to the brim with water and then screwing the top on in such a way as to exclude all air. No degree of violent handling that does not smash the jar will injure the egg.

In regard to the possibility of getting breast cancer from trauma, Dr. Joan Ullyot (Medical World News, 1974) says there is no evidence that repeated trauma can cause malignancy. She suggests that this type of myth has occurred because someone said she was hit on the breast by a baseball bat and got cancer when in reality the lump was already there and was only discovered when she felt the bruised area.

There is little if any evidence to indicate that the child bearing function of women has been adversely affected by athletic participation.[74] According to a survey of 729 Hungarian women athletes, Erdelyi[27] found that menstruation and subsequent obstetrical history were not unfavorably affected. In fact, the length of labor was shorter and the necessity for cesarean section in the athletes was 50 per cent less than for the control group.

In determining the effect of the menstrual cycle on performance, Bilhuber[12] found the cycle had no effect on motor ability and Younger[107] could find no effect on the speed of arm movement or simple reaction time due to the cyclic variations. According to Wyrick[106] the phases of the menstrual cycle have little effect on the physical performance of average women. She also concluded that the majority of women athletes performed about the same during menses, but some performed better during menses and others worse. Ryan[80] states that records have been broken and Olympic medals won by women during menses.

With regard to the effects on the menstrual cycle caused by participation in sports, Ryan has found no evidence, either favorable or unfavorable, about the effect on the cycle due to activity. The Pacific Association of the Amateur Athletic Union[70] examined data from virtually all medical and athletic disciplines and found no evidence that athletic competition has a deleterious effect on girls and women.

Another reason given by Commissioner O'Neill for the inability of women to serve on the beat is that "she has an extra layer of fat on her body which makes her vulnerable to physical attack."[82] Fat is stored in the body in two capacities. Internally it surrounds and supports many structures and organs. Subcutaneous fat is distributed over the surface of the body just below the skin. The functions of the subcutaneous layer are to act as a protective, shock-absorbing cushion for organs and tissues lying beneath it and to serve as a heat insulator for the body.[66] It would seem, therefore, that this extra layer of fat would make a woman more valuable than vulnerable in cases of physical attack.

The role of the sex-related hormones in the storage of adipose tissue is not completely delineated. Comments such as the one by Shaffer[83] that the accumulation of fat is regulated by estrogen seem to give the impression that the level of estrogen in a body somehow controls the amount of fat in the body. More accurately, the sex hormones do have some function in regulating where the adipose tissue on a body is stored. There is quite a lot of variation within women and within men with regard to where adipose tissue is stored. The thickest layers of adipose tissue in women seem to be in the hip region, the thigh, the abdomen, and the calf. Overweight women have thicker layers of adipose tissue but it still locates in the four primary sites. Men tend to distribute adipose tissue rather evenly over various trunk sites. Because older women tend to redistribute their adipose tissue somewhat from the lower limbs to the trunk when their estrogen levels diminish,[66] it does appear that estrogen plays a role in where adipose tissue is located.

The male hormone, androgen, gives a predisposition to higher lean body weight but it does not necessarily follow that estrogen gives a predisposition to a higher percentage of fat.[100] Every person has a certain amount of fat which is essential for proper neural transmission and other functions. Behnke[8] believes that women, because of mammary and sex-specific tissue, should have a higher percentage of essential fat than men.

According to studies by Wilmore and Behnke,[103,104] college-age women have 25.7 per cent of their body weight in fat and college-age men have 14.6 per cent of their weight in fat. After a 10-week weight training program, Wilmore[99] found the female subjects lost 7.5 per cent of their fat weight and the male subjects lost 9.3 per cent. By testing the thickness of subcutaneous fat before and after the weight training, he concluded that for both the women and men there seemed to be a general mobilization of fat and not spot reduction. He also concluded that the changes in body composition from training were not sex specific. He speculates that the substantial differences in percent body fat found between college-age females and males are largely the result of the more sedentary life style of the female.[102]

Since the amount of fat a person carries is primarily a function of the activity level and food intake, it might be expected that women with high activity levels would tend to have a lower percentage of fat. Figure 1 would seem to substantiate this. Elite level gymnasts were found to have 9.6 per cent[72] and 10.1 per cent[73] of their body weight in fat. A sample of twelve runners between the ages of 15 and 32, many of whom were training in excess of 100 miles per week, had an average of about 11 per cent fat.[8] Women competing in college athletics in the late sixties and early seventies fell between 15.5 per cent fat for gymnasts[85] and 20.8 per cent fat for basketball players soon after the rule change to five-player teams.[84] College athletes tested in the middle sixties did not appear to be much different in per cent fat than the typical college student.[21] With regard to the increase in intensity of training and competition which has occurred in the last decade in athletics for college women, these decreases in fat percentage seem to parallel an increase in activity level.

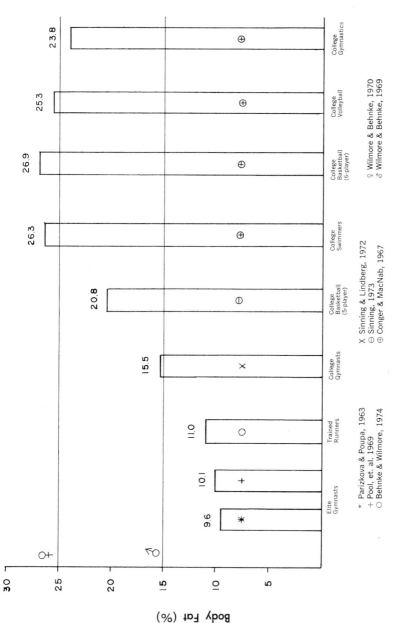

Fig. 1.

Wilmore[110] questions the necessity of the amount of fat women carry and points out that runners and jumpers have been able to decrease their amounts of fat quite dramatically with little apparent harm. He feels that women should be able to approach men in the relative amount of fat carried.[100]

Radiographic methods are used to assess changes taking place among the components of muscle, fat, and bone during growth. Looking at tissue width graphs from roentgenograms[61] it can be seen that girls have a larger amount of fat from the first or second year onward at all four reported sites—the forearm, calf, mid-femur, and hip. Although the values for girls are higher from an early age, the big change in values occurs about the 12th or 14th year. Since this relative increase in fat corresponds temporally with the age of menarche, it has been presumed to be a function of increased estrogen levels. While this theory is not ruled out completely, this increase in fat also seems to correspond with the decrease in activity in most females.

Another reason to prevent women from serving on sector patrol in Philadelphia was given by Stephen Arinson, one of the city's lawyers, "it's not that women can't write traffic tickets. It's a biological difference based on hormones. Estrogen in women doesn't give them muscles."[82]

There are two periods of growth before maturity. Both have major impact on the quantity of muscle tissue found in an adult. The period of growth before puberty is similar in girls and boys since it is unaffected by the sex-related hormones, estrogen and androgen. Postnatal growth of skeletal muscle results mainly from hypertrophy (increase in size) of muscle fibers, rather than from hyperplasia (increase in number) of fibers.[57] Chiakulas and Pauly[20] and Bowden and Goyer[13] suggest that size differences observed in the fibers of different muscles during normal growth are directly related to functional activity. Cheek[19] analyzed muscle biopsies of the gluteus maximus of 26 children. He determined that muscles are not composed of uniformly sized fibers. Also he concluded that boys show increases in fiber size with growth, while girls demonstrate larger fibers at an earlier age but reach their fiber size maximum at about the time their height reaches 130 cm. Goldberg and Goodman[31] examined the relationship between growth hormone and muscular work in rats. They suggested that growth hormone accelerates protein synthesis in muscle and that muscle size is independently determined by growth hormone. Growth hormone appears to act as a biochemical "amplifying system" for the anabolic machinery of a cell and it determines the absolute changes in muscle size which result from changes in muscular work. Bailey, et al.[7] have demonstrated that, in growing rats, exercise is probably one of the extrinsic factors influencing the number of cell nuclei. Thus it appears that the muscularity of a child at puberty is both a function of heredity (the number of muscle fibers) and exercise (the degree of hypertrophy of the fibers). Because exercise also produces protein in muscle, the assumption is that there is a form of feedback looping for active children such that there could be a positive correlation between activity as a child and stature as an adult. Since fiber growth up to puberty does not seem to be related to gender, the observation that the muscle fibers stopped growing in the girls in the Cheek study at the time they reached 130 cm may be related to significant reduction in exercise at that time.

The hormone most responsible for the changes in muscle fiber size from birth to maturity is the human growth hormone. Although adults still have a production of growth hormone from the pituitary gland, it is relatively slight and probably does not have a large interactive effect on muscular hypertrophy in the adult.[64]

It is well documented that in combination with human growth hormone, the sex hormones have an effect on adolescent stature. Since boys are, on the average, larger, with more cells and lean body mass, it is assumed that the androgen group of hormones has a larger effect on hypertrophy than does the estrogen group.

Nearly every tissue in the body is influenced to a certain degree in its development and function by the androgens.[49] The degree to which the respective tissues are affected is probably related to the chemical nature and proportion of the various androgens present in the body and also to the animal species. To have complete knowledge of the mechanism of action of androgen would require information about the sites of action, the nature of changes in specific tissue, the intermediary processes involved, and the mode of participation of the hormone. We lack such knowledge at present.

Although they act in different manners, growth hormone, androgen, estrogen, thyroid, and insulin act anabolically. Growth hormone and anabolic steroids both retain nitrogen but the anabolic steroid is more active in relation to the musculature of the body. Estrogens stimulate growth but mainly in relation to the female organs. In terms of nitrogen balance, androgens cause a positive balance, estrogens a natural balance, and progesterone a negative balance.[52] A positive balance results in protein anabolism and a negative balance in catabolism. Since catabolism is a protein destructive type mechanism, it could have an effect on the protein producing mechanisms to the point of neutralization.

It is known that androgens and anabolic steroids affect increased formation of tissue protein both genitally and extragenitally. In decreasing order of effectiveness anabolic steroids work best on castrated males, females, young males, middle-age males, and old males. Anabolic steroids are responsible for antiestrogenic activity in women.[52]

Laboratory animal studies have demonstrated that castration in the mouse, rat, and guinea pig resulted in a diminished rate of skeletal muscle growth of approximately 10 per cent.[50] After being treated with testosterone the muscles were able to reach normal size. Large doses of testosterone proprionate stimulated the growth of some muscles to slightly above normal.

Although a general decrease of 10 per cent was found in the muscle size of castrated animals, the results were somewhat different for rats and guinea pigs. The rats had a decrease of 10 per cent in virtually all muscles and the skin, while the guinea pigs had losses of about 10 per cent in most muscles but considerably more in others. Most of the muscle changes of the lower body in the guinea pig were in the 10 per cent range but the upper body muscles did not follow that pattern.[50] The muscles in the scapula and forearm regions were about 10 per cent smaller in the castrates, muscles in the chest, body wall and spine were 10 to 20 per cent smaller, muscles in the shoulder and back were 15 to 40 per cent smaller, and muscles in the head and neck were 20 to 45 per cent smaller.

Korner[51] studied the effect of an androgen which possessed protein anabolic activity but little androgenic activity on female rats of 4 months of age. The hormone caused some muscles to grow isometrically with the rest of the body, others to grow faster than the body, and yet others to lose weight and protein content despite the growth of the rat as a whole. The rats treated with the hormone gained 19.5 per cent of their initial body weight, while the controls gained 9.6 per cent. The diaphragm, heart, and quadriceps muscles grew approximately isometrically with the body as a whole, the acromiotrapezius grew faster than the body and the masseter grew more slowly. Of course, these changes are species specific but it does seem to indicate that hypertrophy due to androgen may not be uniform throughout the body. In the male guinea pigs of Kochakian and Tillotson and the female rats of Korner the muscles of the upper body appeared to be more affected by the administration of androgen than the muscles of the lower body.

According to the roentgenographic data of McCammon,[61] the muscle widths of girls and boys is similar at the maximum calf level and mid-femur level from birth through adolescence, while the width at the maximum forearm level increases in favor of the boys at about age 13.

Since the induction of anabolic steroids has accompanied some types of muscular hypertrophy,[50,51] athletes desiring an increased bulk have been taking various dosages and varieties of anabolic steroids without proper supervision. From the literature reported on increase in muscle mass due to administration of anabolic steroids to college-age males, the steroid group was substantially larger in one measurement, substantially smaller in one, and essentially neutral in the other four.[30,88] Since these studies used subjects on exercise programs and exercise is known to facilitate hypertrophy, the importance of anabolic steroids in causing hypertrophy may be overrated.

Since no studies have been conducted on the effect of androgens, either naturally occurring or added, on muscular hypertrophy in women, the hormonal relationship to bulk acquisition is largely conjectural. Brown and Wilmore[15] and Wilmore[99,101] postulate that muscle bulk is due primarily to the presence of the male hormone testosterone. Since women have much lower levels of testosterone, it has been concluded that they are probably not capable of achieving the same degree of hypertrophy as males. Harris[35] states that demands of exercise do not build muscle beyond its genetic and hormonal predisposition. Hormonal secretions of estrogen and androgen vary greatly among individuals resulting in tremendous variance in muscular development within the sexes as well as between the sexes and the implications of this observation have generally not been addressed in sport.

Since testosterone exerts a potent protein anabolic action and is responsible for the maintenance of muscle and bone tissue, Sutton, et al.[90] studied the serum androgen response to physical exercise. Their subjects were female and male swimmers of Olympic standard. All subjects exhibited significant rises in serum androgen level during maximal exercise, but there was no alteration in serum androgen level during submaximal exercise. This suggests that for serum androgen, as well as growth hormone,[89] the rise is related to the intensity of exercise.

There are probably three reasons why the capacity for muscular hypertrophy in the female has been ignored and discounted. (1) The female has relatively less muscle tissue available to undergo hypertrophy. (2) A high intensity of exercise which could cause hypertrophy has been absent in most women. (3) A liberal layer of adipose tissue can do much to obscure any hypertrophy which has occurred.

According to the estimate made by Cheek,[19] females on the average reach maturity with only two-thirds the number of muscle fibers as males. Total body potassium is used as an estimator of muscle tissue since muscle tissue has the highest potassium content of all tissue. In studies thus far, men have been found to have about 50 per cent of their fat-free weight in muscle. Women have 77 per cent of the male total body weight, 72 per cent of the male fat-free weight, and 60 per cent of the male potassium activity.[63] This implies that women have a lower concentration of potassium per fat-free weight. Two hypotheses are offered for the lower potassium ratio in women: either women also have 50 per cent of their body weight in muscle, but with a lower potassium concentration in the muscle or both women and men have similar potassium content for each type of tissue and women have a smaller proportion of muscle in their fat-free weight.

After a 10-week weight training program for college students, Wilmore[99] found that body weight remained stable over the training period but lean body weight increased 1.9 per cent in the women and 2.4 per cent in the men. Using the reported girth and skin-fold measurements at the upper arm, it can be estimated that the women had a muscle diameter hypertrophy of 2.51 mm., while the men had a hypertrophy of 2.33 mm. Although this is hardly enough actual change to cause excitement or concern, it does seem to indicate that women and men can expect similar results from intensive training.

There was a relative similarity between the sexes in leg muscle mass found by Wilmore. He suggests that the female has about the same opportunity as the male to exercise the legs in daily activity such as walking, standing, and climbing stairs. One could argue that the female is probably less active on her legs than the male on his but her relative addition of body fat gives her an overload effect, so she can perform less activity to maintain her muscle size. The fact that neither female nor male subjects were able to generate hypertrophy in the legs following a weight training program can be explained perhaps from a similar finding in laboratory animal studies. The work of Goldspink[32] suggests that muscles which are bimodal in fiber size seem less apt to hypertrophy than muscles which are unimodal. The rectus femoris and hamstring muscles in the human are naturally occurring bimodal muscles and as such would not be expected to demonstrate as much hypertrophy.

Although androgen production in the male at puberty is probably going to insure that the average male will reach adulthood with a larger stature than the average female,* we may reasonably conclude that the relative difference between the averages will diminish and the amount of overlap will increase with a changing cultural expectation of what connotes proper behavior in a young lady. It also seems that the woman who is inclined may undergo intensive training and produce muscular hypertrophy and combine it with a lower level of adiposity so hypertrophy can be seen.

Certainly the presence of sex hormones is a major factor in the ultimate growth of an individual, but the effects of exercise during

---

*Another predisposing factor would seem to be a genetic artifact of social mate-selection wherein the female consistently pairs with a taller male. Ed.

the growing years should also be emphasized. According to Malina,[57] exercise has a stimulating effect on the breadth of local bone tissue, the girth of skeletal muscle, and the linear growth of the upper extremity. Exercise regimens seem to have little if any effect on the total growth of long bones. Sex differences in adult height are due primarily to the fact that boys, on the average, are growing over a longer period of time than girls.[58]

The differences in bone width between girls and boys, illustrated by the data of McCammon, are possibly related to the lower activity level of the girls and differential affects on upper as compared to lower body. The boys have a slightly wider femur but this does not appear until the 15th year. At the maximum calf level the width of the boys' bones begins to exceed the girls' at about the tenth year but the difference is not large. The width of the forearm bones in the boys is greater than the girls' as early as the fourth year and continues to become greater through adolescence.

FITNESS—FOR DUTY AND SPORT

It should be the right of every citizen to have police officers who are physically fit. However, it is difficult to determine what constitutes physical fitness. According to the President's Council on Physical Fitness, it is "the ability to carry out daily tasks with vigor and alertness, without undue fatigue, and with ample energy to enjoy leisure time pursuits and to meet unforeseen emergencies."[76] Since this is quite general, several more measurable components have been suggested to comprise physical fitness. Among these are endurance, body composition, and task-specific components such as strength, flexibility, balance and agility. For most people the two most important facets of fitness are endurance and body composition. Neither a person who is lean but tires easily nor a person who is fat but can last through exercise would be considered to be physically fit. Because strength, flexibility, balance, and agility are infrequently necessary in daily tasks, they are not considered as important to physical fitness as endurance and body composition.

Endurance means using a system of the body under less than maximum stress for a continued period of time. The two primary types of endurance are muscular and cardiovascular. A carpenter would probably have a high muscular endurance in the muscles used in hammering but might not have a high level of cardiovascular endurance. A person who rides a bicycle to work would probably have good cardiovascular endurance but not necessarily enough muscular endurance in the arms to hammer for a continued period. Endurance is specific to the types of stresses which have been imposed and is highly related to the magnitude of those stresses.

An interesting finding was made by Bowie and Cumming[14] in regard to sustained hand-grip in girls and boys. Their subjects ranged in age from 13 to 17 and were asked to hold a hand-grip set at 40 per cent of their maximum gripping strength for as long as possible. The mean gripping time for the boys was 185 seconds, while the mean for the girls was 234 seconds. This seems in direct conflict with the opinion of Antonacci[2] that an all male police wall would be more efficient than a wall of women or a wall of women and men, largely because women were inferior in grip endurance.

The best indicator of cardiovascular endurance is the maximum amount of oxygen that can be supplied to working muscles. This maximum value is referred to as the maximum oxygen uptake or VO_2 max and is usually expressed relative to a person's body weight.

Until the age of 10 to 12 years, girls and boys have virtually identical VO_2 max values. However, by adulthood the average untrained male will have about 30 per cent higher VO_2 max than the average untrained female.[101]

This difference in maximum oxygen uptake should not be taken as proof that males are far superior to females in cardiovascular endurance. The lifestyle of females is much more sedentary than that of males and activity or lack of it can have an effect on VO_2 max values. For example, young female track athletes decreased their VO_2 max by 15.3 per cent after 3 months of inactivity.[24] Six weeks of cross country running increased the VO_2 max in female athletes by 18 per cent.[16]

To get a clearer picture of the actual differences in VO_2 max due to gender, comparisons are made using top level female and male cross country running and skiing athletes. A caution should be made about this type of comparison because distance events are not the same length for females and males and therefore, the type of training involved may be different. The longest race for women in the Olympics is 1500 m. and it was added in 1972. The men race the 1500 m. as well as 5000 and 10000 m. as well as the marathon distance of 26 miles and 385 yards. Since "distance" events for women have not been contested for many years, the performances are still undergoing rapid improvement. Just recently Kazankina of Russia became the first woman to break 4 minutes in 1500 m. when she ran a time of 3:56.0 which is the equivalent of a 4:15 mile.

According to Wilmore,[101] the difference in VO_2 max between the highest recorded value for a male distance runner and the highest value he recorded on a sample of female distance runners for the United States was about 12 per cent. When this difference was expressed relative to lean body mass the difference was only 3.4 per cent.

Since the VO_2 max values are much more divergent between trained and untrained women than between trained and untrained men, this is a probable indication that the sedentary female is much further from her potential than the sedentary male. Because of the newness of distance events for women, the trained female may also be below potential despite the fact that the average VO_2 max of trained females was found to be 25 per cent higher than that of untrained males.[38]

McGill and Luft[63] studied physical performance in relation to fat free weight in women and men. Their conclusion was that women were capable of performing the same maximal work as men relative to their fat free weight despite the fact that the fat free weight of women contains considerably less muscle tissue. They suggest that the efficiency during work by women might be due to a difference in energy metabolism or to a better blood supply.

Of the other facets of physical fitness, body composition has already been discussed and the task-specific components are relatively less important. For instance, Rasch and Burke[76] say that lack of flexibility can limit performance and voluntary correction of postural defects, but experimental evidence indicates that improvements in performance and posture do not result from increased flexibility nearly as often as has been generally supposed. They conclude that flexibility correlates with habitual movement patterns for each person and each joint and that age and sex differences are secondary rather than innate. Also they state that girls and women are more flexible, on the average, than males at the same age. An example of a sex difference is that most women can hyperextend the elbow. However, it should be noted that many gymnasts, weightlifters, and others who frequently perform complete forceful extensions can also hyperextend the joint.

Agility, another of the task-specific components of physical fitness, is generally considered to be the ability to change directions quickly. This item of fitness is highly regarded by the Philadelphia Police Department if their test of physical fitness is any indication. Their test for fitness consists of one item—an agility test. This skill is commonly referred to as a duck walk or waddle. Any male who can duck walk in a moderately straight line for 20 feet is considered to be physically fit enough to serve on sector patrol in Philadelphia. No part of this test involves quickness or direction changing.

Even more highly regarded by the Police Department than agility is the task-specific component of strength. Police Commission O'Neill has stated that a woman "is not as physically strong as a male" as if this renders all women incapable of the physical rigors of police work.

Strength is the capacity of an individual to exert force against some external resistance.[59] It is a necessary component in most athletic endeavors but it does not follow that the best performances are always made by the strongest performers. Strength can be expressed in two manners, relative and absolute. Absolute strength refers to the amount of external resistance that can be overcome by the muscle group involved. If the maximum weight a person could lift in a bench press were 150 pounds, then the absolute strength of the arm extensors would be 150 pounds. If two people with absolute arm extension strength of 150 pounds were desirous of supporting their weight in a hand stand, the person weighing 100 pounds might be able to do it, while the person weighing 200 pounds surely could not. In this example, the absolute strength is relative to the body weight of the individual, since it is being supported or moved. Tasks that involve projecting or supporting oneself are much more dependent on relative strength than absolute strength.

Stress causes certain changes in the chemistry and structure of the body. Some of these changes are signs of damage and others are manifestations of an adaptation reaction to stress. The principle of specific adaptation to imposed demands refers to the extreme adaptability demonstrated by the muscular system in response to stress. In order to develop strength, strength demands must be made on the body. There are many ways to do this in conditioning but the most efficient way is through weight training. According to Harris[35] strength demands do not build muscle beyond the genetic and hormonal predisposition to do so.

Several studies have reported the strength of women relative to men. This can be seen in Table 1. Although the decades and tech-

Table 1.   Absolute Strength

Type of Strength	Ratio, Women:Men	Source
General	.75–.80	Ufland[94]
	.67	Hettinger[40]
	.60	Hettinger[39]
	.60–.80	Astrand[6]
	.41–.50	Berger[10]
Size hel 1 constant	.80	Wyrick[106]
Upper Body	.52–.59	Willoughby[98]
Lower Body	.67	Willoughby[98]
Forearm Flexors	.55	Hettinger[40]
	.49–.53	Wilmore[99]
Finger Flexors	.60	Hettinger[40]
	.57–.61	Wilmore[99]
Hip Flexors & Extensors	.80	Hettinger[40]
	.73–.76	Wilmore[99]

niques of measurement are quite variable, there seems to be somewhat common agreement that the upper body of the female has about 50 to 60 per cent the strength of the male and the lower body has 70 to 80 per cent the strength of a male. When a correction is made for size, the female has about 80 per cent of the strength of a male. The only inconsistency in these reports seems to be with Berger. He reported a range of ratios for general strength when, in fact, his tests were only made on the upper body—push-ups, medicine ball put sitting, bench press, and chinning. The only information given about the subjects was that they were college age.

Another report made by Berger[11] also shows the female to have a much lower percentage of strength than the male with respect to other research. Figure 2 shows a contrast between the results of Berger and Wilmore.[99] The types and methods of testing are not necessarily the same. There are two striking differences observable in this figure. First, there seems to be a homogeneity of female scores and a heterogeneity in the male scores of both researchers. This might be explained by the fact that as a population approaches maximum potential a wider and wider spread among the scores is observed. This can be seen in tests of intellect as well as athletic performance and seems to indicate that there is little variability in mediocrity.

The second observation from Figure 2 is in the variation in the overlap of scores. In only one of the tests did the subjects of Berger overlap and this was a test that included the use of the legs. Although no range of scores was reported by Wilmore, the use of two standard deviations above and below the mean is a conservative estimate for the range. According to this type of treatment of the data, the scores of the females overlapped the scores of the male on every test and in three of the four tests, the mean of the females overlapped the males. The subjects in the Wilmore study were untrained college students. The subjects in the Berger study were police officers in Philadelphia, but absolutely no indication was given about how they were selected.

The previous comparisons have all been made with absolute strength. Comparing relative strength yields some interesting findings. Wilmore[99] found that when leg strength was expressed relative to body weight, the difference between the females and males was reduced to 7.6 per cent. Moreover, when leg strength was expressed relative to lean body weight, the females were 5.8 per cent stronger than the males.

Since there is a positive correlation between male hormone and muscle mass and since there is a positive correlation between strength and muscle mass, some people are supplementing their diets with large doses of male hormones in order to increase their strength.

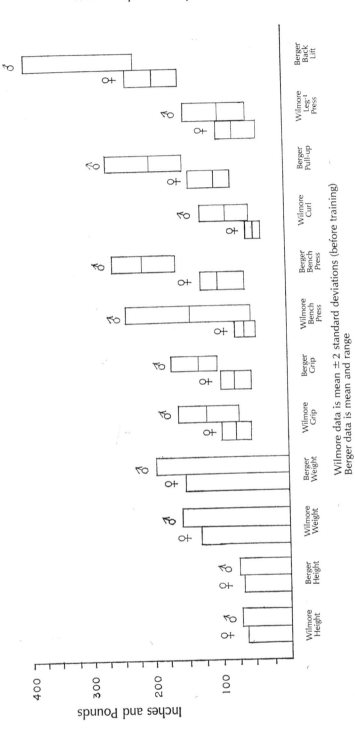

Fig. 2.

However, the relationship among male hormones, muscle mass, and strength is not clear. In three studies which involved male subjects receiving male hormone supplements during the time they followed an exercise regimen, Ward[96] found an increase in strength due to the hormone and Fahey and Brown[30] and Stromme, et al.[88] found no increase in strength by the hormone group over the control group. The latter two studies also measured change in muscle girth. They found changes in strength in the experimental and control groups with virtually no change in muscle girth or hypertrophy. This finding does not support the theory that strength and cross-sectional area of muscle fiber are dependent upon each other. Rather it indicates some psychological or neurological interaction.

An interesting study which attempted to elucidate some psychological or motivational factors in performance involved anabolic steroids. Ariel and Saville[4] informed their subjects (male varsity athletes who trained with weights) that the ones making the most improvement in strength over a 7-week training period would be allowed to take supplemental male hormones while they trained for another 4 weeks. Instead, the subjects were given a placebo. The results clearly indicate that although the subjects continued to improve during the preplacebo period, the improvement during the placebo period was significantly greater. Taking the placebo apparently supplied the necessary psychological benefits to facilitate strength gains above and beyond that which would be expected from a reasonable temporal progression.

Although the effect anabolic steroids have on strength acquisition is probably slight, the effect they have on reflex components of the nervous system may not be. Ariel and Saville[3] tested fractionated reflex time during a 4-week period in which the experimental group took daily dosages of Dianabol, an anabolic steroid. The experimental group showed an increase in reflex latency from 11.21 per cent to 19.74 per cent while the motor time dropped from 88.79 to 80.26 per cent. The mean motor time of 102.28 ms. was reduced to 66.33 ms. and caused a greatly reduced total reflex time. They concluded that the anabolic steroid acted on the central nervous system and the biochemical processes involved in the reflex.

Kochakian[49] has suggested that androgens change the system of cell permeability. A Russian team has found that the increasing muscle mass from compensatory hypertrophy lowered the calcium pump capacity of the sarcoplasmic reticulum.[71]

Burke et al.[17] were able to show a decrease in grip strength after the age of 30 which corresponds to the decline of 17-ketosteroid output in the male. Although the loss of strength could be caused by a reduction in androgen production, Espenschade and Eckert[29] postulate that this explanation would not account for a similar strength loss in women. They suggest that in ageing there is an increase in the amount of collagen filling up the spaces between the muscle fibers. Such "dead" material added to the muscle structures would tend to reduce the effective strength of the muscle.

Improvements in strength are made by applying strength demanding stressors to the muscular system. Although weight training is the best method known for making rapid gains in strength, activities such as sports, games, and dancing also apply stressors of varying intensities. In a hierarchical arrangement of strength production, people who participate in sports, games, or dance would be expected to fall between those who do not participate at all and those who do weight training. Conger and Macnab[21] were able to demonstrate in their study of female college students that the athletes were stronger than the non-athletes on a variety of measures. Since small and weak people tend to deselect themselves from athletic activity, large and strong people tend to predominate. It should be no surprise, then, that athletes are stronger than those who choose not to participate. However, Conger used athletes from the intercollegiate system of the middle sixties who might be characterized more by their interest than their skill. Her sample of athletes was not statistically different than the non-athletes on body weight and the athletes averaged 65 inches in height to the non-athletes 64 inches. It appears that the practice and playing of varsity sports helped make the athletes stronger than the non-athletes.

Wilmore[99] examined the increases in strength of untrained college females and males due to a weight training program. The subjects met twice a week for 40-minute periods for 10 weeks. Except in the curl where the females and males improved 10.6 and 18.9 per cent respectively, the women had greater improvements than the men. The women improved 12.8, 28.6, and 29.5 per cent, while the men improved 5.0, 16.5, and 26.0 per cent on grip strength, bench press, and leg press. It might also be noted that the final absolute value of the females on the leg press was similar to the initial value for the men.

Brown and Wilmore[15] analyzed the strength improvements made by five young females who were nationally ranked in throwing events of track and field. After 6 months of weight training their strength in the bench press improved by 15 to 44 per cent and in the half-squat by 16 to 53 per cent. The strength levels achieved by these athletes are much higher than any others reported. The bench press values ranged from 115 to 187 pounds and the half-squat from 215 to 575 pounds.

Since it has been clearly demonstrated that women have less strength on the average than men, several people are willing to speculate on the reasons. Willoughby[98] has an idea why women have 80 per cent of the muscle mass of men but can only bench press about half the weight of men. His three theories, none of which are supported in research, are that: (1) the oxygen carrying capacity of the blood in relation to the body weight is only 69 per cent as efficient in women; (2) the cross-sectional strength of muscle tissue is weaker in women; and (3) women receive a less powerful nervous stimulus.

Although the oxygen carrying capacity of blood is not as inferior in women as Willoughby would indicate, this capacity is of only secondary or even tertiary importance in strength. It is of primary importance in endurance or aerobic activities, but strength displays are anaerobic in nature and no replacement of oxygen is necessary during the task.

Ikai and Fukunaga[45] found no significant difference between the scores of females and males with respect to strength per cross-sectional area of muscle tissue. Morris[67] found that the women had 99 per cent of that of men on scores of cross-sectional area relative to leg strength. The subjects of Ikai and Fukunaga, adolescent and young adult Japanese females and males, demonstrated a slight but non-significant difference (92 per cent) in favor of the males on arm flexor strength per area. Morris found a difference of 78 per cent in favor of the males on arm flexion strength per area. This difference could be partially in technique of measurement. Ikai and Fukunaga used ultrasonic photography, while Morris used limb circumference corrected for subcutaneous fat and soft tissue radiography. Her percentages of area for each muscle were taken from cross-sectional tissue drawings of male cadavers.

Related studies involve correlating muscle girth, limb girth, or calculated cross-sectional area with strength produced by the associated muscle group. Rarick and Thompson[75] correlated calf muscle size (area and breadth) with ankle extensor strength in 7-year-old children. The correlations for the boys were .58 to .63, while the correlations for the girls were .22 to .52. They found that the size of the calf muscle was 5 per cent larger in the boys, but they had 13 per cent more strength than the girls. Royce[79] found low to moderate correlations of .24 to .65 for young adult males in calculated cross section of muscle to maximum strength. To examine the relationship between hypertrophy and strength, Wilmore[99] computed correlations between absolute strength and girth size. For the men the values ranged from .63 to .77 and for the women the values ranged from .09 to .42.

If subjects had equal motivation and equal training (and presumed efficiency in fiber firing), then there should be an almost perfect correlation between cross-sectional area of muscle and strength produced. The fact that the females have much lower correlations than the males may reflect both low levels of motivation and low levels of training. Wilmore[102] states that the changes taking place during strength acquisition are not presently clear. The traditional view was that hypertrophy was responsible for manifestations of higher levels of strength. He thinks this theory is inadequate in explaining how a 99-pound woman could lift an automobile off her son trapped underneath. His speculation is that strength may be a neurological phenomenon. Apparently athletes use less than 20 per cent of their fibers after training. Until we discover how to use 100 per cent of the muscle fibers available, it will be theoretically possible for a person with fewer fibers, trained to use a higher percentage of fibers, to match in strength a person with more fibers not trained to utilize them.

Hettinger[40] feels that the trainability of women is lower than of men. He says that with equal training stimulus men will increase more in strength and at a faster rate than women. According to the results of Wilmore,[99] the women were able to increase strength faster than the men on three of four measures. Though it is difficult to assess neural stimulus as Willoughby suggests, the response to training stimulus appears to be at least as favorable for women. The indication is that women and men can expect similar results from intensive training.

Wilmore feels that the quality of muscle is identical in females and males, i.e. the contractile properties and the ability to exert force. He attributes to use the similarities between the sexes in lower body strength when related to body size and attributes the differences in upper body strength to lack of use in the female. Since he assumes the muscles of the lower and upper body react in the same manner to training stimulus, he postulates that the female has the same potential for strength development as the male of comparable size.

There seem to be several factors preventing females from being as strong as males in the upper extremity—even when the most favorable modes of comparison are used. When considering an "average woman," the lack of shoulder development at puberty creates a situation in which producing force from the arms is more problematic from a biomechanical standpoint. Cultural expectations diminish the chance an average girl has of using her arms and shoulders as early as the fifth year. Girls and women are conditioned not to display strength. There is evidence that through puberty muscles grow first in size and later in strength.[29] Since strength is somewhat dependent on appropriate practice and the adolescent environment ridicules practice for girls, this period has probably the most profound impact on the lack of strength in most women. Most women reach adulthood without ever having done much work with their upper bodies; men seem to have much more experience. This would appear to have a great effect on adult size and strength.

Willoughby[98] states that the performance of women is less than that of men because the women receive a less powerful nervous stimulus, but the responsiveness of the neuromuscular system is not measured by strength of stimulus. Instead, reaction time and movement time are used. Reaction time is the length of time it takes an individual to perceive a stimulus and initiate a response to it. Movement time refers to the speed with which an individual can move a limb through space, irrespective of reaction time. With the use of electromyographic equipment, reaction time can be split or fractionated into pre-motor and motor reaction times. The pre-motor phase starts with the stimulus and ends with the first sign of electrical activity in the muscle to be used. The motor reaction time is the time from the onset of electrical activity in the muscle until the muscle has built up enough contractile force to start the limb moving. Historically, reaction time studies have not used the fractionating technique so when differences are discovered, there is no indication of which phase, if either, is more responsible for the differences.

Sportswomen have been found to have faster reaction times than non-sportswomen.[105,107] Scarborough[81] found physically active women to have faster discriminatory reaction times than women who were not physically active. Varsity intercollegiate athletes had significantly faster movement times than women who were non-athletes.[107,108] In comparisons between females and males who were not athletes, the trend is for the males to be none to slightly faster in reaction time and none to dramatically faster in movement time.[37,41,44,91] Unfortunately, comparisons of reaction and motor times of sportswomen and sportsmen have not been made. The indications are that people who are active have a quicker response in movement and also a quicker motor reaction time. The differences found between women and men appear to be more a function of activity level than gender.

MECHANICAL FACTORS

There are several biomechanical factors which can influence performance. Among these are mass, moment of inertia, limb length, and center of gravity. These parameters affect the production of force, velocity, and acceleration which, in turn, influence throwing, kicking, running and virtually all types of movement. Although a person has definite structural limitations, these biomechanical factors can be manipulated in various ways to produce a wide range of performances.

It is almost impossible to dichotomize these factors due to gender. In general, women will have less mass, smaller moments of inertia, shorter limbs, and lower centers of gravity, but these characteristics overlap considerably between the sexes. A heavy person with short arms could be either a female or a male.

Because people have been willing to extrapolate characteristics of the average person to all persons, there are some misconceptions with regard to how biomechanical factors influence performance. An example of this involves center of gravity. The center of gravity is an imaginary point within the body at which the weight of the body is said to be balanced or concentrated. The location of the center of gravity helps to determine balance; lowering the center of gravity improves balance. According to Cotton[23] the location of the center of gravity in the average man is 56.7 per cent of his height above ground and for the average woman, it is 56.1 per cent of her height. This difference of 0.6 per cent has been given as the reason females have better balance. If the center of gravity of an average female and an average male of the same height were computed, the difference would be less than half an inch. This is probably not enough to make a critical difference in balance in favor of the female, especially when considerations are taken for mass and base of support. Since heavier objects have more stability and objects with large bases of support have more stability, it is quite possible to theorize that the male should possess better balance due to more mass and bigger feet.

It has been suggested that women who participate in the high jump should not use the Fosbury Flop (backward, headfirst) method because their center of gravity is too low. The implication was that women should jump feet first because their mass was concentrated in that end of their body. Although there are no reports on the location of the center of gravity in female and male athletes, there is no reason to believe that the results found in average females and males would be radically different from those found in athletes. If the center of gravity is 56 per cent of the standing height above the ground, that means the mass is concentrated in the upper half of the body. Since the location of the center of gravity is similar in females and males, there seems to be no justification in advocating one style of jumping for one gender and a different style for the other.

Another misconception concerning jumping is the idea that men can "hang in the air" and women cannot. Regardless of the definition of "hang in the air", this is analogous to saying tennis balls can hang in the air and baseballs cannot. Any object which is projected upwards slows down until it reaches an instantaneous stop and then picks up speed as it returns earthward. Since the object is traveling slowly near the high point, it seems to be almost motionless or to "hang in the air". Regardless of how high an object is projected, the time spent within 3 inches of the high point, or the time when the object appears to hang in the air, is 0.25 seconds. While it may be true that many men can jump higher than many women, the time spent hanging in the air will be 0.25 seconds for persons of either gender.

An expert witness for the City of Philadelphia stated that males would show greater ability in jumping over an obstacle while giving chase to a law breaker.[2] This was predicated on the lower center of gravity and less muscle strength of the female. While neither of these facts are denied, their marginality should be emphasized. A difference in center of gravity of one half inch is unlikely to be a determining factor in obstacle jumping. According to Wilmore[99] the relative leg strength of females is 7.6 per cent less than males and the relative strength to lean mass is 5.8 per cent greater. Muscle strength might prove the difference in an obstacle jumping contest but probably not in common chases.

The moment of inertia, or resistance to rotary movement, is an important quantity in performance. It is a linear function of mass and a quadratic function of distance of mass distribution from the axis of rotation. Virtually all movement is composed of sequences of rotary motion of body segments around the joints. These rotations cannot occur until the muscles are able to generate enough force to overcome the inertia, or resistance to movement, of the limbs. Speed of movement is also influenced by moment of inertia. For the speediest movement, the mass should be distributed as close as possible to the axis of rotation or joint. Women have one advantage and two disadvantages with respect to moment of inertia. Generally, the limbs of females are shorter than males. Since the resistance to movement is squared due to distance of mass, people with short limbs have less inertia to overcome, provided the mass is smaller. The disadvantages are somewhat correctable. Adding mass to a limb increases its inertia. Females tend to carry more fat than males and much of this is distributed in the limbs. Since the fat is not contributing to move the limb but rather retards the movement, having less fat facilitates movement. Speed of movement is also a function of strength. Having a low moment of inertia is of no advantage if the strength is also low. Therefore, speed of movement could be improved considerably by reducing fat deposits and undergoing strength training.

In skills which involve projecting an object, such as throwing or kicking, the velocity of projection is equally dependent on the speed of the body segment and the length of the body segment. Of course, coordinating the segment is of critical importance. If coordination were held constant, a person with a shorter limb would have to have greater speed of movement to achieve the same projection velocity as a person with a longer limb. Few comparisons have been made between women and men, but the results seem to indicate that men have higher limb velocities and accelerations and also higher projection velocities. A person with short, fat weak arms will not be good at throwing. A person with short, lean, strong arms and coordination from practice might be good at throwing.

Skills which involve contact, such as hitting a pitched ball or golf ball, are dependent on momentum. Mass and velocity are equal contributors to momentum. Thus a light object must be traveling faster to cause the same results as a heavier object. Light people must also travel faster for equivalent results when the body contributes to the performance.

Biomechanics, the study of the application of mechanical principles to human movement, is related to kinanthropometry, the study of human movement having to do with the measurement of size, shape, proportion, composition, maturation, and gross function. The easiest way to relate biomechanics and kinanthropometry is through sports because it is possible to evaluate performance in this area.

At the championship level, several factors such as skill, training, opportunity, motivation, and intelligence must be at near optimal levels. Some sports, particularly those with a highly specific and rigid biomechanical demands, seem to require specific prerequisites of physique.

From their analysis of male competitors in several events at the Mexico City Olympics (1968), Hebbelinck and Ross[36] found highly significant differences among the sports on the anthropometric variables of height, weight, arm length, leg length, biacromial breadth, and biiliocristal breadth. They concluded that there were unique characteristics associated with various events. This can be seen for both females and males in Table 2. The gymnasts and divers are smaller and lighter than the swimmers, canoers, and sprinters and the weight throwers are taller and heavier.

Not only are there pronounced size differences between sports, but even within a given sport classification, absolute size is often associated with success. In the highly select company of Olympic competitors the finalists, medalists, and winners tend to be systematically taller and heavier than their peers in the sprints, hurdles, jumping events and throwing events.[68]

According to Hebbelinck and Ross,[36] secular trends such as differing genetic pools of talent, changing technique, and differing opportunity for participation may have an effect on the stature of the competitors. In comparing the male athletes of 1928 with modern male athletes, the modern athletes are taller in events in which height has a biomechanical advantage, the modern athletes are both taller and heavier

Table 2.   Anthropometric Comparisons of Participants in Mexico City Olympics (1968)

		Ht.	Wt.	Arm Length	Leg Length	Trunk Length	Biacromial	Biiliocristal
Gymnasts	♀	157	50	52.3	72	47.5	35.2	25.5
	♂	167 .94*	62 .81	55.7 .94	76.5 .94	50.6 .94	40.0 .88	26.7 .96
Divers	♀	160	52	53.4	74.5	48	36.5	26.5
	♂	172 .93	65 .80	58.5 .91	79 .94	51.3 .94	40.2 .91	27.4 .97
Swimmers	♀	164	57	55.3	76	49.5	37.2	27.0
	♂	179 .92	72 .79	60.6 .91	82 .93	53.5 .93	41.2 .90	28.1 .96
Canoers	♀	163	61	54.2	75.5	49.3	38	27.8
	♂	178 .92	74 .82	60.6 .89	83 .91	52.8 .93	41.7 .91	28.9 .96
Sprinters	♀	165	56	55.3	77.5	49	36.8	26.2
	♂	175 .94	68 .82	60.4 .92	82.5 .94	51.6 .95	40.3 .91	26.7 .98
Weight Throwers	♀	171	73	56.3	80	51.4	38.4	30.0
	♂	187 .91	103 .71	64.0 .88	86.5 .92	57.2 .90	44.6 .86	30.6 .98

* Female to male ratio

in events in which both are advantageous, and there is no trend for height in events in which increased height has no biomechanical advantage, such as gymnastics. Another trend is for both female and male swimmers to be leaner than their earlier counterparts.

Shape, or the outer morphological configuration, appears to be a selective factor in many sports. However, size and shape together may be of prime importance in the biomechanical interpretation of various sports performances. Although there are often proportional differences which can give mechanical advantages in performance, Hebbelinck and Ross suggest that absolute size is far more important biomechanically than proportions are. Carter[18] states that champion performers at various levels of a given sport exhibit similar patterns of body size and somatotype, with patterns tending to become narrower as the levels of performance increase.

At the elite level there is a high degree of similarity in proportions of all the competitors in a given event. When height and weight benefit performance, there is a high positive correlation between size and success. It is interesting to compare the proportions of the average female with the average male in several Olympic events. Table 2 shows an extreme similarity between the participants in each event. The measurements of length are particularly consistent. Consider the case of the gymnasts: in height, arm length, leg length, and trunk length the females are 94 per cent of the size of the males. There is a slightly different trend in the width measurements. Across all sports the biacromial width of the females is about 90 per cent that of the males and the biiliocristal width is about 97 per cent. Therefore, in terms of proportions the females are slightly smaller but almost identical to the male competitors in their event. The most striking difference is in weight; the females weigh only 80 per cent of the weight of the males.

Given the pattern of increases in the stature of the participants in many events over the years, it will be interesting to follow the secular trends with relation to females to see if their size changes as a function of increased opportunity to participate. Perhaps alternative techniques will be developed which will favor anatomical structures which are not replicas of the classical mold. It is possible that a "new classical model" could be a shape which is more commonly identified with females than with males.

The Olympic events which have been analyzed are rather narrow in the variety of talents that are necessary to the performance. Some require strength and balance, others require force production or velocity. As the specificity of the task increases, the size range of successful performers decreases. In activities which have widely varying demands and the constant application of interactive strategy, the size of the participants is not confined to a specific model. Tennis, for example, involves many types of movements and strategies, and the size of championship players ranges from Billie Jean King and Ken Rosewall to Margaret Court and Stan Smith. Presumably the demands of police work would be better compared to tennis and variety rather than shot putting and narrowness. If so, the size of police officers should not need to be fixed at the arbitrary level of 67 inches and 140 pounds.

Although this size standard set for police officers is probably intended to prevent physically inadequate people from holding potentially dangerous jobs of protection, it can be ridiculously exclusive of both males and females. No one would dispute that Olympic weight lifters possess the strength to be beat patrol officers but many would be excluded from this job by virtue of their height. For instance, Phil Gripaldi has been the most consistent world class lifter for the United States in the early seventies. His weight is 198 pounds but his height is less than 67 inches. Another man who might be adequate for police tasks is Joe Bost, the 1976 Eastern Collegiate Grand Champion in Judo. Although Bost won his title by besting a man standing 6 feet 6 inches tall and weighing 376 pounds, he is too small to be a police officer (by Philadelphia standards) since he weighs 139 pounds and stands 5 feet 3 inches.[56]

PERFORMANCE

Women have been prevented from becoming beat patrol officers in Philadelphia in the past because they have not challenged the city on its size standard and in the present because the city presumes they cannot perform police-oriented tasks. The belief of the city, relative to performance ability of women, is reflected by the statement of the counselor for Philadelphia, who said, "Nobody says that women can't perform to some degree. But they can't safely and efficiently perform."[82] If some studies indicate that women were poor performers, the question becomes why? Is this really a genetic necessity?

According to nationally administered fitness tests, girls and boys have virtually the same scores in running and jumping until about the age of 12.[29] Laboratory and field tests indicate that American girls seem to reach peak performances in strength at about the age of 12.5.[5,83] After the age of 12, boys continue to improve, while girls tend to plateau or actually decrease their skill. The diminishing scores of the girls signals a life-long physical decline that does not occur in males until the age of 22 to 25.[65]

Because of this performance peak in average 12-year-old girls, many prominent people have selected the age of 12 as the point at which physical capacities are maximized for females. An example of the trend to youthful record setters is the fact that the average age of the American female swimmers was 15½ years in the 1964 Olympics.[92] According to Klafs and Lyon

> "The constant setting of new records and top-level performances by very young girls indicate what exercise physiologists, supported by many reputable studies, have long maintained that girls 12-15 years old are at their physiological peak and are both socially and psychologically more trainable than at any other time. Certainly the current record-breaking spree helps bear out this contention."[39]

Harris[35] indicates, in disagreement with the youthful peak theory, that half the finalists in the 1952 Olympics were married and had children, many were over the age of 35, and at least two were grandmothers! Although many precocious athletes compete internationally at young ages, few who continue training reach their peaks in their early teens. Madeline Manning Jackson set the American record for the 800 m. run in 1976 at the age of 28. Martha Watson competed in the long jump in her fourth Olympic games in 1976. Irena Szewinska, a 30-year-old Polish wife and mother, set a world and Olympic record in the 400 m. dash at the Montreal Olympics. Swimmers have tended to be younger than runners but the two most successful American women swimmers in Montreal were Shirley Babashoff, 19, and Wendy Boglioli, 21.

One reason girls seem to reach peaks in performance around the twelfth year is that this is also the age of menarche for many girls. Wilmore[101] suggests that this imparts pressure to stop running around and to start becoming a young lady. Rather than a physiological phenomenon, he sees it as an artifact of social or cultural restrictions imposed on females.

This argument for the diminution of activity and subsequent drop in performance due to social and cultural factors operating relative to menarche has some support. If girls had individual pressure to modify their play activities as they reached the age of menarche, then one would expect late maturing girls to be better performers. Espenschade[28] found girls who were later in maturing to be superior physical performers. Females competing in a national collegiate track and field championship were found to have reached menarche 1.35 years later on the average than a group of non-athletic controls.[60] According to a study of Hungarian athletes and non-athletes, there was no difference in the two groups in the age of menarche.[26]

Although these studies merely show a relationship between maturity and performance, not cause and effect, it is interesting to note that the relationship for males is exactly the opposite. Good performance in males is linked to early maturity.[60] In noting this reversal between the role of maturity in the performance of girls and boys, the researchers advance two possible theories—one cultural and one anthropometric. Culturally they recognize the tendency for girls to date rather than play games after menarche. But they also suggest the anthropometric argument that body composition changes occur at menarche that would hinder successful performance. This would mean that the last girls to undergo changes would be the most successful and, therefore, encouraged to continue in sports. According to Malina[59] early maturity is linked to endomorphy in girls and mesomorphy in boys. Since most tests of performance tend to favor mesomorphs the most and endomorphs the least, there is credence in the anthropometric argument. However, enough women make dramatic improvements in performance after the early teens to suggest that cultural and social restrictions also play a large part in creating the false adolescent peak in performance.

Since existing evidence indicates that females in general become inferior to males in general in the performance of physical tasks after the age of 12, the questions become how inferior the females are and how much of this gap is necessary. As new attitudes are adopted, more females will have the opportunity to participate on a rigorous level and close the gaps that now exist in performance.

To make fair comparisons of performance, events or skills need to be chosen that have equivalence in training, motivation, equipment, and structural composition. For these reasons, Olympic swimming, running, and jumping should be the best available. The differences in times and distances and the percentage of comparison between females and males for the 1968 and 1976 Olympics are given in Tables 3 and 4. From Table 3 it can be seen that in each of the swimming strokes the women compared more favorably as the distance becomes longer. Wyrick[105] suggests this may be partially due to the better buoyancy of females. Except for the shorter butterfly and longer freestyle and breast stroke, the best female time was 88 to 89 per cent of the best male time. The most favorable comparison was 91.6 per cent. The running events showed a reversal in trend from the swimming in that the comparison was weaker as the distances became longer. The jumping ratios were considerably worse than the swimming and running.

In looking at the swimming results in Table 4, it can be seen that the event with the most favorable comparison in 1968, the 200 m. breast stroke, has become the worst of 1976. Most of the other strokes show ratios over 90 per cent with a high of 93.2 per cent in the 400 m. individual medley. All five of the running events show comparisons in the 90 to 91 per cent range. Even the jumping event ratios made improvement from the 1968 results.

Table 3. Performance Ratios in Mexico City Olympics (1968)

Event		♀	♂	♀ / ♂ %
Freestyle	100*	1:00.0	52.8	88.0
	200	2:10.5	1:55.2	88.3
	400	4:31.8	4:09.0	91.6
Breaststroke	100	1:15.8	1:07.7	89.3
	200	2:42.4	2:28.7	91.6
Butterfly	100	1:05.5	55.9	85.3
	200	2:24.7	2:08.7	88.9
Backstroke	100	1:06.2	58.7	88.7
	200	2:24.9	2:09.6	89.4
Track	100	11.0	9.9	90.0
	200	22.5	19.8	88.0
	400	52.0	43.8	84.2
	800	2:00.9	1:45.4	87.2
Field	High Jump	5'11⅝"	7'4¼"	81.2
	Long Jump	22'4½"	29'2½"	76.6

From Klafs & Lyon[48] p. 50.
*Olympic events are in meters

Table 4. Performance Ratios in Montreal Olympics (1976)

Event		♀	♂	♀ / ♂ %
Freestyle	100*	55.65	49.99	89.8
	200	1:59.26	1:50.29	92.5
	400	4:09.29	3:51.93	92.8
Breaststroke	100	1:10.86	1:03.11	89.1
	200	2:33.35	2:15.11	88.1
Butterfly	100	1:00.13	54.35	90.4
	200	2:11.41	1:59.23	90.7
Backstroke	100	1:01.83	55.49	89.7
	200	2:13.43	1:59.19	89.3
IM	400	4:42.77	4:23.68	93.2
Track	100	11.01	10.06	91.4
	200	22.37	20.23	90.4
	400	49.29	44.26	89.8
	800	1:54.94	1:43.50	90.0
	1500	4:02.13	3:36.87	89.6
Field	High Jump	6'3¾"	7'4½"	85.6
	Long Jump	22'2½"	27'4¾"	81.1

*Olympic events are in meters

Table 5. Comparisons of Best Times by Country in Montreal Olympics (1976)

Event		USA ♀	USA ♂	USA % ♀/♂	GDR ♀	GDR ♂	GDR % ♀/♂
Freestyle	100	56.81*	49.99‡	88.0	55.65‡	53.93	96.9
	400	4:10.46*	3:51.93‡	92.6	4:09.89‡	4:02.20	96.9
Backstroke	100	1:06.01	55.49‡	84.1	1:01.83†	57.22	92.6
	200	2:17.27*	1:59.19‡	86.8	2:13.43‡	2:08.02	96.0
Butterfly	100	1:01.17*	54.35	88.9	1:00.13‡ tie	55.09	91.6
	200	2:12.90	1:59.23‡	89.7	2:11.41†	2:00.02	91.3

* American record
† Olympic record
‡ World record

The trend of improvement in the 400 m. freestyle has been dramatic. In the 1924 Olympics the winning time for men was 16 per cent faster than for women. In 1948 the difference was reduced to 11.6 per cent and in 1972 the world records differed by only 7.3 per cent.[100] Don Schollander won the race in the 1964 Olympics in 4:12.2 which would have been fast enough in 1976 for the bronze medal in the women's race![47]

Although the females have gained in comparison to the males over the years, the extent to which these gains can continue is unknown. A valid comparison should only be made in situations where the training and coaching opportunities are equal. As of now the opportunities for females and males in swimming, for instance, have not been comparable. In looking at Table 5, it can be seen that the best times for the American women at Montreal were almost all American records, but they were almost all in the high eighties in percent difference. A more equitable comparison might be made between the female and male swimmers from East Germany. That country has made a concerted effort to produce gold medalists and their training and coaching methods seem to be quite comparable for their females and males.[46] From Table 5 the best times for the East German females and males at the 1976 Olympics show the women to be in the 91 to 93 per cent range for some races but also as high as 96 per cent (once) and 97 per cent (twice) in other races. Therefore, it is probably premature to select an upper limit for comparisons between females and males in performance.

Actually, there are some running and swimming events which seem to favor women. When races extend beyond 2 hours women seem able to make up the difference and as the time becomes longer, they even begin to excel. The best time recorded for swimming the English Channel was broken twice in 1976 by two different women. Tina Bischoff swam it in 9 hours 3 minutes[86] and then Wendy Brook swam it in 8 hours and 56 minutes.[87] The best times for both the 50 mile run[42] and 50 mile swim were recorded by women.[97] Natalie Cullimore has won the Amateur Athletic Union open supermarathon run of 100 miles.[65]

Since it can be demonstrated that women can compare quite favorably with men on rigorous tasks, it is presumed that they could also compare favorably on the less rigorous tasks performed by police officers. If the criteria for selection to the police force becomes a Police Officer Olympics, then probably there would be a large portion of men on the force. But if the criteria is such that all people who can perform the duties are eligible, then there should be no automatic limitation on women serving as police officers.

Similarly, in traditional sports which require great size and strength, those people who are larger and stronger (predominantly males) will continue to have an advantage. Many non-traditional, recreational, and competitive sports depend on assets which are not based on size and strength. Success in these events could result from such factors as training, coaching, motivation, and strategy.

REFERENCES

1. Adrian, M.: Sex differences in biomechanics. in *Women in Sport: A National Research Conference.* D. V. Harris, ed. University Park, Pennsylvania State University Press, 1972.
2. Antonacci, R. J.: Analysis of teaching the body-contact skills and its probability of success and performance between men and women during the process of subduing a male. Unpublished study, Temple University, 1976.
3. Ariel, G. and W. Saville: The effect of anabolic steroids on reflex components. *Medicine and Science in Sports, 4,* 120, 1972.
4. Ariel, G. and W. Saville: Anabolic steroids: the physiological effects of placebos. *Medicine and Science in Sports, 4,* 124, 1972.
5. Asmussen, E.: Growth in muscular strength and power. in *Physical Activity: Growth and Development,* G. L. Rarick, ed. New York, Academic Press, 1973.
6. Astrand, P. O.: Human physical fitness with special reference to sex and age. *Physiol. Reviews, 36,* 307, 1956.
7. Bailey, D. A., R. D. Bell and R. E. Howarth: The effect of exercise on DNA and protein synthesis in skeletal muscle of growing rats. *Growth, 37,* 323, 1973.
8. Behnke, A. R. and J. H. Wilmore: *Evaluation and Regulation of Body Build and Composition.* Englewood Cliffs, New Jersey, Prentice-Hall, Inc., 1974.
9. Bellis, C. J.: Reaction time and chronological age. *Soc. Exper. Med. Proc. 30,* 801, 1932-1933.
10. Berger, R. A.: Comparison between college age females and males on strength and power. Unpublished study, Temple University, 1974.
11. Berger, R. A.: Comparison between female and male police officers on muscle strength. Unpublished study, Temple University, 1975.
12. Bilhuber, G.: The effect of functional periodicity on the motor ability of women in sports. Master's thesis, University of Michigan, 1927.
13. Bowden, D. H. and R. A. Goyer: The size of muscle fibers in infants and children. *Arch. Path. 69,* 188, 1960.
14. Bowie, W. and G. R. Cumming: Sustained handgrip in boys and girls: variation and correlation with performance and motivation to train. *Res. Quart. 43,* 131, 1972.
15. Brown, C. H. and J. H. Wilmore: The effects of maximal resistance training on the strength and body composition of women athletes. *Medicine and Science in Sports, 6,* 174, 1974.
16. Brown, C. H., J. R. Harrower, and M. F. Deeter: The effects of cross country running on pre-adolescent girls. *Medicine and Science in Sports, 4,* 1, 1972.
17. Burke, W. E., W. W. Tuttle, C. W. Thompson, C. D. Janney, and R. J. Weber: The relation of grip strength and grip-strength endurance to age. *J. Applied Physiol., 5,* 628, 1953.
18. Carter, J. E. L.: The somatotype of athletes—a review. *Human Biology, 42,* 535, 1970.
19. Cheek, D. B.: *Human Growth: Body Composition, Cell Growth, Energy and Intelligence.* Philadelphia, Lea & Febiger, 1968.
20. Chiakulas, J. J. and J. E. Pauly: A study of postnatal growth of skeletal muscle in the rat. *Anat. Record, 152,* 55, 1965.

21. Conger, P. R. and R. B. J. Macnab: Strength, body composition, and work capacity of participants and non-participants in women's intercollegiate sports. *Res. Quart., 38,* 184, 1967.
22. Corbitt, R. W., D. L. Cooper, D. J. Erickson, F. C. Kriss, M. L. Thornton, T. T. Craig: Female athletics: a special communication from the committee on the medical aspects of sports of the American Medical Association. *J. Physical Education and Recreation, 46,* 45, 1975.
23. Cotton, F. S.: Center of gravity in man. *Amer. J. Phy. Anthropol., 18,* 401, 1933.
24. Drinkwater, B. L. and S. M. Horvath: Detraining effects on young women. *Medicine and Science in Sports, 4,* 91, 1972.
25. Edwards, L. F.: *Concise Anatomy,* 2nd Ed. New York, McGraw-Hill Book Co., 1956.
26. Erdelyi, G. J.: Gynecological survey of female athletes. *J. Sports Medicine and Physical Fitness, 2,* 174, 1962.
27. Erdelyi, G. J.: Women in Athletics. Paper presented at American Medical Association 2nd National Conference on the Medical Aspects of Sports. Chicago, 1971.
28. Espenschade, A. S.: Motor performance in adolescence including the study of relationships with measures of physical growth and maturity. *Monograph of Social Research in Child Development, 5,* 1, 1940.
29. Espenschade, A. S. and H. M. Eckert: *Motor Development.* Columbus, Ohio, Charles E. Merrill, 1967.
30. Fahey, T. D. and C. H. Brown: The effects of an anabolic steroid on the strength, body composition, and endurance of college males when accompanied by a weight training program. *Medicine and Science in Sports, 5,* 272, 1973.
31. Goldberg, A. L. and H. M. Goodman: Relationship between growth hormone and muscular work in determining muscle size. *J. Physiol. 200,* 655, 1969.
32. Goldspink, G.: The proliferation of myofibrils during muscle fiber growth. *J. Cell Science, 6,* 593, 1970.
33. Goldspink, G. and K. F. Howells: Work-induced hypertrophy in exercised normal muscles of different ages and the reversibility of hypertrophy after cessation of exercise. *J. Physiol., 239,* 179, 1974.
34. Hale, C. J.: Affidavit, Docket No. AJ05SB–0493, State of New Jersey, Department of Law and Public Safety, Division of Civil Rights, No. 12, p. 4.
35. Harris, D. V.: Conditioning for stress in sports. Paper presented at the Sixth Annual Symposium, Medical Aspects of Sports. New York, 1973.
36. Hebbelinck, M. and W. D. Ross: Kinanthropometry and biomechanics. in *Biomechanics IV,* R. C. Nelson and C. A. Morehouse, eds. Baltimore, University Park Press, 1974.
37. Henry, F. M.: Influence of motor and sensory sets on reaction latency and speed of discrete movements. *Res. Quart., 31,* 448, 1960.
38. Hermansen, L. and K. L. Anderson: Aerobic work capacity in young Norwegian men and women. *J. Applied Physiol., 20,* 425, 1965.
39. Hettinger, T.: Muskelkraft und muskeltraining bei frauen und männern. *Arbeitsphysiology, 15,* 201, 1953.
40. Hettinger, T.: *Physiology of Strength.* Springfield, Charles C Thomas, 1961.
41. Hodgkins, J.: Reaction time and speed of movement in males and females of various ages. *Res. Quart., 34,* 335, 1963.
42. Horvath, S. M.: Effects of exercise. *Science, 184,* 977, 1974. 1958–1965. *J. Health, Physical Education, and Recreation, 47,* 23, 1966.
43. Hunsicker, P. A. and G. G. Reiff: A survey and comparison of youth fitness: 1958–1965. *J. Health, Physical Education, and Recreation, 37,* 23, 1966.
44. Ikai, M.: Work capacity of the Japanese related to age and sex. *J. Sports Medicine and Physical Fitness, 6,* 100, 1966.
45. Ikai, M. and T. Fukunaga: Calculation of muscle strength per unit cross-

sectional area of human muscle by means of ultrasonic measurement. *Internationale zeitschrift für angewandte physiologie einschliesslich arbeitsphysiologie, 26, 26,* 1968.

46. Kirshenbaum, J.: Assembly line for champions. *Sports Illustrated, 45,* 57, July 12, 1976.

47. Kirshenbaum, J.: Theirs was a Midas stroke. *Sports Illustrated, 45,* 18, Aug. 2, 1976.

48. Klafs, C. C. and M. J. Lyon: *The Female Athlete: Conditioning, Competition, and Culture.* St. Louis, C. V. Mosby Co., 1973.

49. Kochakian, C. D.: Mechanisms of androgen actions. *Lab. Investig., 8,* 538, 1959.

50. Kochakian, C. D. and C. Tillotson: Influence of several C_{19} steroids on the growth of individual muscles of the guinea pig. *Endocrinol., 60,* 607, 1957.

51. Korner, A.: The influence of methylandrostenediol on the protein fractions and adenosinetriphosphatase activity of muscles of the rat. *J. Endocrinol., 13,* 90, 1955.

52. Kruskemper, H. L.: *Anabolic Steroids.* New York, Academic Press, 1968.

53. Larson, R. L. and R. O. McMahon: The epiphyses and the childhood athlete. *JAMA, 196,* 607, 1966.

54. Lee, M.: The case for and against intercollegiate athletes for women and the situation as it stands to-day. *APER, 29,* 13, 1924.

55. Lockhart, R. D., G. F. Hamilton and F. W. Fyfe: *Anatomy of the Human Body.* Philadelphia, J. B. Lippincott Co., 1965.

56. Lyon, B.: Big belt fits a little man. *Philadelphia Inquirer,* July 1, 1976, p. C-1.

57. Malina, R. M.: Exercise as an influence upon growth: Review and critique of current concepts. *Clinical Pediatrics, 8,* 16, 1969.

58. Malina, R. M.: Adolescent Changes in Size, Build, Composition and Performance. *Human Biology, 46,* 117, 1974.

59. Malina, R. M.: Anthropometric correlates of strength and motor performance. in *Exercise and Sport Sciences Reviews,* Vol. 3, J. H. Wilmore and J. F. Keogh, eds. New York, Academic Press, 1975.

60. Malina, R. M., A. B. Harper, H. H. Avent and D. F. Campbell: Physique of female track and field athletes. *Medicine and Science in Sports, 3,* 32, 1971.

61. McCammon, R. W.: *Human Growth and Development.* Springfield, Charles C Thomas, 1970.

62. McCloy, C. H.: A stuly of landing shock in jumping for women. *Arbeitsphysiologie. 5,* 100, 1931.

63. McGill, F. and U. C. Luft: Physical performance in relation to fat free weight in women compared to men. in *Physiological Aspects of Sports and Physical Fitness.* Chicago, American College of Sports Medicine and the Athletic Institute, 1968.

64. McKerns, K. W.: *The Sex Steroids: Molecular Mechanisms.* New York, Appleton-Century-Crofts, 1971.

65. *Medical World News:* The compleat athlete? (sic) May 24, 1974. p. 35–44.

66. Moody, D. L.: Fat—fact and fallacy. in *DGWS Research Reports: Women in Sports,* D. V. Harris, Ed. Washington, D. C., American Association of Health, Physical Education and Recreation, 1971.

67. Morris, C. B.: The measurement of the strength of muscle relative to the cross section. *Res. Quart., 19,* 295, 1948.

68. Owen, J. W.: Heights and weights of athletes in the Olympic games in Mexico City. *Brit. J. Sports Medicine, 4,* 289, 1970.

69. Oyster, N. and E. P. Wooten: The influence of selected anthropometric measurements on the ability of college women to perform the 35-yard dash. *J. Amer. College of Sports Medicine, 3,* 130, 1971.

70. Pacific Association of the Amateur Athletic Union: Study of the effect of athletic competition on girls and women. 3rd ed. San Francisco, Pacific Association of the Amateur Athletic Union, 1960.

71. Panchenko, L. F., M. K. Alier, and F. Z. Meerson: Condition of the sarcoplasmic reticular calcium pump in compensatory hypertrophy function and hypertrophy of the skeletal muscle. *Byull. Eksp. Biol. Med., 77,* 55, 1974.
72. Parizkova, J. and D. Poupa: Some metabolic consequences of adaptation to muscular work. *Brit. J. Nutrition, 17,* 341, 1963.
73. Pool, J., R. A. Binkhorst and J. A. Vos: Some anthropometric and physiological data in relation to performance of top female gymnasts. *Internationale zeitschrift für angewandte physiologie einschliesslich arbeitsphysiologie, 27,* 329, 1969.
74. Rarick, G. L.: Competitive sports for girls: Effects on growth, development and general health. in *DGWS Research Reports: Women in Sports,* D. V. Harris, Ed. Washington, D.C., American Association of Health, Physical Education, and Recreation, 1971.
75. Rarick, G. L. and J. A. J. Thompson: Roentgenographic measures of leg muscle size and ankle extensor strength of seven-year-old children. *Res. Quart., 27,* 321, 1956.
76. Rasch, P. J. and R. K. Burke: *Kinesiology and Applied Anatomy.* 5th ed. Philadelphia, Lea & Febiger, 1974.
77. Ritchey, S. J., G. J. Schonholtz and Ms. Thompson: The dashboard femoral fracture. *J. Bone and Joint Surg., 40–A,* 1347, 1958.
78. Rose, D. L.: The effect of the obliquity of the shaft of the femur upon speed of running and vertical jumping ability. Master's Thesis, The Pennsylvania State University, 1959.
79. Royce, J.: Use of body components as reference standards for basal metabolic rate. *Res. Quart., 29,* 60, 1958.
80. Ryan, A. J.: Gynecological considerations. *J. Physical Education and Recreation, 46,* 40, 1975.
81. Scarborough, K. L.: Central processing of adult females of divergent age and activity levels. Unpublished Ph.D. dissertation, The University of Texas, 1973.
82. Schaffer, J.: Police cite 'God's-wisdom' against women. *Philadelphia Inquirer,* Feb. 8, 1976, p. B1–2.
83. Shaffer, T. E.: Physiological considerations of the female participant. *Women in Sport: A National Research Conference,* D. V. Harris, Ed. University Park, Pennsylvania State University Press, 1972.
84. Sinning, W. E.: Body composition, cardiovascular function, and rule changes in women's basketball. *Res. Quart., 44,* 313, 1973.
85. Sinning, W. E. and G. D. Lindberg: Physical characteristics of college age women gymnasts. *Res. Quart., 43,* 226, 1972.
86. *Sports Illustrated.* For the record. *45,* 71, Aug. 16, 1976.
87. *Sports Illustrated.* For the record. *45,* 119, Sept. 13, 1976.
88. Stromme, S. B., H. D. Meen, and A. Aekvaag: Effects of an androgenic-anabolic steroid on strength development and plasma testosterone levels in normal males. *Medicine and Science in Sports, 6,* 203, 1974.
89. Sutton, J. R., J. D. Young, L. Lazarus, J. B. Hickie and J. Maksvytis: Growth hormone responses during physical exercise. *Australian Ann. Med., 18,* 84, 1969.
90. Sutton, J. R., M. J. Coleman, J. Casey and L. Lazarus: Androgen responses during physical exercise. *Brit. Med. J. 1,* 520, 1973.
91. Takano, K. and H. Frijiyoshi: A study on timing in sensory motor performance viewed from the developmental stages. *J. Sports Medicine and Physical Fitness, 5,* 50, 1965.
92. Thomas, C. L.: The female sports participant: some physiological questions. in *DGWS Research Reports: Women in sports,* D. V. Harris, ed. Washington, D.C. American Association of Health, Physical Education, and Recreation, 1971.
93. Torg, B. G. and J. S. Torg: Sex and the little league. *The Physician and Sports Medicine, 2,* 45, 1974.

94. Ufland, J. M.: Einfluss des lebensalters, geschlechts, der konstitution und des berufs auf die kraft verschiedener muskelgruppen; über die dynamometrischen werte bei mannern und bei-frauen. *Arbeitsphysiology, 7,* 251, 1933.
95. Ulrich, C.: Women and sport. in *Science and Medicine of Exercise and Sport,* W. R. Johnson, ed. New York, Harper & Brothers Publishers, 1960.
96. Ward, P.: The effect of an anabolic steroid on strength and lean body mass. *Medicine and Science in Sports, 5,* 277, 1973.
97. Wennerberg, C.: Wind, waves, and women. *Science, 185,* 102, 1974.
98. Willoughby, D.: The comparative strength of men and women. *Iron man, 34,* 30, 1975.
99. Wilmore, J. H.: Alterations in strength, body composition, and anthropometric measurements consequent to a ten-week weight training program. *Medicine and Science in Sports, 6,* 133, 1974.
100. Wilmore, J. H.: Exploding the myth of female inferiority. *The Physician and Sports Medicine.* 2, 54, 1974.
101. Wilmore, J. H.: They told you you couldn't compete with men and you, like a fool, believed them. Here's hope. *Women Sports, 1,* 40, 1974.
102. Wilmore, J. H.: Body composition and strength development. *J. Physical Education and Recreation, 46,* 38, 1975 .
103. Wilmore, J. H. and A. R. Behnke: An anthropometric estimation of body density and lean body weight in young men. *J. Applied Physiol., 28,* 25, 1969.
104. Wilmore, J. H. and A. R. Behnke: An anthropometric estimation of body density and lean body weight in young women. *Amer. J. Clin. Nutrition, 23,* 267, 1970.
105. Wyrick, W.: Effects of exercise, championship level competition, and winning or losing on simple reaction time. Unpublished research report, The University of Texas, 1972.
106. Wyrick, W.: Biophysical perspectives. in *The Amreican Women in Sport,* E. W. Gerber, J. Felshin, P. Berlin and W. Wyrick. Reading, Massachusetts, Addison-Wesley Publishing Company, 1974.
107. Younger, L.: A comparison of reaction time and movement time measures of women athletes and non-athletes. Doctoral thesis, Michigan State University, 1956.
108. Younger, L.: A comparison of reaction and movement times of women athletes and non-athletes. *Res. Quart., 30,* 349, 1959.

In considering the interrelation of society, sport, and the female body, we can benefit from investigating the process by which the female perceives her own body. Sharon Mathes addresses this issue in a chapter which is aimed most directly at individuals who are researched-oriented. There are intriguing questions also for those who interact daily with girls and women in physical education classes and sport teams.

Of particular interest may be the finding that while women athletes appear to acknowledge widely a *social stigma* attached to participation in sport, they also report more positive feelings toward their own bodies than do other women. It appears that these athletes transform what might be a debilitating attitude into strength. If this thought process were better understood, it might prove to be a valuable tool for others.

C.A.O.

Chapter 3

BODY IMAGE AND SEX STEREOTYPING

Sharon Mathes

Historically, the concept of body image (body schema, postural model of the body, perceived body, body ego, body boundary, etc.) was broadly defined and applied in the context of psychological, psychiatric and neurological theory. Schilder[57] stressed the relationship between body image and aspects of functioning in both normal and abnormal personalities. He defined body image as "the picture of our own body which we form in our mind, that is to say the way in which the body appears to ourselves." Head[36,37] introduced the notion of body schema (unconscious model of oneself against which all body movements and postures are judged) to explain disorders of movement and sensation. And Fisher and Cleveland[19] examined the nature of an individual's conceptions of body image boundaries (perception of the exterior of the body) and the relationship to psychosomatic symptomatology, patterns of group behavior and modes of physiological response.

While the early work on atypical populations was interesting, it was the proposed interrelationship between body image and movement that was necessarily intriguing to those studying human movement. Clinical work in neurology[21,37] suggested that various skills and capacities might be dependent upon a well-organized body image. Schilder postulated that "only as man is aware of the attitude and orientation of his body do his other perceptions find meaning."[57]

"When knowledge of our body is incomplete and faulty, all actions for which this knowledge is necessary will be faulty too. We need body image in order to start movement."[57]

These concepts were translated into a variety of hypothetical questions by those studying human movement. Does body image influence the acquisition of movement skills? Are skill decrements or differences in individuals' skill attainment explained by varying or changing body images? Is the choice of movement experiences in which individuals participate due to the nature of the person's body perception? It seemed reasonable that the more highly skilled person using the body as an instrument of interaction in a movement media would have a more clearly defined concept of the body. It seemed logical that where there were difficulties in motor performance that this could be due to a lack of clear differentiation of the body. And it seemed possible that body image influenced the choice of sports in which individuals participated.

A major obstacle to answering these questions has been the vague and equivocal definitions and conceptions of body image. Too often there has been a confounding or direct perception of the physical appearance of the body with those thoughts, images, attitudes and affects regarding the body.[75] When Hunt states:

"Probably limited effort patterns will accompany a rigid body image and inappropriate or inaccurate patterns will occur with an ill defined image."[41]

it is difficult to determine if she is referring to direct perception of the body or the expanded concept which includes emotional attitudes toward the body developed in social interactions. When Kephart,[44] Doman and Delacato[12] advocate motor activities to develop "body sense," do they refer to the perceptual capabilities associated with right-left differentiation or to the enhancement of a child's awareness of his body and its relationship to others? Cratty[8] on the one hand suggests the introduction of activities to retarded and neurologically impaired children to develop their body image (perception of body parts, objects in space, right and left). On the other hand he points out that the extent to which the developing youngsters are "comfortable" with their bodies influences their willingness to experience a variety of movement patterns in space.

While body image has both somatic and psychic, conscious and unconscious components, the failure by researchers to satisfactorily define and examine these components has led not only to confusion in the literature but a failure to scientifically substantiate seemingly logical hypotheses.

PERCEPTUAL CORRELATES OF BODY IMAGE

Those who have separated body perception from feelings and attitudes toward the body have asked if people differ in knowledge of varying body dimensions. Is there a relationship between knowledge of the body and ability to use that body in a movement media? What influence does movement have on perception of the body?

A growing body of data concerning perception of the body indicates that people show consistent patterns of estimating body size despite wide variations in measurement conditions.[2,3,14,15,62,63,64] The assumption underlying these investigations is that the personal body is a perceptual object and that body part size judgments reflect theoretically "central stable processes that operate under available information in such a way as to produce a relatively constant pattern of size experience."[62]

A relationship of body image to movement is suggested by Fuhrer and Cowan's[20] findings that subjects have a reduced tendency to underestimate body part size under light and dark conditions when that body part was moved. Movement seemed to facilitate perception of the body. However, Hester's[38] work with 20 male subjects under normal illumination failed to support the concept that active movement produces proprioceptive cues which enhance the individual's ability to make judgment of body parts being moved. Consistent with the findings of Shontz,[62,63] who found that neither standing or sitting conditions nor active or passive participation by subjects influenced judgments of body or non-body stimuli, Hester's research does not support the view that induced muscular tension creates an enhancing effect upon size judgments of body and non-body objects.

Hart[32] used a gross motor skill in order to investigate the accuracy with which 7-year-old boys were able to estimate their shoulder width under static and dynamic conditions. With subjects walking on a treadmill she found that no significant difference existed between estimates made in static or dynamic situations. Like Alvarez,[1] Hart found that dynamic conditions produced estimations which were significantly larger than the measured size of the body. But she noted that subjects also overestimated shoulder width in static conditions.

Using a population of athletes (30) and non-athletes (30) Strati[73] compared static estimates of arm span, standing height, shoulder span, extended height and hip width. While athletes tended to underestimate (arm span and two height measures), there was no significant difference in the underestimation patterns of athletes and non-athletes.

It seems empirically logical to believe that knowledge of the size of body parts extended into space influences the capability "to move into position in any of the game, sport, dance, aquatic, or gymnastic situations."[79] However, this cannot be supported by existing research literature.[1,25,32,73]

Schilder,[57] Gesell,[22] Piaget[56] and Kephart[44] stress the importance of visual manipulative movement in the structuring of body image. But existing research does not corroborate the belief that movement enhances perceptual judgments about the body. Active judgments and judgments made by active populations (athletes) are not significantly different from static or non-athletic estimates of body dimensions.

The limited amount of experimental evidence substantiating the relationship between perception of the body and movement could be due to a host of experimental variables. A relationship may exist but can only be found by continued research. The literature contains many isolated studies, but few done by one researcher who persistently pursues answers to questions the research has raised. The lack of scientific validation may lie in the failure to painstakingly manipulate the variables involved. Hester[38] points out that differences in body estimation may be a function of when the subject moves. In Fuhrer and Cowan's[20] study subjects estimated their body while they moved. Hester's[38] subjects estimated following active conditions. The varying controls across studies may be further complicated by the degree and duration of the movement experienced by the subjects. Movement of subjects ranged from extending a body part through the range of motion for 15 seconds[38] to running 30 feet prior to making body estimates.[1]

The lack of research support may be due to an error in theory pertaining to the interrelationship of body perception and movement. Perception of the body may be one of a multitude of factors influencing performance. The lack of clear research evidence may reflect an overestimation of the influence of body perception. What an athlete lacks in body perception may be compensated for in reaction time, body build, strength or cognitive understanding of the task. Body perception may not account for a significant enough amount of the motor performance in normal individuals to ever be seen in differences in athletic and non-athletic populations.

PSYCHO-SOCIAL CORRELATES OF BODY IMAGES

The failure to confirm positive relationships between perceptual aspects of body image and movement could also be a function of an inappropriate separation of somatic and psychic qualities of body image. Hunt suggests that body image is "more than fact and reality, it is also fantasy, with feelinges and attitudes derived from the value system of the society in which it develops."[41] Perhaps the psychosocial correlates of body image cannot be separated from the perceptual because of the degree to which an individual's awareness of his body is influenced by socially formed attitudes toward his body.[9]

Schonbuch and Schell[58] attempted to analyze the influence that the social importance of the body might have on the accuracy of perception of the body. They asked whether individuals who noticeably deviate from the average in terms of physique might judge their bodies differently from those with normal physiques. Is the judgment by extreme physique groups of body size and shape affected by the judgments of others? They hypothesized that over- or underweight persons may have been so convinced by the comments of others concerning physical deviance that they would, by judgmental "contrast", estimate themselves to be more deviant than they are. Or they reasoned the physically deviant person might, by a process of "assimilation" to the most frequently appearing individuals of normal physique, judge their own physique closer to average than it really was. Either hypothesis predicted a greater error of judgment by the more deviant than average physique person. Analyzing 60 male college subjects they found both the overweight and underweight groups made incorrect judgments significantly more than did the normal weight group. Both underweight and overweight subjects tended to overestimate body size and shape in comparison to the normal weight population. The authors speculate that the overweight subjects seem to magnify (contrast) the degree of their stigma of being fat, while the underweight subjects minimize (assimilate) their differences in body appearance by rating themselves closer to normal. In the same vein Cremer and Hukill[9] found with a female undergraduate population (102) that the greater the deviation in weight from that considered "desirable" in terms of height and age, the greater the difference between perceived body contour lines and real ones. Using a battery of tests, results showed that the greater the deviation (from socially acceptable standards) in body size or configuration, the greater the difference which appeared between perceived and real body outlines. This work suggests that perception of body size and contour may be more than reporting what is objectively definable (height, weight, arm length, shoulder width). To some degree body perception may be a function of the reactions of others which have become incorporated into the recipient's own body concept.

This research supports Schilder's theory that an individual's attitude toward the different parts of the body can be to a great extent determined by the interest other persons take in that body.[57] Do people have characteristic ways of regarding body builds? Is there a definable range of consistent reactions to particular body configurations?

Accumulating research suggests that a particular body type is capable of eliciting rather common reactions from adults and children in the form of descriptions of personality and behavior traits.[4,70,74,78] The mesomorph body image is associated with socially positive behavioral descriptions, whereas the endomorph and ectomorph are regarded negatively. These stereotypic reactions have been found in boys and girls as young as 5 years of age,[48] elementary school boys and girls,[5,35,53,70] college men and women,[49,55] and middle-aged male adults.[66] Subjects have responded to silhouettes, Sheldon's somatotype photographs and photographs and drawings of same age and sex physique types. While a majority of the research has involved subjects relating to male physique types, researchers[55,71] have found female physiques are also socially stereotyped. In analyzing sex differences Stewart, Tutton and Steele[71] have found that men are more consistent in stereotyping certain concepts than women. Studying the reactions of

50 university students (25 men) to female physiques they found men were more consistent in stereotyping six concepts, while women were more consistent on only one concept. They concluded, however, that since significant stereotyping in 14 of the 15 concepts was found, that sex differences are specific to certain concepts and do not reflect a general sex difference. In an elementary school population of 75 girls in grades one through five, however, Caskey and Felker[5] found that the ectomorph received the socially favorable adjectives, while the mesomorph received only those favorable adjectives which were related to the physical. Kurtz[46] has reported similar results in a study of attitudes toward body build with college students. Men preferred the mesomorphic body type, while women preferred the ectomorphic body type. Jourard and Secord[42,43] in analyzing the degree of satisfaction (body-cathexis) of men and women for parts of their body found also that men value large size of body parts, while women with the exception of bust generally value small body part size.

Of what interest is the social stereotyping of body image literature to the movement educator? If, as Hunt[41] proposes, "cultural values dictate goodness and badness to the body and its behavior thereby fostering feelings about body parts and their movement" then the literature on stereotyping would suggest a number of hypotheses in relation to movement and body build. Do the existing physique social stereotypes extend to movement activities? Is there a particular physique associated with sport? Will individuals with certain body builds tend to avoid activities that are inconsistent with their physiques? If a mesomorphic physique is associated with sport, but valued by men and not women, does this create certain conflicts and anxieties for the sportswoman? Will an individual's feelings toward the body influence performance?

One of the recurring personality traits associated with physique literature has been activity orientation. Kretschmeyer[45] described one of his physique types as "athletic", while Sheldon labeled "somatotonia" the temperament trait cluster of assertiveness of action, high energy, competitive aggressive and directness of manner. While Sheldon's theory of genetic inheritance, physique, and temperament was seriously criticized in terms of methodology[6,67] and statistical procedures[40] there has been an upsurge of interest in reapplication of the Sheldonian paradigm which is based on a social learning hypothesis.[39]

"The social learning hypothesis stipulates that people in a child's socializing environment expect specific behaviors or personality traits to be associated with specific body builds and that these stereotypes are transmitted so that a child will conform to the expectations of his somatotype in the course of his development."

A number of researchers have reported active description traits such as need for play (Sanford, 1943) leader in play,[76,77] activeness in games,[26] motor responsiveness,[23,24] high athletic ability,[4] associated with the muscular or mesomorphic body build. Endomorphs, on the other hand, have been described by traits such as love of eating, desire for comfort and relaxation, athletic inability,[4] laziness, weakness, good naturedness.[78] The ectomorph has fallen somewhere between the previously mentioned extremes and has been viewed as serious and unhappy,[26] aesthetic,[23,24] lacking in desire for physical exercise and adventure,[6] lethargic, aversive to gross motor play.[76] Thus it appears that the stereotypic qualities assigned specific body builds do extend to the movement media. The more muscular physique is associated with movement activities.

Harris[28] postulates that individuals will repeat movement experiences that are compatible to their body image and reject completely or fail to repeat movement experiences that are in conflict with their body image.

"Many individuals avoid swimming because they are too uncomfortable psychologically in a swim suit. Wearing a leotard for dance may produce a conflict with body image of an individual to the point that avoidance is the only solution to the conflict."

The psychological discomfort of which Harris speaks could be the discrepancy between the individual's body build and the physique deemed appropriate to participate in that movement activity. The fat individual might be as likely to avoid swimming because the suit seems more appropriate for the muscular body build, as the muscular person would be to avoid the leotard that seems more suited for the slim, aesthetic physique. While some empirical evidence supports these contentions, existing research does not unequivocally substantiate that "undoubtedly the body image influences choice and participation in sports."[28]

Research evidence is at best limited and at worst indirect and inconclusive. Sugerman[74] studying 102 college males found athletic participation correlated with mesomorphy. However, his measure of sophistication of body concept was based on a vaguely defined figure drawing test. Felker[17] found no significant interaction effect between heavy body build, fathers' interest in sports and self-concept of 72 sixth grade and 48 eighth grade boys. He did find that boys with differing body builds differ in self-concept in the sixth grade but not in the ninth. Mathes[53] found with 180 subjects representing three body types and three grades (first, third, sixth) that all physique groups assigned with similar frequency a greater number of active scores to a same age and sex mesomorph silhouette. However, when assigning active or passive qualities to themselves all physique groups assigned themselves more active than passive scores. When viewing a same age and sex photograph of a child being active or passive, all groups chose significantly more often the active photograph as representing what they would like to do. Kurtz[46] on the other hand found that the mean activity dimensions on the Semantic Differential was significantly larger for men than women. He could only speculate that most girls, at least those from the middle class, come to recognize that it is not lady-like to be as rough and active as their twin brothers. Darden[10] compared body image, body-cathexis, and self-cathexis variables among college male athletes in football (65), basketball (12), baseball (26), weightlifting (15), swimming (18), and gymnastics (9). While he found differences within teams, he found no significant differences between the combined team sports and combined individual sports. In particular no significant difference existed among the athletic teams on the body image variable. In comparing mean scores of athletes with those obtained from "typical" college male populations they found that the gymnasts most resembled the average college male and the weight lifters and basketball players seemed to be the most deviate in terms of positive feelings toward 40 body parts and functions. But these two athletic populations did not differ significantly from the other athletic groups.

It does not seem at this time that sufficient research evidence exists to substantiate the claim that body build significantly influences sport selection or that individuals with certain physiques tend to avoid activities that are inconsistent with their physiques.

It does seem that a mesomorphic physique stereotype is associated with sport and that male children,[13,70] and college men[11] prefer to look like the mesomorphic image. But what about the woman athlete? If muscular physique is associated with sport participation, what does this mean for the sportswoman?

Many authors suggest that the female athlete experiences role conflict when she enters the male dominated realm of sport.[27,33,34,60] To be female and an athlete have been contradictory social positions with conflicting role expectations. One area of conflict centers around body build. Athletes report across sports a preoccupation with their appearance and a concern with avoiding the "masculinization" of the body that some postulate inevitably follows sports participation.

"Vicki Foltz, as a 27-year-old married woman probably one of America's finest long distance runners was asked in an interview whether she had any 'feminine hang-ups' about running. She responded, 'Yes, I have lots of hang-ups. You wouldn't believe it. I always worry about looking nice in a race. I worry about my calf muscles getting big. But mostly I worry about my hair. . . . I suppose it's because so many people have said women athletes look masculine. So a lot of us try, subconsciously maybe, to look as feminine as possible in a race. There's always lots of hair ribbons in the races!"[60]

Research that goes beyond a descriptive level is limited in this area. Snyder and Spreitzer[69] asked 510 randomly drawn surburban and urban females on a self-administered questionnaire "In your opinion, would participation in any of the following sports enhance a girl's, woman's feminine appearance". The ranking of "yes" responses to the sports listed were swimming, 67 per cent; tennis, 57 per cent; gymnastics, 54 per cent; softball, 14 per cent; basketball, 14 per cent; track and field, 13 per cent. The "yes" responses never exceed 67 per cent (tennis) and decreased steadily as the sports become less associated with the female role. Sherif[61] reporting her work and that of Garman and Harres concurs as she states:

"In the research done by Garman, Harres, and Sherif on femininity and athletics, player characteristics appear to be an important factor affecting attitudes toward the desirability of a sport. This is substantiated by the high correlations between somatic differences and preference ranking as shown by Garman. Also, it seems that sports like softball which utilize the more masculine skills of throwing, batting, and running are far less desirable for female athletic competition than gymnastics which emphasize delicacy and gracefulness."

The work of these authors seems to support in part Metheny's theories[54] concerning the social acceptance of women athletes. Those activities which include body contact with an opponent, application of force to some heavy object, projecting the body through space over long distances, and cooperative face to face competitions are rated less frequently as enhancing girl's or women's feminine qualities. Conversely, the most acceptable competition (and thus less contradictory to the female role) seems to be that which involves presenting the body in an aesthetically pleasing pattern, use of manufactured devices to facilitate bodily movement and use of a light implement and/or light object such as a tennis racket, and maintenance of a spatial barrier with an opponent.

Keeping in mind earlier work[42,43] which suggested females value more than males the ectomorph physique and small body size, it would appear that the woman athlete in force producing, contact sports might face conflict about her physique and her particular role in sport. This conflict might well vary by sport. Snyder and Kivlin[68] report when analyzing responses of 328 Women National Intercollegiate Championship participants that differences exist by sport in answer to the question "Do you feel there is a stigma attached to women who participate in the sport you specialize in?" Fifty-four per cent of the basketball players, 47 per cent of the track and field participants and 38 per cent of the swimmers and divers, and 27 per cent of the gymnasts answered "yes" to the question about stigma. The control population of 275 college women had 65 per cent responding "yes" to the question "Do you feel there is a stigma attached to women's participation in sports?" Why do basketball players feel more stigmatized than gymnasts? Is the emphasis in gymnastics on the development of balance, grace and skill in an aesthetically pleasing manner more in keeping with the female sex role? Does the running, scrambling, combative quality of basketball make its participants feel more discrepant from the usual feminine role? The degree of the "stigma" which relates specifically to subjects' feelings about their body cannot be determined. But it might be asked whether such differences exist in attitude toward the body between athletes and non-athletes as well as between various sports groups.

Surprisingly the work of Snyder and Kivlin[68] suggests that women athletes have more positive feelings toward their bodies than non-athletes. Using a modification of the Secord and Jourard Body Image Scale they compared college women (275) and intercollegiate championship participants (328) in basketball, gymnastics, swimming, diving, track and field. They found that women athletes have more positive feelings toward their bodies than non-athletes especially on key items for athletes such as energy level and health. In comparing the athletic population of basketball players and gymnasts they found the basketball player as positive as the gymnasts on 21 of the body image measures. Basketball players were significantly more positive than gymnasts on two measures (appetite, arms) and gymnasts significantly more positive than basketball players in relation to two measures (posture, waist). The authors contend that their data refute the negative expectations associated with athletic participation for women.

"The findings of this study raise serious doubts about the stereotypes regarding women athletes. Comparisons of women athletes and nonathletes on measures of psychological well-being and body image show more positive self attitudes of athletes. . . . Thus, even though women athletes have frequently received negative sanctions, their participation in sports has apparently been psychologically satisfying and rewarding. Perhaps the social costs of athletic participation by women today are not as great as previously, and contemporary changes in broadening of sex roles are reflected in the positive findings regarding the women athletes."[68]

Could it be that the sportswoman has, through the demands placed on her by the role conflict in sport, become very secure and positive about herself and her body? Or might it be that the perception being tapped is a measure of an acceptability of her body for use in sport and not in a social setting? Might different responses be obtained from athletes if you asked them to differentiate between feelings of positiveness, negativeness and neutralness in varying context? Do athletes have special concerns about their bodies that rise in prominence in the social context of sport?

"The female athlete feels very unfeminine when she enters the male-dominated sports world. If she shows any athletic ability or correct technique, she is not praised for her ability or correct technique but because she can 'move like a man.' . . . It makes me question my own femininity—the very roots of my being. If I am a women, why do I enjoy sport? Why do I participate?"[34]

With the limited amount of research in this area it is too early to reject the hypothesis that women athletes have different and perhaps more negative attitudes toward their bodies than non-athletes. When large numbers of athletes and non-athletes indicate that sport "detracts from being feminine" and that a "stigma" is associated with sport participation and yet indicate they feel positive about their bodies and social role, then further analysis is demanded. Additional work which considers the athlete's feelings about her body in various social situations needs to be conducted. Analysis needs to be made of the stimulus words referring to the body to see if they are appropriate to the potential concerns of the athletes about their bodies. Athletes speak of worries about being muscular, large, thick, mannish. These concerns may not be tapped when they respond to generalized stimulus words such as body build, profile, and sex. A woman athlete might be highly positive in response to the label "body build" and still be concerned in competition about appearing masculine. The research instrumentation needs to deal more specifically with the anxieties that athletes have expressed about their bodies.

REFERENCES

1. Alvarez, J.: Body width estimations by six-year-old boys under static and dynamic conditions. Unpublished master's thesis, Purdue University, 1968.
2. Barton, M. I. and S. Wapner: Apparent length of body parts attended to separately and in combination. *Perceptual Motor Skills, 20,* 901, 1965.
3. Boraks, F. C.: Sex differences in body cognition. Unpublished doctoral dissertation, University of Kansas, 1962.
4. Brodsky, C.: *A Study of Norms for Body Form Behavior Relationships.* Washington, D. C.: Catholic University Press, 1954.
5. Caskey, S. R. and D. W. Felker: Social stereotyping of female body image by elementary school age girls. *Res. Quart., 42,* 251, 1971.
6. Child, I. L.: The relation of somatotypes to self ratings on Sheldon's temperamental traits. *Journal of Personality, 18,* 440, 1950.
7. Clifford, E.: Body satisfaction in adolescence. *Perceptual and Motor Skills, 33,* 119, 1971.
8. Cratty, B. J.: *Psychology and Physical Activity.* Englewood Cliffs, New Jersey, Prentice-Hall Inc., 1968.

9. Cremer, A. G. and M. A. Hukill: Relationship between weight-height ratios, other body measurements, and self perception of body contours. *Res. Quart., 40,* 30, 1969.
10. Darden, E.: A comparison of body image and self-concept variables among various sport groups. *Res. Quart., 43,* 7, 1972.
11. Darden, E.: Masculinity-feminity body rankings by males and females. *J. Psychol., 80,* 205, 1972.
12. Delacato, C. H.: *The Diagnosis and Treatment of Speech and Reading Problems.* Springfield, Charles C Thomas, 1964.
13. Deno, E.: Self-identification among adolescent boys. *Child Development, 24,* 259, 1953.
14. Dillon, D. J.: Estimation of perceived body size. *Perceptual and Motor Skills, 14,* 219, 1962.
15. Dillon, D. J.: Measurement of perceived body size. *Perceptual and Motor Skills, 14,* 191, 1962.
16. Douty, H. I., J. B. Moore and D. Hartford: Body characteristics in relation to life adjustment, body image and attitudes of college females. *Perceptual and Motor Skills, 39,* 499, 1974.
17. Felker, D. W.: Relation between self concept, body build and perception of fathers' interest in sports in boys. *Res. Quart., 39,* 513, 1968.
18. Felker, D. W. and R. S. Kay: Self-concept, sports interests, sports participation, and body type of seventh and eighth-grade boys. *J. Psychol., 78,* 223, 1971.
19. Fisher, S. and S. Cleveland: *Body Image and Personality.* Princeton, New Jersey, Van Nostrand Company, Inc., 1958.
20. Fuhrer, M. J. and C. O. Cowan: Influence of active movement, illumination and sex on body part size estimates. *Perceptual and Motor Skills, 27,* 979, 1967.
21. Gerstmann, J.: Psychological and phenomenological aspects of disorders of body image. *J. Nervous and Mental Disorders, 126,* 499, 1958.
22. Gesell, A.: *Studies in Child Development.* New York, Harper & Bros., 1948.
23. Glueck, S. and E. Glueck: *Physique and Delinquency.* New York, Harper & Bros., 1956.
24. Glueck, S. and E. Glueck: *Unraveling Juvenile Delinquency.* Cambridge, Massachusetts, Harvard University Press, 1950.
25. Greenlee, J. C.: The estimation of body height, object height, and motor performance by six-year-old boys. Unpublished master's thesis, Purdue University, 1967.
26. Hanley, C.: Physique and reputation of junior high school boys. *Child Development, 22,* 247, 1951.
27. Harris, D. V. (Ed.): DGWS research reports: Women in sports. Washington, D.C., AAHPER, 1971.
28. Harris, D. V.: *Involvement in Sport.* Philadelphia, Lea & Febiger, 1973.
29. Harris, D. V.: Women and sport: A national research conference. In *Penn State HPER series no. 2.* University Park, Pennsylvania, Pennsylvania State University Press, 1972.
30. Harris, M. B., S. Ramsey, D. Sims and M. Stevenson: Effects of uniforms on perceptions of pictures of athletes. *Perceptual and Motor Skills, 30,* 59, 1974.
31. Harris, M. B. and S. A. Ramsey: Stereotypes of athletes. *Perceptual and Motor Skills, 39,* 705, 1974.
32. Hart, B.: Size estimation as a measure of body image of the movement performer. *Res. Quart., 42,* 391, 1971.
33. Hart, M. (Ed.): *Sport in the Socio-Cultural Process.* Dubuque, Iowa, Wm. C. Brown Co., 291–302, 1972.
34. Hart, M.: Stigma or prestige: The all American choice. In McGlynn, C. H. *Issues in Physical Education.* Palo Alto, California, National Book Press, 214–220, 1974.

35. Hassan, I. N.: The body image and personality correlates of body stereotypes. Unpublished doctoral dissertation, Indiana University, 1967.
36. Head, H.: *Aphasia and Kindred Disorders of Speech.* London, Cambridge University Press, 1926.
37. Head, R.: *Studies in Neurology.* London, Hodder Stonghton, Ltd. and Oxford University Press, 1920.
38. Hester, G. A.: Effects of active movement on body-part size estimates. *Perceptual and Motor Skills, 30,* 607, 1970.
39. Hopkins, B.: Body Build Stereotypes. In H. T. A. Whiting (Ed.), *Readings in Sports Psychology.* Lafayette, Indiana, Balt Publishers, 1972.
40. Humphreys, L. G.: Characteristics of type concepts with special reference to Sheldon's typology. *Psychological Bulletin, 54,* 218, 1957.
41. Hunt, V.: Movement behavior: A model for action. *Quest,* Monograph 11, 69, 1964.
42. Jourand, S. and P. F. Secord: Body-cathexis and the ideal female figure. *J. Abnormal and Social Psychol., 50,* 243, 1955.
43. Jourand, S. M. and P. F. Secord: Body-cathexis and personality. *Brit. J. Psychol., 46,* 130, 1955.
44. Kephart, N. S.: *The Slow Learner in the Classroom.* Columbus, Ohio, Charles E. Merrill, 1966.
45. Kretschmer, E.: *Physique and Character.* (translated by W. J. H. Sprott). London, Routledge and Kegan Paul, 1925.
46. Kurtz, R. M.: Body image: Male and Female. *Sociological Abstracts, 18,* 24, 1970.
47. Kurtz, R. M.: Sex differences and variations in body attitude. *Journal of Consulting and Clinical Psychology, 33,* 625, 1969.
48. Lerner, R. M. and E. Geller: Body build identification, preference, and aversion in children. *Developmental Psychology, 1,* 456, 1969.
49. Lerner, R. M.: Some female stereotypes of male body-build behavior relations. *Perceptual and Motor Skills, 28,* 363, 1969.
50. Lerner, R. M.: The development of stereotyped expectancies of body-build relations. *Child Development, 40,* 137, 1969.
51. Lerner, R. M. and S. J. Korn: The development of body build stereotypes in males. *Child Development, 43,* 912, 1972.
52. Lerner, R. M., J. R. Knapp and K. B. Pool: Structures of body-build stereotypes: A methodological analysis. *Perceptual and Motor Skills, 39,* 719, 1974.
53. Mathes, S.: Social stereotyping of body image and movement orientation. Unpublished doctoral dissertation, Purdue University, 1972.
54. Methany, E.: Symbolic forms of movement: The feminine image in sports. In *Connotations of Movement in Sports and Dance.* Dubuque, Iowa, Wm. C. Brown Co., 1965.
55. Miller, A. R. and R. A. Stewart: Perception of female physiques. *Perceptual and Motor Skills, 27,* 721, 1968.
56. Piaget, J.: *The Construction of Reality in the Child.* New York, Basic Books, 1954.
57. Schilder, P.: *The Image and Appearance of the Human Body.* New York, John Wiley & Sons, Inc., 1950.
58. Schonbuch, S. S. and R. E. Schell: Judgements of body appearance by fat and skinny male college students. *Perceptual and Motor Skills, 24,* 999, 1967.
59. Schonfield, W. A.: Inadequate masculine physique as a factor in personality development of adolescent boys. *Psychometric Medicine, 12,* 49, 1950.
60. Scott, J.: Men and women in sport: The manhood myth. In G. McGlynn (Ed.), *Issues in Physical Education and Sport.* Palo Alto, California, National Press Books, 1974.
61. Sherif, M.: Girls compete? DGWS research reports: Women in sports. In D. Harris (Ed.), Washington, D.C., *AAHPER,* pp. 31–36, 1971.

62. Shontz, F.: Body-part size judgement in contrasting intellectual groups. *J. Nervous and Mental Disorders, 136,* 368, 1963.
63. Shontz, F.: Some characteristics of body-size estimation. *Perceptual and Motor Skills, 16,* 665, 1963.
64. Shontz, F.: A conceptual and methodological approach to research on body part size judgements. Paper read at Houston State Psychiatric Institute, Houston, Texas, 1965.
65. Shontz, F.: Influence of measurement conditions on size estimates of body parts. *J. Personality and Social Psychology, 1,* 469, 1965.
66. Sleet, D. A.: Physique and social image. *Perceptual and Motor Skills, 28,* 295, 1969.
67. Smith, H. C.: Psychometric checks on hypothesis derived from Sheldon's work on physique and temperament. *J. Personality, 17,* 310, 1949.
68. Snyder, E. E. and J. E. Kivlin: Women athletics and aspects of psychological well-being and body image. *Res. Quart., 46,* 191, 1975.
69. Snyder, E. E. and E. A. Spreitzer: Family influence and involvement in sports. *Res. Quart., 44,* 249, 1974.
70. Staffieri, R. J.: A study of social stereotype of body image in children. *J. Personality and Social Psychology, 7,* 101, 1967.
71. Stewart, R. A., S. J. Tutton and R. E. Steele: Stereotyping and personality: I. Sex differences in perception of female physiques. *Perceptual and Motor Skills, 36,* 811, 1973.
72. Stewart, R. A., G. E. Powell and S. J. Tutton: Subjective factors in social stereotyping and impression formation. *Perceptual and Motor Skills, 37,* 867, 1974.
73. Strati: Body Image and performance. In D. Harris (Ed.), *Women and Sport: A national research conference.* Penn State HPER series #2, 1972, 61-70.
74. Sugerman, A. A. and F. Garonian: Body type and sophistication of body concept. *J. Personality, 32,* 380, 1964.
75. Traub, A. and J. Orbach: Psychophysical studies of body image. *Arch. General Psychiatry, 11,* 53, 1964.
76. Walker, R. N.: Body build and behavior in young children: I. Body build and nursery school teachers' ratings. *Monographs of the Society for Research in Child Development, 27,* 1, 1962.
77. Walker, R. N.: Body build and behavior in young: II. Body build and parents' ratings. *Child Development, 34,* 1, 1963.
78. Wells, E. and B. Siegel: Stereotyped somatotypes. *Psychological Reports, 8,* 77, 1961.
79. Woods, M. D.: An exploration of developmental relationships between children's body image boundaries, estimates of dimensions of body space and performance of selected cross motor tasks. Unpublished doctoral dissertation, Ohio State University, 1966.

Section 2

SOCIETY, SPORT, AND SEXUALITY

In this section, two authors offer withering critiques of traditional stereotypic sexuality and deny its validity and desirability. The third author reports a research study illustrating a specific effect of women athletes coping with traditional femininity.

Oglesby and Duquin express great concern for the health and well-being of individuals seeking to live out simplistic, social expectations in today's world. They agree that the historical perspective of sport has emphasized the "masculine" principle. Both opt for a future where understandings of sexuality and sport are dramatically altered.

Pat Del Ray's study investigates Felshin's concept that women athletes, aware of the "masculine" perspective in sport, defensively protect their perceived femininity by espousing an apologetic. The apologetic involves verbalizations of traditional, conservative views of femininity which are offered to neutralize the feared "masculinizing" of the sport experience. Del Ray concludes that the apologetic will disappear when the androgynous view of sport, described by Oglesby and Duquin, becomes transcendent.

C.A.O.

Chapter 4

THE MASCULINITY/FEMININITY GAME: CALLED ON ACCOUNT OF . . . .

Carole A. Oglesby

The polarized, sex stereotyped world which we have been carefully taught is, for women, a place of subordination and spiritual slavery conjoined with deification and distrust of our own sensual being. For many, this a world of nothingness. Each has an opportunity to exercise existential courage. The offering of an alternative to that world is an act of being in the face of nothingness.

In this essay, an alternative is presented which is consistent with sport feminist philosophy and arises out of an ultimate concern for the actualization of all human beings. An entree to this alternative is gained by making a distinction between style and stylization in sport. Style is an authentic way of being; in sport, style is manifested in various strategic decisions made and in the meanings attached to movement.[19] Style is difficult to verbalize. Mal Andrews comes bull's-eye close in a quotation and verse concerning black experience and sport. "We live in our movements and style in our actions in a performing sense."

> On style: You don't know what IT is,
> You just know that IT is.
> You can't describe IT.
> All you can do is feel that
> I GOT IT; HE GOT IT; SHE GOT IT; WE GOT IT;
> WE GON DO IT; HE AIN'T GOT IT; THEY AIN'T GOT IT.[1]

In an existential ethical sense, the implication in Felshin and Andrew's writing is clear that having style (experiencing being authentically) is good.

Stylization, on the other hand, is a displacement of authentic experiencing and choosing; it is a replacement of personal style in favor of patterns imposed by others and understood on the basis of external outcomes. Stylization is rigid, stereotypic and, to some degree, false.[19]

Within this framework we shall explore two themes: (1) that traditional masculinity-femininity definitions, which will be referred to as stereotypic sexuality, are examples of social stylizations rather than personal style; (2) traditional sport has been a social mode (a socialization process) for the particular stylization of sexuality which is normative in our society. Carolyn Heilbrun states the case succinctly in *Women Studies: An Interdisciplinary Journal:* "The world we inhabit (I would add, create) is excessive, indeed obsessive, in its sexual polarization. There are men and women in the world and dividing them into quarterbacks and cheerleaders has been disastrous."[38]

Finally, a sketch is provided of a viable alternative to stereotypic sexuality. One might ask why a viable alternative is so painfully long in coming. Indeed some suggest that the lack of such an alternative proves that one is unnecessary or even unnatural (that is, counter to "Man's" nature).

George Kelly, in *The Psychology of Personal Constructs*, offers another explanation for this delay.[29] Kelly suggests one of the crucial elements of human life is the capacity to represent the environment through choices; to place alternative constructions on the environment. A person interprets the world through constructs, which may not fit well with reality but are better than nothing at all. "In seeking improvement in a construct system the person is repeatedly halted by fear of damage to the whole system which may result from the alteration of a construct . . . in which the personal investment is large."[29] It seems obvious that one's construct of sexuality would have high personal investment and hence be threatening to consider altering in radical terms. Kelly suggests that another condition unfavorable to construct alteration is the absence of a "laboratory" in which to "experiment" with the new construct. It may be that sport, with its separateness from real life and its subtle guise of unimportance, may provide just the laboratory for the "trying on" of new masculinity-femininity concepts. In part 1, analysis procedures will be followed in which the nature of stereotypic sexuality is identified and a two-part case is made for the rejection of these traditional notions of gender identity.

SEPARATION FROM OLD STRUCTURES

Stereotypic Sexuality

The first step in this analysis is to identify and describe stereotypic sexuality, traditional masculinity-femininity in our society. With Kelly we view these definitions as hypothetical constructs whose goodness of fit with something called "true masculinity-femininity" is not only unknown but is irrelevant. We cannot know "true masculinity-femininity" so what we are seeking is sexuality definition which brings happiness and self-actualization to ourselves and others.

We must immediately disavow the idea that traditional masculinity-femininity, as measured by social science methods, is dependent upon biological sex. John Money has stated, "psychosexual differentiation can take place in opposition to genetic sex, hormonal sex, gonadal sex, and morphology."[40] Traditional masculinity-femininity, as usually measured, is dependent upon gender role identity, is analogous to imprinting in some animals, and initially develops approximately simultaneous with language. Money describes gender identity in this fashion,

"It is all that distinguishes males from females; patterns of skills, occupations, dress, adornments, gestures, demeanor, emotional expression, erotic fantasies, and sexual behavior. These patterns show such wide cultural variation that they are generally assumed . . . culturally determined. The problem of determining true masculinity-femininity is one on which few scientists agree."[40]

Table 6. Traits of Stereotypic Sexuality

Masculine	*Feminine*
Task leader	Emotional support
Aggressive	Teasing
Tenacious	Insistence on rights
Ambitious	Obedience
Original	Friendliness
Free-ranging	Passive-dependent
Competent	Nurturant
Tough	
Independent	Various research studies
Objective	(see bibliography)
Masculine	*Feminine*
Aggression	Passive
Penetration	Receptive
Change	Stable
Objectivity	Subjective
Logic	Intuitive
Dissection	Integrated
Analysis	Synthesis
Apartness	Togetherness
	Bazin and Freeman
Life risker—	Life giver—
Active	Passive
Aggressive	Submissive
Public	Private
Cultural	Natural
Rule-governed	Idiosyncratic
Instrumental	Expressive
Goal-oriented	Chaotic
Organized	Disorganized
Dominating	Subordinate
Competitive	Cooperative
Controlled	Uncontrolled
	Ortner

Parsons, from Smith College, continues in the same vein. "We have reviewed the research on early behavioral sex differences and only aggression occurs with regularity and even aggression is not always a consistent factor. The bulk of studies with significant sex differences have focused on reports of perceived sex role related behavior rather than response style differences."[42]

It appears that if one reviews pop and high culture, as did Bazin and Freeman (Martin[38]) and Ortner (Duquin[15]) or asks people to report how males and females are "s'posed to be", a fairly consistent picture of bi-polar, dichotomous traits emerges. Three models of this type of trait configuration are included on Table 6.

Rejecting the Stereotype

The traits on these lists represent the familiar patternings, the stereotypic constructs. To dramatically alter these patterns means revising our thought systems. Why is such a revision important enough to justify the turmoil?

I suggest there are two bases for the assertion that concepts of stereotypic sexuality must be actively rejected: (1) technical weaknesses of research data purporting to demonstrate genetic bases for sex differences of this nature; (2) the basis of demonstrable damage to individuals experiencing alienation from legitimate aspects of themselves.

Technical Weaknesses of Research Data

There are four kinds of weaknesses which will be briefly presented.

1. Projective tests, theoretically designed to reveal deep and pervasive aspects of personality, cannot be utilized to consistently discriminate sex differences in responses. This finding was reported by Baughman, DeWit, Maccoby and Jacklin, and Sanford.

2. It is common to find a high degree of overlap in distributions of data on sex differences (Fig. 3). Witkin, for example, reports rod and frame tests results with the following statement, "The differences between the sexes, though clear cut and consistent, tend to be small compared to the range of individual differences within each sex."[55] The validity, interpretations, and applications may be questioned of so-called sex differentiated distributions wherein a considerable percentage of the low-mean sex outstrips the other sex in score (see Chapter 2 for further examples).

3. It is common to find imprecise language which identifies secondarily learned patterns as "sex differences" in a context which implies biogenetic causation. As an example let us consider the field dependence findings on women which some have suggested to be related

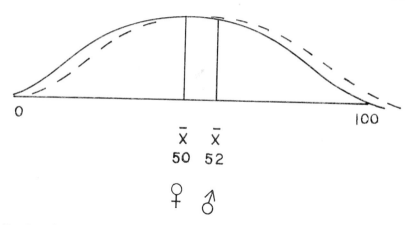

Fig. 3.   Theoretical Example of Overlapping Distributions.

to inherent perceptual organization. Barclay and Consumano,[2] reporting a study on black and white boys, with and without fathers, hypothesized that boys without fathers would be higher in field dependence (feminine trait) than boys with fathers. Their hypothesis was borne out but in a footnote they reported that the black youths (with or without fathers) were significantly higher in field dependence than whites. The researchers concluded that the "passive orientation" which the victimized black youths had apparently adopted, accounted for the results. Maccoby,[36] in *The Potential of Women*, gives a fuller exposition of the manner in which "passive orientation" may account for much of the "sex difference" data, of both a physical and psychological nature.

4. Construct validity—What do the items that discriminate between men and women really mean?

Most M–F scales are composed of vocational choices, hobbies, goodness of conduct items. What do we know about sexuality when we know a person prefers baths to showers? Landers reported female physical education majors as less feminine than education majors in scores on the MMPI and the Gough Scale of Psychological Femininity. Only 2 of the 11 item categories accounted for the differences with the education majors reporting more restraint/caution and more religious beliefs than did the physical education majors. Is this femininity?

Sanford and Friedan comment on findings wherein increases in education for women correspond with drops in femininity scores. Friedan asks abrasively, "What is femininity if it can be destroyed by an education which makes the mind grow?"[20] Sanford says of the Vassar seniors who gave more "masculine" responses than did the freshman, "She is not in reality (editor's note, as contrasted with the

unreality of the test) less feminine. She is more flexible and broad thinking; imagining herself taking a greater variety of roles."[45]
Technical considerations such as these suggest at least partial rejection of the produced data as objective bases for stereotypic sexuality.

Psychological Damage Due to Stereotypic Sexuality

Of greater seriousness and more powerful as justification for revising constructions of masculinity-femininity are the systematic and pervasive incidences of damage to males and females as a consequence of these stereotypic definitions.

The weapon of damage is alienation of self, from self. As Bazin and Freeman point out, "Men are not the embodiment of the masculine principle nor women the embodiment of the feminine. True human personality is androgynous." (Martin[38]) Lest you infer that such a position is a recent development of radical feminists, read Talcott Parsons,[43] Nevitt Sanford[45] and Frank Beach.[4]

"At the same time the 'parent oneness' is differentiated into mother/father, the self is bifurcated into masculine/feminine. This does not involve a difference by presence or absence of certain critical factors but by differences in organization of what are qualitatively the same factors. We deduce a bisexuality of the child independent of Freud's constitutional bisexuality."[43]

In proposing that so-called masculine-feminine traits exist in all personalities, Sanford says of a man having a strong feminine component in personality, "His masculine identity was secure enough so that he could permit himself the indulgence of sublimated femininity . . . rather than being denied or displaced . . . it was a source of creative urge."[45] Beach, in *Sex and Behavior*, speaks about the general handling of cross-sex traits. "Gender role qualities that belong to the opposite sex are usually viewed as unacceptable and are often not recognized by the person possessing them."[4]

Thus we see outlined the model of alienation and denial which we universally experience to varying degrees. The period of greatest stress due to alienation varies for the two sexes. It appears that the patterns and values of childhood are oriented around what we have called the feminine principle. Consequently this is the time when males suffer most from the alienation of denial of self. The patterns and values of adolescence and adulthood center around what we have called the masculine principle and this is the period of greatest damage to women. In terms of the quantity of years, woman's self-alienation is longer (hence worse) than man's; however, the data of developmental psychology point out the lifelong effects of childhood experiences.

Boyhood/Childhood Alienation

As examples of the alienation-producing effects of traditional masculine-feminine definitions for boys, research data are presented describing boys' intense need to demonstrate they are "not feminine" and data on polarized sex roles and male violence.

Freudian and developmental identification theorists postulate that boys and girls identify with (and hence imitate) their mothers initially. The degree to which boys have to struggle to avoid and deny this 'feminine aspect' of themselves may be interpreted in studies by Emmerich, Lefkowitz, and Fauls. Kathryn Johnson, sociologist from Purdue University writes, "Boys are increasingly aware of the demands of masculinity and have anxiety about being 'good children' and 'real boys' at the same time. Anxieties about assuming masculinity and denying femininity makes girls a natural target for in-group/out-group phenomena. . . . as do boys who do not display masculinity."[25] Hartley and Hardesty, Koch, and Sutton-Smith all suggest that the sanctions for sissiness are much greater than those for tomboyishness.

The effects of polarized sex roles on male patterns of violence and aggression are discussed by Komisar, Kanter, Roszak, Bazin and Freeman, and Schimel. In the interest of time let us review only a small section of Schimel's article in *Contemporary Issues in Sport Psychology* entitled Sporting and Gaming Aspects of Love and War.

"During the heavy U.S. involvement in the Vietnamese war, a statement was made that we would bomb them back to the Stone Age. In this one notes an exhibition of strength, potency, virility. . . . and a psychiatrist notes a parallel to the behavior of small boys. Small boys struggle to retain a sense of play, playfulness, and humor. In a world they never made, in which they have small skills for coping and which highlights their true impotence to influence affairs; they strike poses, they imitate invincible heroes, they mow down enemies with bursts from imaginary sub-machine guns, they wipe out with their H-bombs. They save themselves and their mothers and their self-esteem. There are men who remain children and who bring the passions and wonder of the child to the brute force of sport and war."[48]

Womenhood/Adulthood Alienation

To document this case adequately would be to subsume the whole outcry of the women's movement and is impossible. The enforced denial of those qualities reflecting what we have called the masculine principle has brought psychological damage to women on a savage scale. Fauls, Weisstein, Cohen, Friedan, de Beauvoir, and Daly comment on the alienation of traditional femininity from adult competency values. Komarovsky, Dixon, Schoeppe, Coleman, Sutton-Smith, and Webb have all alluded to the outer-directedness of qualities of traditional femininity and the social devaluation of these qualities. Horner and others have focused on achievement problems and fear of success. Many studies are just now turning to the effects on women of their status as targets of direct discrimination, prejudice, and tokenism. Truly, alienation of self from self exacts its toll from men and women, boys and girls, in our society. As the Roszaks ask in the preface to *Masculine-Feminine,* how do we call off the deadly game?

IDENTIFICATION OF NEW STRUCTURES

To call off the game, we must have what Roszak calls "a changed society with changed definitions of sexuality."[44] Felshin, in Triple Option for Women in Sport also proposes the radical view that change for men and women in sport is predicated on change for men and women in society.[18] Alice Rossi calls for a hybridization of society wherein dominant (masculine) and minority (feminine) values are both changed.[44] Is it possible that sport may provide the arena/laboratory where human beings can practice calling off the masculinity-femininity game? That is exactly what is proposed but the task will not be easy. Sport has existed too long as a primary social mode for the stylization of stereotypic sexuality. Felshin states, "The dramatic equation of sport has yielded a stylistic and social formula for manhood . . . the athletic and masculine models (of competition, power, and dominance) are interchangeable."[19]

This isomorphism between traditional sport and masculinity, however, makes sport a perfect vehicle (the not-so-tragic flaw) to utilize in bringing down the false and debilitating construct which immobilizes us.

Sport as Androgyny Training

We call off the masculinity-femininity game in sport by recognizing and publicizing that sport is *not* masculinity training, nor femininity training but androgyny training. All the qualities of fully functioning human beings are potentially communicable/reinforceable in sport. In other papers, the author has proposed that sport is an ambiguous context in which the noble or the base in human personality and spirit may be expressed.[41] Similarly, sport is inherently ambiguous as to sexuality training but it may provide an environment for the development of all desirable human qualities—those of the so-called masculine and feminine principle. This is the truth which we in sport are in a unique position to propose as a replacement for the myth of dichotomous sexuality training. For example, we have long proposed that sport participation can assist the development of independence and dominance (two qualities of the so-called masculine principle).

Table 7. Androgyny and the Experiencing of Sport

Female Athletes	Male Athletes
Joan Joyce (SI, Sept, 73), "I set up private challenges for myself. I play sports seriously."	Herzog on attaining Annapurna, "I was stirred to the depths of my being. Never had I felt happiness like this—so intense, yet so pure" (Quest, 1968).
Billie Jean King (WomanSport, Apr, 75), "What I really liked was that all the women superstars were really gutsy."	Slusher—"Athletes hang loose but tough . . . they relax and let sport turn them on" (Slusher: 1967).
Esther Williams (WomanSport, Apr, 75), "Men like to think they are the only ones who fight for principle . . . I kept fighting until a beautiful thing happened."	Beisser—"In his relation with his teammate, he found something akin to closeness of mothering" (Beisser: 1967). He continues, "The redeeming factor in this player's life was his freedom in sport to express otherwise constricted physical desires."
Galina Shavrova (WomanSport, Apr, 75), "In our country, men and women are treated equal in sport . . . We (women) need to be strong to build the mother country." Of Elvira Saadi, Russian gymnast: "The crowd seemed awed by her strength."	Ogilvie and Tutko—"relationship with the coach is *trust* in a caring and competent authority figure" (Ogilvie & Tutko: 1966).
Alexandra Mezey (WomanSport, Apr, 75), "In our raft we are swooped right into the foamy white water which seems to put us at a momentary standstill before dunking us with an avalanche of water. It is sheer excitement."	Bill Virdon (SI, Sept, 1973), "I thanked them for the wonderful years they gave me. I couldn't leave them without that. That clubhouse is filled with some mighty fine men."
Of Mary Jo Peppler (WomanSport, Apr, 75), ". . . she turned out to be the second coming of Babe Didrickson except bigger, faster, stronger, and maybe smarter."	Mike Andrews (SI, Oct, 1973), "I don't think I ever had ovation before in my life. It gave me chills."
Of Karen Logan (WomanSport, Apr, 75), ". . . you could watch her walking from 30 feet away and understand something of her pain and determination."	O. J. Simpson (SI, Oct, 1973), "I've cried with these guys . . . now I want to drink champagne with them."
Of Cathy Rigby (WomanSport, Apr, 75), "Cathy Rigby turned out to be a fierce, friendly, modest woman who performed with more courage and determination than almost anyone else."	Wilt Chamberlain (SI, Oct, 1973) "During my European travels, I've found the people there particularly warm. The men are not afraid of touching each other. I think that can be a very supporting thing in coaching."
Debbie Meyer (WomanSport, Apr, 75), As her arms stuck out of the sleeves of the gift sweat suit, "you'd think they never saw anyone with shoulders before."	Bruce Crampton (SI, June, 1973), "Affection; it's the key to the whole thing. You get affection when you show it. It's the only way."
Nancy Kasson (WomanSport, Dec, 74), of the Women's National Road Champion Bike Race . . . "This race would not determine who was gutsy in the corners or who could climb like a goat . . . it would go to the one who could pedal hard and who was not troubled by the heat and humidity."	Gayle Sayers (I *Am Third*), ". . . he was my back-up man and I needed him. When I was tired I depended on him for a rest. . . He was a comfort to me during the 1969 exhibition season. . . he built up my morale."

I believe it is equally possible to demonstrate that sport can and does assist the development of such qualities as dependence and subordination. In softball or baseball, when the squeeze play is on, the runner at third base breaks running with the pitch trusting/depending that the batter will do what she/he must to make the play successful. In the many sacrifice situations (and scores of other instances) a player learns the benefits of subordination of personal glory to team victory.

In Table 7 are reproduced numerous examples of athletes' reports of experiencing/reflecting "cross-sex" traits. It should be emphasized that males and females experience the full complement of human qualities in athletic competition. Why have we been so unaware of the potential of sport for the development of so-called feminine values? A simple explanation would be that almost all males participate or are interested in sport and the duality of stereotypic sexuality has crippled our ability to perceive the role of the development of so-called feminine qualities in men and boys; it has crippled our ability to perceive the role of the development of so-called masculine qualities in women and girls. Sport experiences can enable us to revise and improve our constructs of sexuality. What such construct has a better goodness of fit with the experiences of male and female athletes than our present duality?

Sexuality as a Quality of Interaction

Though utilizing a variety of labels, researchers like Bem and Loevinger appear to postulate three general stages of sexuality awareness: (1) the undifferentiated gender identity stage prior to age 2 to 3 years; (2) conformance period of dichotomous trait sexuality; (3) androgyny or condition of balance of various personality qualities. To call this condition of balance "androgyny" is still to support the notion of a correlated set of traits associated with masculine and feminine principles and is, in some respects, unsatisfactory.

Can we conceive of masculinity/femininity as a construct which is trait-free? The terms would then have reference to a quality of interpersonal interaction alone. Human sexuality is defined, for our purposes, as a quality of interaction between the sexes, such that: masculinity is the level of effectiveness and satisfaction experienced when a male interacts with females; femininity is the level of effectiveness and satisfaction experienced when a female interacts with males. The meaning of this definition may become more clear if resultant postulates are enumerated.

1. Sexuality is a self-perception: a male develops a sense of the effectiveness and satisfaction experienced in interaction with females. This is labeled by him as masculinity. A female develops a sense of

the effectiveness and satisfaction experienced in interaction with males. This is labeled by her as femininity.

2. There is no notion of masculinity except as a male relates to females and there is no notion of femininity except as a female relates to males. The connotative meaning of these two words is radically narrowed by using them in this fashion.

3. The notion of "loss of masculinity" would imply the loss of the capacity to interact effectively and satisfactorily with females; the notion of "loss of femininity" would imply the loss of the capacity for interaction with males.

4. Since sexuality is defined as a quality of human interaction, the application of the term masculine or feminine as adjectives to describe objects would be inaccurate; for example a "feminine sport" or a "masculine toy" would be phrases utterly devoid of meaning.

5. By definition, males cannot be "feminine" (for that signifies a a quality of interaction women experience with men) nor can females be "masculine."

6. The "most masculine male" will be that individual who interacts most effectively (in task orientation) and most satisfactorily (in an emotional orientation) with females in the greatest variety of roles. The "most feminine female" will be that individual who interacts most effectively and satisfactorily with males in the greatest variety of roles.

The devising of a new definition for masculinity/femininity and the identification of a few postulates related to it was a mind-bending personal experience. Not surprisingly, the response often elicited by its presentation sounds suspiciously like Peggy Lee's classic "Is that all there is?" With full knowledge of the inadequacy of this definitional effort to aid in the solution of the problem of sexuality in our society, it is still offered in a spirit of hopefulness. If we can make permeable the construct of sexuality, rid it of a false cloak of supernatural origin, we can create and live new definitions.

We are in need of a construct which, in its brilliance and order, would expose and shatter the androcentric prison which destroys women.

But as scientists we have read too much and observed too much to honestly propose that women suffer more from this aberration of our society. Little boys cry and fathers and brothers die before they should, at the hands of androcentrism.

If we are truly in professions in the service of humankind, we must take the power in our hands. . . . the power we have to change our heads and change the world. We cannot begin the process with infants only and hope that by the time they grow up the change will have occurred painlessly. Without dramatic changes in adult society, the

4

world of children will not change. We cannot begin the processes with girls and women only and hope that they can help men and boys to change painlessly. As de Beauvoir has observed, "The forest must be planted all at once." We must plant it now. We must face the responsibility that if we are not active planters and growers, we are destroyers.

REFERENCES

1. Andrews, Mal: Physical education and sports: Business as usual vs. by any means necessary. *Issues in Physical Education and Sport*, National Press Books, University of San Francisco, 1974.
2. Barclay, Allan G. and D. R. Consumano: Testing Masculinity in Boys without Fathers. *Transaction*, 7, 18, 1970.
3. Baughman, E. Earl and Samuel Guskin: Sex Differences on the Rorschach. *J. Consulting Psychol.*, 22, 400, 1958.
4. Beach, Frank A.: *Sex and Behavior*. New York, John Wiley & Sons, 1965.
5. Bem, S. L.: Sex role adaptability: one consequence of psychological androgyny. *J. Personality and Social Psychol.*, 31, 634, 1975.
6. Bennett, Edward M. and Larry Cohen: Men and Women: Personality Patterns and Contrasts. *Genetic Psychology Monograph*, 59, 101, 1959.
7. Bernard, H. W. and Wesley Huckings: *Readings in Human Development*. Boston, Allyn and Bacon, Inc., 1967.
8. Boring, Phyllis: Little League: For Boys Only, testimony in favor of Little League Bill, H.R. 8864, Congressional Hearings, Spring, 1974.
9. Brim, Orville: Family Structure and Sex Role Learning by Children. *Sociometry*, 21, 1, 1958.
10. Cohen, Mabel: Personal identity and sexual identity. *Psychiatry*, 29, 1, 1966.
11. Coleman, James S.: *The Adolescent Society*. Glencoe, Illinois, Free Press, 1961.
12. DeBeauvoir, Simone: *The Second Sex*. New York, Alfred A. Knopf, 1957.
13. DeWit, Gerard: *Symbolism of Masculinity and Femininity*. New York, Springer Publishing Co. Inc., 1863.
14. Dixon, Marlene: The rise of women's liberation, *Masculine Feminine*. New York, Harper Colophon Books, 1969.
15. Duquin, Mary: The philosophic effects of culture on women's experience in sport. Unpublished paper, University of Pittsburgh, 1975.
16. Emmerich, Walter: Parental Identification in Young Children. *Genetic Psychol. Monograph*, 60, 57, 1959.
17. Fauls, L. B. and Walter Smith: Sex Role Learning of 5 years olds. *J. Genetic Psychol.*, 88, 105, 1956.
18. Felshin, Jan: Triple Option for Women in Sport, *Quest XXI*, NAPECW and NCPEAM, Jan. 1974.
19. Felshin, Jan: Sport, Style, and Social Mode. *J. Physical Education Recreation*, 46, 31, 1975.
20. Friedan, Betty: *The Feminine Mystique*. New York, W. W. Norton and Co., 1963.
21. Gagnon, John: Sexuality and Sex Learning in the Child. *Psychiatry*, 28, 3, 1965.
22. Gerber, Ellen: My Body, Myself. Unpublished paper, 50th Annual Convention of Texas Association for Health, Physical Education, Recreation, Dallas, Nov. 29, 1973.
23. Hartley, Ruth and Francis Hardesty: Children's Perception of Sex Roles in Childhood. *J. Genetic Psychol.*, 105, 43, 1964.

24. Horner, Matina: Femininity and successful achievement: A basic inconsistency. *Feminine Personality and Conflict,* Belmont, Brooks/Cole, 1970.
25. Johnson, Kathryn: Development of Human Values Through Sport: A Sociological Perspective. *Proceedings of National Conference,* Springfield College, Washington, D.C., American Association of Health, Physical Education, Recreation, 1974.
26. Jourard, Sidney: *The Transparent Self.* New York, D. Van Nostrand Co., 1971.
27. Kagen, Jerome and Howard A. Moss: Stability of Passive and dependent Behavior from Childhood through Adulthood. *Child Development, 31,* 577, 1960.
28. Kanter, Rosabeth: Women in organizations: change agent skills. *New Technology in Organizational Development,* National Training Lab Institute, 1974.
29. Kelly, George: *Psychology of Personal Constructs.* New York, W. W. Norton and Co. Inc., 1955.
30. Koch, H. L.: Sissiness and Tomboyishness in relation to Sibling characteristics. *J. Genetic Psychol., 88,* 231, 1956.
31. Komarovsky, Mirra: Functional analysis of sex roles. *American Sociological Review,* Aug. 1950.
32. Knopf, Irwin J. and T. W. Richards: Child's Differentation of Sex as Reflected in Drawings of Human Figure. *J. Genetic Psychol., 81,* 99, 1952.
33. Landers, Daniel: Psychological Femininity and the Prospective Physical Educator. *Research Quarterly, 41,* 164, 1970.
34. Lansky, Leonard: The Family Structure Also Affects the Model. *Merrill-Palmer Quartery,* April, 1967.
35. Lefkowitz, M. M.: Some relationships between sex role preference of children and other parent and child variables. *Psychological Reports, 10,* 43, 1962.
36. Maccoby, Eleanor: Women's Intellect, *The Potential of Women.* New York, McGraw-Hill Book Co., Inc., 1963.
37. Maccoby, Eleanor and Carol Jacklin: *The Psychology of Sex Differences.* Stanford, Calif., Stanford University Press, 1974.
38. Martin, Wendy (ed.): *Women's Studies: An Interdisciplinary. J., 2,* 1974.
39. Mead, Margaret: *Male and Female.* New York, New American Library, 1964.
40. Money, John (ed.): *Sex Research: New Developments.* New York, Holt, Rinehart & Winston, 1965.
41. Oglesby, Carole: The Saga of Nellie Namath, *Development of Human Values Through Sport,* Proceedings of the National conference, Springfield College, Washington, D.C., American Association for Health, Physical Education, Recreation, 1974.
42. Parsons, A.: Socialization of Sex Roles. Unpublished paper, Smith College, Northampton, Massachusetts, 1975.
43. Parsons, Talcott and Robert F. Bales: *Family, Socialization, and Interaction Process.* Glencoe, Ill., Free Press, 1955.
44. Roszak, Theodore and Betty Roszak: *Masculine/feminine.* New York, Harper Colophon Books, 1969
45. Sanford, Nevitt: *Self and Society.* New York, Atherton Press, 1966.
46. Sayers, Gayle: *I am Third,* New York, Bantam Book, 1970.
47. Schoeppe, Aileen: Sex Differences in Adolescent Socialization. *J. Social Psychol., 38,* 175, 1953.
48. Schimel, John: The Sporting and Gaming Aspects of Love and War. *Contemporary Issues in Psychology of Sport,* Chicago, Athletic Institute, 1940.
49. Sears, Robert A., Lucy Rau, and Richard Alpert: *Identification and Child Rearing.* Stanford, California, Stanford University Press, 1965.
50. Sherif, Carolyn: The Social Context of Competition. Unpublished paper, *Conference on Sport and Social Deviancy,* State University of New York, Brockport, 1971.
51. Slusher, Howard: *Man, Sport and Existence.* Philadelphia, Lea & Febiger, 1967.

52. Sutton-Smith, Brian, B. G. Rosenberg and E. F. Morgan, Jr.: Development of Sex Differences in Play Choices During Preadolescence. *Child Development, 34,* 119, 1963.
53. Webb, Allen P.: Sex role preference and adjustment in early adolescents. *Child Development, 34,* 609, 1963.
54. Weisstein, Naomi: Psychology constructs the female, or the fantasy life of the male psychologist, *Roles Women Play,* Brooks/Cole, 1971.
55. Witkin, H. A.: *Psychological Differentiation.* New York, John Wiley & Sons, 1962.

Chapter 5

THE ANDROGYNOUS ADVANTAGE

Mary E. Duquin

Within the past decade, sport has undergone a variety of judicial analyses. Critics have explored the areas of sport ethics, economics, politics, racism and sexism.[18,25] Currently, one of the most controversial and dramatic issues in sport is that of female equality in opportunity and involvement in the sport experience.

The history of sport is generally one of masculine domination.[47] Such domination results from cultural patterns and perceptions which determine not only who participates in sport but how sport is conducted and experienced. However, male dominated sport is becoming an antiquated concept in many corners of the sport world, and today's emphasis on the growth and expansion of women's involvement in sport has important implications for how sport will be perceived and conducted in the future.

The more interesting areas of investigation involve questions concerning how sport involvement could affect women, how female involvement in sport could change society's perception of sport, and how society's perception of sport influences the number of women attracted to the sport experience.

The basic issues of how cultural perception and psychological motivations relate to the general perception of sex roles and psychological well-being will be explored. Then three different cultural perceptions of sport, sport perceived and conducted as an agent of masculine orientation, sport perceived and conducted as an instrumental activity suitable for both sexes and sport perceived and conducted as an androgynous activity, will be examined in greater detail.

SOCIO-PSYCHOLOGICAL PERCEPTIONS OF SEX ROLES

The socially distinct roles played by men and women lead societies to label certain behaviors and traits as masculine and certain others as feminine. This bipolar view of behavior has both historical and cross-cultural significance.[37] Generally, the traits needed to fulfill a given sex role are considered desirable for that sex.[3] Thus, for example, in many cultures the child-rearing domestic female must be able to perform expressively. Expressive behavior is characterized by the capability to be understanding, sympathetic, affectionate, compassionate and tender. These traits, together with others such as sensitivity, warmth and shyness, combine to form a social image of femininity. Likewise, in many cultures the publicly oriented male must perform instrumentally, that is, be independent, assertive, ambitious, aggressive, and willing to take risks. Thus, a socially "masculine" or instrumental image is described in terms of leadership, dominance and competitive tendencies.

The fact that societies generally ascribe instrumental traits to males and expressive traits to females does not assure the validity or desirability of such ascriptions. Nevertheless, the subsequent belief that sex-typed socialization of individuals contributes to psychological well-being and healthy social adjustment has usually followed.[5] In some societies such segregation of sex roles may function efficiently. However, the more complex the society is, that is, the greater number of roles which must be learned, the more dubious the efficiency of such a system, and the greater the likelihood of sex-typed role conflict.

The participation of women in sport has often been cited as an example of this role conflict.[24] Various writers have claimed that the role of the expressively-oriented female is in conflict with the role of the instrumentally-oriented athlete.[53] Some writers have even proposed that female participation in sport robs males of the right to sport as an agent of masculine orientation.[19,50] The implicit assumption here is that psychological health and social adjustment rests on the maintenance of instrumentality as a male preserve and expressiveness a female preserve. Recent developments in social psychology, however, have stressed the need to reassess the definition of psychological well-being as it relates to the practice of sex-typing.[3,10,31] Research on highly sex-typed individuals has provided evidence which supports the belief that a high degree of sex role development is not conducive to behavioral flexibility and does not necessarily facilitate general social or psychological well-being.[4]

Studies on females have shown that high femininity is associated with poor adjustment, low social acceptance, and high anxiety.[14,22,49] Research on high masculine adult males has shown them to have high anxiety, and neuroticism and low self-acceptance.[23,34,35] Maccoby[31] has summarized the research on the effect of sex-typing on intellectual development and has found that greater intellectual development seems to be associated with cross sex-typing. In describing cross sex-typing Bem[2] states, "In girls, impulsiveness and aggressiveness are positive factors, whereas fearfulness and passivity are negative factors. In boys, the pattern of correlations is exactly the reverse." Cross sex-typed individuals have been found to have higher creativity, higher spatial abilities and higher overall intelligence.[31]

The benefits of cross sex-typing have important implications for interpreting the research regarding female participation in a culturally perceived cross sex-typed activity such as sport. High scores on the personality dimensions of autonomy and achievement orientation so often reported for female athletes provide evidence as to the ability of these women to be instrumentally oriented.[9,17,36] Further research suggests, however, that although female athletes see themselves as instrumental in sport situations, they see themselves as typically feminine (expressive) in social situations.[32,38] Although some research has found female athletes to score below the norm on some feminine traits,[26] typical measures of masculinity and femininity tend to polarize male and female attributes, rendering impossible the recognition of individuals who perceive themselves as both instrumental *and* expressive, (i.e., androgynous).[4] The psychological rubric "androgyny" describes those persons who perceive themselves as being both instrumental *and* expressive, both assertive *and* yielding, both masculine *and* feminine.[4]

Proceeding with a firm belief in the existence of androgynous persons, Bem[6] constructed the Bem's Sex Role Inventory (BSRI) which places masculinity and femininity in two dimensions, thus allowing for the identification of the androgynous individual. On the BSRI scale individuals score masculine, feminine or androgynous according to the degree of difference between their masculinity and femininity scores. Using the BSRI to classify individuals masculine, feminine or androgynous, Bem[4] tested the assumption that sex-typing contributes to psychological well-being and behavioral flexibility. Bem tested the hypothesis that sex-typed individuals would tend to exhibit defensive trait-like consistency in their responses to situations which call for behavior in conflict with their perceived sex role expectations (i.e., feminine, or masculine). Androgynous individuals as Bem hypothesized are expected to exhibit behavioral flexibility by performing effectively in both the instrumental and expressive domains.

The experimental results of Bem's research[5,8] found that given an instrumental task, males and females who scored androgynous or masculine on the BSRI performed significantly better than males and females who scored feminine. When given an expressive task, Bem found that androgynous and feminine individuals performed better than masculine individuals.

In a further study on the avoidance of cross-sex behavior, Bem[7] found that sex-typed individuals were more likely than sex-reversed or androgynous individuals to prefer sex-appropriate activity and to resist sex-inappropriate activity. Results also indicated that when required to perform a cross sex-typed activity, the sex-typed individuals experienced the most discomfort and felt the worst about themselves.

As a whole, Bem's research shows that individuals with androgynous capabilities are more likely to possess behavioral flexibility and psychological well-being in today's complex society.

An important sports education problem, stemming from androgyny research, concerns the vital need to develop in feminine females a sense of instrumentality. In addressing this problem three important issues must be raised. The first concerns how females might come to feel instrumental. An understanding of this issue is suggested by self perception theory which states that,

> "Individuals come to 'know' their own attitudes, emotions and other internal states partially by inferring them from observations of their own overt behavior and/or the circumstances in which this behavior occurs."[3]

This suggests that the process of socialization can work in both directions, i.e., "I am what others tell me I should be" and "I am the way I see myself behave."

According to self-perception theory, females may come to view themselves as being capable of instrumental activity if they observe themselves engaging in instrumental activities.

The second issue concerns what activities may facilitate instrumental development. Assuming sport provides instrumental experiences and research shows that females benefit psychologically if their sense of instrumentality is nourished, then sport could and should make a significant contribution to the development of female instrumentality.

The final problem concerns how to induce females to engage in instrumental activities given that "feminine" females avoid participation in such cross sex-typed activities.

In attracting females to the sport experience, one of the more important aspects to consider may be the way sport is perceived. Such perception may influence both the type and number of females attracted to the sport experience. In addition, how sport is conducted influences the kind and quality of experience provided by the sport encounter.

As a result of various social forces (e.g., the Women's Movement, Civil Rights Movement) U.S. culture is slowly evolving its view of sport, especially as it relates to female participation. The direction of change is from a perception of sport as an "agent of masculine orientation" to a perception of sport as an "instrumental" activity open to and desirable for both sexes. A third and more desirable perception of sport as an "androgynous" activity, that is, an activity which requires and fulfills both instrumental and expressive tendencies is proposed.

The following sections explore these three cultural perceptions of sport, and the effects of these perceptions on the type and number of females attracted to the sport experience.

SPORT AS AN AGENT OF MASCULINE ORIENTATION

Literature in the fields of psychology and sport psychology give much support to the view that sport and athletics are generally perceived as a male sex-typed activity.[15,27] Everything from children's textbooks to the toys parents buy for their children attests to the perceived masculine orientation of sport.

Experiments on parents indicate that male infants are physically stimulated, thrown about and played with more roughly than their female counterparts. Although there is no physical rationale to justify differential treatment, parents treat female infants as if they were more fragile. Research involving older children finds that parents give male children more autonomy and freedom to explore the environment than female children. These freedoms correlate highly with non-verbal and spatial abilities in which boys, on the average, excel girls.[16,27]

One of the most extreme sex differences found in childhood occurs in play behavior. Boys and girls discover early what are considered appropriate games, toys and playmates for their sex. In nursery school boys tend to play in larger groups than girls and tend to aggress and roughhouse more than girls. By second grade both girls and boys classify athletics as a masculine activity.[45]

Parents also encourage and reward sex-typed behavior as illustrated in the types of toys they buy for their girls and boys and the kind of clothing in which they dress their children. Little girls are often clothed in dresses which are inappropriate for vigorous physical play.

In elementary textbooks the masculine image of activity is reinforced. Child, Potter and Levine[13] discovered that girls in these books risk little and gain little. The passivity ascribed to females causes them to be portrayed as lazy far more often than males. Investigating California State Series texts, Kidd[28] found sexual role dramatized in the following way:

> "Mark! Janet. . . .! " said Mother
> "What is going on here?"
> "She cannot skate," said Mark
> "I can help her.
> I want to help her.
> Look at her, Mother.
> Just look at her.
> She is just like a *girl*.
> She gives up."
>
> Mother forces Janet to try again.
>
> "Now you see," said Mark.
> "Now you can skate.
> But just with me to help you."

These books reinforce in the minds of girls *and* boys that sport, vigorous activity and risk-taking are appropriate behaviors for males but not for females. As Bem[3] states, "When females appear, they are noteworthy primarily for what they do *not* do. Boys in these stories climb trees and fish and roll in the leaves and skate. Girls watch, fall down, and get dizzy."

Within the framework of this perception the female psyche is perceived as too weak or nervous for the strain of sport competition and the female body is described as inefficient or unsuited for sports.[11] Participation of females in sport is seen somehow to lower the quality of sport participation and spectatorship.[20] The results of perceiving sport as an agent of masculine orientation has serious consequences for the conduction of sport programs.

The primary indication that sport is being conducted as a male sex-typed activity is the greatly different status accorded male and female sport programs. The higher priority given male sport programs as regards facilities, equipment, publicity, coaches' salaries, training, awards, and budget indicates that sport is being perceived as an activity considered primarily for males.

Perceiving and conducting sport as a sex-typed activity has significant effects on both males and females as well as on the profession of physical education itself. Much professional time has been devoted to discussing, debating, deciding and then dictating what females should and should not be allowed to do in the realm of sport. Certain sports and sport events are deemed inappropriate or even illegal for female participation.[33] For example, females are restricted from pole vaulting, high hurdles, hammer-throw and long distance Olympic swimming and running events. Inappropriate sports include wrestling, football and ice hockey.

Females are artificially limited, before the fact, by rules based on preconceived notions of what is appropriate or even what is humanly possible for them to achieve. Males, however, are allowed to repeatedly redefine their human limits by striving to achieve beyond known boundaries.

Physical education curricula are also affected by sex role expectations. Typical of curricula which espouse a philosophy based on fulfilling pupil needs, the California State Department of Education's Physical Education Framework[12] advocates that girls spend a greater percentage of their time in dance than boys and that boys spend a greater percentage of their time in team sports and physical fitness activities. Conditioning exercises for "figure control" and improvement of "posture" are also a special recommendation for girls.

These curricula recommendations are usually suggested without the benefit of any substantiating physiological research data. Why boys need team sports more than girls and why girls need dance more than boys is not explained. What does seem to be a logical result of this lopsided curricula, however, is that physical education programs produce many rhythmical females who bemoan the fact that they are destined to dance alone!

Such sex biased curricula are based on traditional notions of what males and females should learn. This curriculum bias is akin to a U.S. history course which requires that only the girls learn about the suffrage movement and only the boys learn about the World Wars, because that is where their interests lie. As Wilson[51] so aptly questions, "Do we or do we not have a subject matter" in physical education.

Wherever sex bias infiltrates, curricula and teachers alike are affected. Another effect of sex typing sport as masculine is that physical abilities and coordinations become associated with males and, as a result, teachers often expect much less of their female pupils in the early grades and, in turn, come to offer less to them in the upper grades. Although the literature does not support physiological sex differences which would significantly affect physical skill performance in the pre-pubescent child, teachers and tests will often set much lower standards for girls or expect less from them.[52] And as teacher expectation research has shown, often what a teacher expects of a child is exactly what occurs, be it good performance or poor performance.[40]

Within the sex-typed view of sport, girls are more likely to come to view their bodies as passive objects to be adorned rather than as active and able agents to be used to control and direct their destiny. Consequently, females are less likely to develop their physical potentials. Sex-typing sports and sport proficiency as masculine tends to set up the masculine standard as the norm. Thus if a girl runs or bats a ball correctly, she is said to "Run like a boy" or "Bat like a guy." Females come to learn that correct and coordinated movement patterns are associated with males and that uncoordinated and inefficient movement patterns are associated with females i.e., "He runs like a girl—help him". Some girls come to accept this standard for feminine movement and ability as normal and consequently have a poor concept of themselves in sport performance situations.[42] This attitude can detrimentally affect movement patterns and physical attributes and thus severely handicap women with regard to their perceived or actual ability to operate, by choice or by chance, independently without the protection or assistance of a male.

Sport perceived and conducted as an agent of masculine orientation thus appears to have a number of negative consequences for females. However, one final characteristic of this sport perception is important to mention. Sport perceived as an agent of masculine orientation is conducted as a highly instrumental activity characterized by a strong emphasis on the participant's autonomy-power capabilities and the end results achieved. Sport conducted with such extreme instrumental orientation is likely to develop the characteristic of high masculinity. That is, sport, untempered by a sufficient concern and sensitivity to people and processes, is likely to be characterized by arrogance, exploitation and callosity. The traditionally unexpected involvement of women in sport has resulted in women avoiding the roles of sport victim or victimizer, roles which often characterize activities conducted with extreme instrumental orientations.

IMPLICATIONS FOR FEMALE PARTICIPATION

The major result of perceiving sport as an "agent of masculine orientation", that is an instrumental activity suitable only for males, is that a majority of females will not desire prolonged or serious participation in such an activity. This fact has been substantiated by research which has found that the importance of participating in sport declines drastically for girls around puberty.[16,46] The important issue of female performance in sport and female attraction to sport must be considered when evaluating the effects of sport perception.

Using Bem's psychological categories, predictions can be made about how psychologically predisposed each group of females is toward high performance in sport. Holding physical potential constant, both androgynous and masculine females should be able to perform well on a cross sex-typed activity like sport. The psychologically "feminine" female, however, given the same physical potential for performance, would not be expected to perform as well. Because of her sex typing she would likely experience psychological conflicts which would inhibit her performance.

If one assumes that people are attracted to those activities they perceive as being compatible with their own psychological frameworks, then it is possible to determine how attracted each female group is to the sport experience. Bem's data suggest that "feminine" females, when given a choice, would reject sport as an activity they would enjoy performing because they perceive sport as a cross sex-typed activity and would therefore feel uncomfortable performing instrumentally.

Table 8 illustrates the expected female attraction to and performance in sport perceived and conducted as a masculine activity. Masculine and androgynous women are expected to be moderately attracted to such sport and are expected to perform well. Feminine women, however, are expected to have a low attraction and low performance in sport.

Table 8. Sport Perceived as an Agent of Masculine Orientation

Females Classified on the BSRI	Expected Performance	Expected Attraction
Masculine	High	Moderate
Androgynous	High	Moderate
Feminine	Low	Low

In summary, sport, when perceived as an instrumental, cross sex-typed activity has little overall appeal to women and has a low appeal to the feminine female who, in fact, has the greatest need for experiencing such instrumental activities.

SPORT AS AN INSTRUMENTAL ACTIVITY FOR BOTH SEXES

The cultural perception of sports as an instrumental activity open to and desirable for females is a growing but not yet established perception. This perception enlarges upon the sex-typed perception of sport as an agent of masculine orientation by advocating that females can and should benefit from the instrumental sport experience. An important aspect of this perception of sport is the right of women to develop their physical potentials, appreciate their physical abilities and enjoy the mastery of their bodies in sporting activity.

Another aspect is the equalitarian approach to sport which claims that *if* participation in sport is going to mold leaders, build stamina, heighten competitive spirit, produce physical fitness, create mental toughness and put students through college, then girls, as well as boys, should have equal opportunity to participate in sport and gain such benefits. However, sport perceived as an instrumental activity for both sexes is based upon and includes more than just the value of equalitarianism. Viewing sport from this perspective affects the sex-typed value of instrumentality.

The effect of changing the perception of sport from a sex-typed activity to a sex neutral activity has some intriguing psychosocial consequences.

Society has traditionally expected males to be instrumental, not expressive and females to be expressive, not instrumental. Perceiving sport as an instrumental activity open to and desirable for both sexes in effect says instrumentality is a valuable trait for both males and females. This neutralization of instrumentality as a male preserve does not in any way neutralize expressivity as a female preserve. Thus, under this perception males are still expected to be solely instrumental, while females are expected to be both instrumental and expressive.

The perception that instrumentality is important for both sexes has the effect of elevating the status of instrumental traits and behaviors over expressive traits and behaviors. One further step results in the subtle assumption that instrumentality is *the* only "orientation for a healthy adult to possess."[10]

As an instrumental activity, sports focus is a product versus process orientation. Instrumental sport is primarily concerned with the ends achieved. This instrumental perspective is successfully portrayed in common locker room slogans such as those reported by Snyder.[43] These slogans deal with themes of aggressiveness, competitive spirit, stamina, and discipline, all important aspects of instrumental sport.

> Win by as many points as possible
> Give 100 per cent or get out
> We issue everything but guts
> Be good or be gone
> Winning beats anything that comes in second
> No one likes a loser
> A moral victory is like kissing your sister
> Live by the code or get out
> They ask not how you played the game but whether
>   you won or lost
> No one ever drowned in sweat
> Be a doer not a tryer
> We don't want excuses we want results

Women's orientation to sport has traditionally not been this highly instrumental. In fact, research on sex differences in achievement motivation and task competence[48] indicates that women "do not especially learn to value assertive competence above other goals" especially those of affiliation or acceptance by others. Females are more oriented toward "doing something for its own sake without concern for payoff value, becoming absorbed in the task whatever its difficulty," whereas the male orientation is toward "power of winning over the demands of an external task," toward "performance that requires assertiveness via power, autonomy and achievement." Researchers do, however, suggest that given consistent exposure to socially evaluative settings, females are likely to adopt the more instrumental orientation.[48]

Sport conducted as an instrumental activity valuable to both sexes is as stated previously, a philosophically equalitarian approach to sport and is characterized by a sexually equal apportionment of sport opportunities and materials. Recent legislation, such as Title IX of the Educational Amendments Act of 1972, reflects the legal efforts to bring about comparable sport programs in terms of curricular offerings, facilities, equipment, scholarships, competitive opportunities, budget, training and coaching.

Because the perception of sport as an instrumental activity for both sexes is an evolving cultural perception, implications of this perception must necessarily be predictive in nature.

One significant consequence an instrumental orientation of sport for both sexes has, is that programs for women would be created where previously no sport programs existed. Institutions which do provide programs for females may have to alter their programs to establish parity with the existing men's programs. Men's programs *may* be comparable with the women's programs; however, given the greater instrumentality, higher status and culturally valued support of men's programs, legal pronouncements would likely have the effect of requiring women's programs to model themselves on the men's programs or show just causes for the differences in their programs.

Sport, conducted as an instrumental activity, would give primary attention to the more talented and serious sport pursuer as opposed to the less instrumental more expressive participant. Thus interscholastic and intercollegiate sport programs would have higher priority than intramural sport programs. Whereas, in the preceding perception, sports was pursued by nearly all boys as a masculinizing experience, instrumental sport for both sexes would patronize those highly talented individuals of both sexes. Thus poorly skilled boys may find less pressure and possibly less opportunity to participate in intramural sport when financial limitations require assessment of program importance. Conducting sport as an instrument activity open to females would tremendously alter the present sport establishment. Institutions would support women in their desire to explore and expand their physical potentials, pursue sport careers and exhibit pride in their physical capabilities.

Society would construct reward systems for women who have the capabilities and talent to "make it" in the realm of instrumental sport. Physical abilities would be rewarded for both sexes. However, with instrumentality the overriding principle of sport, males may still be considered to be more instrumental in sport because of their general ability to outperform females in those sporting activities involving power, speed and strength. In any case, instrumental sport will require that women, like men, be able to "sell" their sport ability to the public. Finally, sport conducted from this perspective would be likely to enlighten men to the sporting abilities of women, upgrade the quality of female sport performance and improve the overall physical potential of those women attracted to the sport experience.

IMPLICATIONS FOR FEMALE PARTICIPATION

Again the assessment must be made as to which females would be attracted to sport perceived as an instrumental activity and how well

Table 9. Sport Perceived as an Instrumental Activity for Both Sexes

Females Classified on the BSRI	Expected Performance	Expected Attraction
Masculine	High	High
Androgynous	High	High
Feminine	Low	Low–Moderate

they would perform. Bem's data[5,7] would support the hypotheses that masculine and androgynous women would react as they did to sport as a cross sex-typed activity. Both androgynous and masculine women should perform well and be attracted to sport as an instrumental activity for females. Given that sport is defined as an instrumental activity open to *both* sexes, the "feminine" females should have a low to moderate attraction to sport but their actual performance in sport would still likely be low in comparison to masculine and androgynous women. Table 9 is a synopsis of these implications.

The feminine female perceiving sport as an instrumental experience would still have a difficult time finding her way into the sporting experience. If participation in sport becomes part of the social identity of a girl's peer group, then the feminine girl may be pressured into participating and may thus be exposed to instrumental experiences. However, if only successful participants are given the rewards of sport and her level of performance is low, she may decide to change her friends in order to avoid the unrewarding sport experience. In any case, repeated failure in sport would not be conducive to maintaining her involvement. The status of sport in the individual peer group, the individual's ability to perform instrumentally and the attraction of the sport experience all mediate in determining the feminine females' involvement in sport.

THE FUTURE OF SPORT: ANDROGYNY

Androgynous sport is perceived as an activity in which both instrumental and expressive behaviors are experienced, where agency and communion can merge.[6] Western culture perceives sport as primarily instrumental. The question to ask is whether only instrumental qualities are inherent in sport or whether Western societies have merely inhibited or ignored what might be termed the more expressive aspects of the sport experience. According to an androgynous perspective, sport can involve the following expressive experiences:

1. Moving with child-like joy and cheerfulness
2. Experiencing passive, defensive, yielding movements

3. Moving and responding to others by understanding what they are communicating non-verbally
4. Moving delicately, tenderly, gently
5. Becoming aware and sensitive of others, their presence, their movements, their emotions
6. Creating beauty with movement, sensing the aesthetic nature of human movement
7. Sensing the introspective quality of becoming absorbed in one's bodily movements and feeling at one with one's body.

Perceiving sport this way is possible because sport is basically human movement and human movement has an infinite variety of qualities. The instrumental view of sport does not necessarily encourage the recognition or emphasis of these other experiences. An androgynous view of sport recognizes the importance of both the sport process and the sport product.

Historically and philosophically the majority of women leaders in physical education have directed their programs for girls from what may be termed an expressive perspective. Product (i.e. winners, stiff competition, high level performance, dedicated training) was ideally to play a subordinate role to process.[11] Given this expressive ideal as the goal, but aware of the product orientation of sport as males played it, (in practice), many female sport encounters were probably quite androgynous.

Some present day organizations are attempting to combine this process-product orientation of sport. The Escelen Sport Institute is one example of an organization which is conducting sport from a more androgynous perspective. An expert from the Escelen Sport Center News states:

> Western Culture is goal and competition oriented. Many of us over-emphasize these aspects and in the process lose the sense of present-time involvement. With it we lose the intense joy of immediacy and the kind of focus that allows for supreme performance, no matter what the activity. One of the greatest challenges to modern man is finding personal balance.[44]

The traditional Eastern orientation to sport is also a more process-product approach which emphasizes body awareness, sensitivity, meditation, and joy. The path of sensitivity to the expressive element in sport culminates in quality performance.[41] Authors writing on the humanistic movement in sport have also urged that present day instrumental sport become more attuned to the individual, to the expressive element in sport, and to the zestful process of sport itself.[39] There are many indications that sport is being experienced as an androgynous activity. The participant feels a sense of fulfillment when participating, as well as when winning. She feels joy, strength, thrill, competence and control when sporting whether in practice or competition. She performs ethically, drawing her ethics from her own self-conscience, with standards which if necessary could rise above a coach's instructions. She performs with confidence and comradeship. She thinks deeply of the balance between means and ends, between seriousness and play. And she thinks it important to live fully all moments in sport. This kind of sport may be difficult to experience if teammates, opponents and coaches approach sport from a totally instrumental perspective. It may also be difficult to experience given the research on overjustification effects,[30] if money, scholarships and extrinsic incentives are perceived as improving the total sport experience. Extrinsic motivations may benefit instrumental sport but may retard the experience of androgynous sport.

Critics may fear that conducting sport as an androgynous activity may result in a deterioration of the quality of sport performance. However, the Eastern perspective and writers, such as Leonard[29] who are familiar with Eastern philosophy, do not predict a lower performance but rather a higher quality more harmonious sport response. The quality of the sport experience would also be enhanced by a mutually respectful and honest relationship between athlete and coach. In addition, sport programs would provide for social as well as competitive experiences between teams and participants. Androgynous sport would provide a mechanism by which the values and viewpoints of the athlete could be recognized and considered in decisions which affect the sport participant and the conduction of sport. Finally, the sport experience would be conducted so as to make operational both instrumental and expressive values thereby providing an enticing and creative medium of human expression for both sexes.

IMPLICATIONS FOR FEMALE PARTICIPATION

Bem's research would support the hypothesis that androgynous and masculine women would both be able to perform well in androgynous sport, although depending upon the specific sport's expressive requirements, androgynous females may perform better. In considering attraction to sport, both masculine and androgynous females should be attracted to sport with the androgynous females being likely to exhibit the stronger attraction. Finally, the feminine woman, who at last has found a substantial expressive component in sport, would for the first time, be expected to perform moderately well. Feminine females would also be expected to show a moderate attraction to androgynous sport (Table 10).

Androgynous sport would be expected to appeal to the largest number of female participants. Those females who perceive them-

Table 10.   Sport Perceived as an Androgynous Activity

Females Classified on the BSRI	Expected Performance	Expected Attraction
Masculine	Moderate–High	Moderate–High
Androgynous	High	High
Feminine	Moderate	Moderate

selves as highly expressive would be able to feel that sport is an activity which could fulfill expressive needs. Likewise, androgynous sport would also appeal to those females who enjoy seeking out instrumental activities.

Returning once again to Bem's conclusion,[6] if it is true that "what separates women from one another is . . . whether their sense of instrumentality or agency has been sufficiently nourished . . ." then, as a means of attracting feminine females to engage in instrumental activities, androgynous sport would appear to be the most attractive perception of sport.

EPICENISM: A STEP BEYOND ANDROGYNY

The androgynous person is one who is able to perform and feel instrumentally and expressively. And sport, viewed androgynously, allows for both instrumental and expressive activity. However, as Bem[6] states:

> The concept of androgyny contains an inner contradiction and hence the seeds of its own destruction . . . the concept of androgyny necessarily pre-supposes that the concepts of masculinity and femininity themselves have distinct and substantive content. But to the extent that the androgynous message is absorbed by the culture the concepts of masculinity and femininity will cease to have such content and the distinctions to which they refer will blur into invisibility. Thus when androgyny becomes a reality, the concept of androgyny will have been transcended.

Thus, the step beyond androgyny is epicenism, the quality of being held in common by both sexes. When society reaches the perceptual point of epicenism, behavior, including sport behavior, will have no gender. Sport will then be perceived as human activity.

REFERENCES

1. Bem, D.: *Self Perception Theory.* New York, Academic Press Inc., 1972.
2. Bem, S. and D. Bem: *Homogenizing the American Woman: the Power of an Unconscious Ideology.* Unpublished manuscript, 1972, P. 8.

3. Bem, S.: Psychology looks at sex roles: where have all the androgynous people gone? Paper presented at the UCLA Symposium on Women, Los Angeles, May 1972.
4. Bem, S.: The measurement of psychological androgyny. *J. Consulting and Clin. Psychol., 42,* 155, 1974.
5. Bem, S.: Sex role adaptability: one consequence of psychological androgyny. *J. Personality and Social Psychol., 31,* 634, 1975.
6. Bem, S.: Beyond androgyny: some presumptuous prescriptions for a liberated sexual identity. Paper presented at the National Institute of Mental Health Conference on New Directions for Research in the Psychology of Women, Madison, Wisconsin, May, 1975.
7. Bem, S. and E. Lenney: Sex typing and the avoidance of cross-sex behavior. *J. Personality and Social Psychol., 33,* 48, 1976.
8. Bem, S., W. Martyna and C. Watson: Sex typing and androgyny: Further explorations of the expressive domain. *J. Personality and Social Psychol., 34,* 1016, 1976.
9. Bird, E. J.: A review and evaluation of the assessment of aggression among women athletes as measured by personality inventories. Proceedings of the fourth Canadian symposium on psycho-motor learning and sport psychology. Waterloo, Ontario, Canada, October, 1972, Pp. 353–364.
10. Broverman, I. K., D. M. Broverman, F. E. Clarkson, P. S. Rosenkrantz and S. R. Vogel: Sex role stereotypes and clinical judgements of mental health. *J. Clin. and Consulting Psychol., 34,* 1, 1970.
11. Burchenal, E.: A constructive program of athletics for school girls: policy, method and activities. *Amer. Physical Education Review, 24,* 272, 1919.
12. California State Physical Education Framework, Sacramento, California, 1973.
13. Child, S., E. Potter and E. Levine: Children's textbooks and personality development: an exploration in the social psychology of education. In J. Posenbleth and W. Allensmith, (Ed.), *Causes of Behavior: Readings in Child Development and Educational Psychology.* Rockleigh, New Jersey, Allyn, 1960.
14. Cosentino, F. and A. Heilbrun: Anxiety correlates of sex-role identity in college students. *Psychology Reports, 14,* 729, 1964.
15. Cratty, B.: *Social Dimensions of Physical Activity.* Englewood Cliffs, New Jersey, Prentice-Hall Inc., 1967.
16. Cratty, B.: *Psychology and Physical Activity.* Englewood Cliffs, New Jersey, Prentice-Hall, Inc., 1968.
17. Dayries, J. and R. Grimm: Personality Traits of Women Athletes as measured by the Edwards Personal Preference Schedule. *Perceptual and Motor Skills, 30,* 229, 1970.
18. Edwards, H.: *Sociology of Sport.* Homewood, Illinois, The Dorsey Press, 1973.
19. Fisher, A.: Sports as an agent of masculine orientation. *The Physical Educator, 29,* 120, 1972.
20. Gilbert, B. and N. Williamson: Sport is Unfair to Women. *Sports Illustrated.* May 28, 1973, Pp. 88–98.
21. Gilbert, B. and N. Williamson: Are you closed minded? *Sports Illustrated.* June 4, 1973, Pp. 45–55.
22. Gray, S.: Masculinity-femininity in relation to anxiety and social acceptance. *Child Development, 28,* 203, 1957.
23. Harford, T., C. Willis and H. Deabler: Personality correlates of masculinity-femininity. *Psychological Reports, 21,* 881, 1967.
24. Hart, M.: Stigma or prestige: the all American choice. In G. McGlynn (Ed.), *Issues in Physical Education and Sports.* Palo Alto, California, National Press Books, 1974, Pp. 214–220.
25. Hoch, P.: *Rip Off the Big Game.* Garden City, New York, Doubleday and Co., Inc., 1972.

26. Ibrahim, H.: Comparison of temperament traits among intercollegiate athletes and physical education majors. *Res. Quart., 38,* 615, 1967.
27. Kagan, J. and H. Moss: *Birth to Maturity.* New York, John Wiley and Sons, Inc., 1962.
28. Kidd, V.: Now you see, said Mark. *New York Review of Books.* September, 35, 1970.
29. Leonard, G.: Winning isn't everything, it's nothing. *Intellectual Digest,* October, 1973.
30. Lepper, M. R., D. Greene and R. Nisbett: Undermining children's intrinsic interest with extrinsic reward: a test of the overjustification hypothesis. *J. Personality and Social Psychol., 28,* 129, 1973.
31. Maccoby, E. E.: Sex differences in intellectual functioning. In E. E. Maccoby (Ed.), *The Development of Sex Differences.* Stanford, California, Stanford University Press, 1966, Pp. 25–55.
32. Malumphy, T.: Personality of women athletes in intercollegiate competition. *Research Quarterly, 36,* 610, 1968.
33. Metheny, E.: Symbolic forms of movement: the feminine image in sports. In *Connotations of Movement in Sport and Dance.* Dubuque, Iowa, Wm. C. Brown Co., 1965, Pp. 43–56.
34. Mussen, P.: Some antecedents and consequents of masculine sex-typing in adolescent boys. *Psychological Monographs, 75,* No. 506, 1961.
35. Mussen, P.: Long-term consequents of masculinity of interests in adolescence. *J. Consulting Psychol., 26,* 435, 1962.
36. Neal, P.: Personality traits of US women athletes who participated in the 1959 Pan-American Games as measured by EEPS. Master's thesis, University of Utah, Salt Lake City, Utah, 1963.
37. Ortner, S.: Is female to male as nature is to culture? In M. Rosaldo and L. Lamphere, (Eds.), *Woman, Culture and Society.* Stanford, California, Stanford University Press, 1974, Pp. 67–87.
38. Rector, J.: Selected personality variables in social and competitive situations as perceived by female athletes. Masters of Science thesis. Pennsylvania State University, 1971.
39. Scott, J.: Sport and the radical ethic. In G. McGlynn, (Ed.), *Issues in Physical Education and Sport.* Palo Alto, California, National Press Books, 1974, Pp. 155–162.
40. Silberman, C.: *Crisis in the Classroom.* New York, Random House, 1971.
41. Smith, A.: The Zen approach to sports. *Psychology Today, 9,* 48, 1975.
42. Smith, H. and M. Clifton: Sex differences in expressed self concepts concerning the performance of selected motor skills. *Perceptual and Motor Skills, 14,* 71, 1962.
43. Snyder, E.: Athletic dressing room slogans as folklore; a means of socialization. *International Review of Sport Sociology,* 89–100, 1972.
44. Spino, M.: Sports and the energy body. *Escelen Sports Center News, 1,* 1973.
45. Stein, A. and J. Smithells: Age and sex differences in children's sex role standards about achievement. *Developmental Psychology, 1,* 252, 1969.
46. Tyler, S.: Adolescent crisis: sport participation for the female. In D. Harris (Ed.), *DGWS Research Reports: Women in Sports, 2,* 27, 1973.
47. Van Dalen, M. and B. Bennett: *A World History of Physical Education.* Englewood Cliffs, New Jersey, Prentice-Hall, Inc., 1958.
48. Veroff, J., L. McClelland and D. Ruhland: Varieties of Achievement Motivation. In M. Mednick, S. Tangri, and L. Hoffman (Eds.), *Women and Achievement.* Washington, D. C., Hemisphere Publishing Corp., 1975, Pp. 172–205.
49. Webb, A.: Sex role preferences and adjustment in early adolescents. *Child Development, 34,* 609, 1963.
50. Werner, P.: The role of physical education in gender identification. *The Physical Educator, 29,* 27, 1972.

51. Wilson, B.: The battle between the sexes in physical education. *The Physical Educator, 29,* 139, 1972.
52. Wyrick, W.: The physiological support system. In E. Gerber, J. Felshin, P. Berlin and W. Wyrick (Eds.), *The American Woman in Sport.* Reading, Massachusetts, Addison-Wesley Publishing Co., 1974, P. 475.
53. Zobel, J.: Femininity and achievement in sports. In D. Harris (Ed.), *Women and Sport: a National Research Conference.* Pennsylvania State HPER Series No. 2, 1972, Pp. 203–224.

Chapter 6

THE APOLOGETIC AND WOMEN IN SPORT*

Patricia Del Rey

Felshin[2] suggested that an "apologetic" in the woman athlete operates to maintain femininity and therefore reduce the cognitive dissonance she may experience. The female athlete is a social anomaly, according to Felshin, and as a result may attempt to emphasize her femininity, while expressing a strong commitment to sport participation. Emphasizing femininity may take the form of dressing in sex-appropriate ways, not taking sports seriously, pursuing the so-called more acceptable sports, or in any way reaffirming the feminine values of the society. Given the existence of apologetics, when sport is pursued it is never taken too seriously and at all times the female athlete strives to conform to desirable feminine characteristics. Female athletes will do everything to maintain their own femininity and thus avoid threatening their image. All this is done it would seem, to reduce cognitive dissonance. Other authors have reported the dissonance experienced by the female athlete. Harris[4] found that the female athlete experiences dissonance between her social self and her competitive self. That is, female athletes have viewed themselves as having different and often antithetical qualities on and off the playing field. In social situations the self-reports of female athletes have not differed from the non-athlete. However, the athlete's self-perception in a competitive situation has differed greatly from the non-athlete's overall self-perception. There seemed to be a dichotomy within the female athlete illustrating the dissonance between society's stereotypic view of acceptable female behavior and the qualities necessary for successful participation in a competitive sport.

Moreover, Griffin,[3] using the semantic differential, found that the least valued roles for college students were the female athlete and the female professor. The most highly valued role was that of girl friend and mother. In examining the semantic space between concepts she found the most distance between the female athlete and the ideal

*This chapter is reprinted with permission from D. M. Landers and R. W. Christina (Eds.), *Psychology of Motor Behavior and Sport, Vol. II.* Champaign, Ill., Human Kinetics Publishers, 1977.

woman. These findings are understandable, since the qualities necessary for the ideal woman would certainly not be the same as those necessary for athletic competition: aggression, physical strength, high physical and emotional endurance, strong desire to achieve.

High anxiety has been found in women athletes by Kane.[6] It would seem that this anxiety is the expression of the inner conflict between desires to fulfill her own expectations and her desires to fulfill the expectations outlined by society. Horner[5] has identified the female's conflict between her competitive desires and her desire to fit into society as a double bind. Performance in sport especially intensifies this conflict because athletics is one area that has been historically appropriate for males only. Thus, for the female athlete it is not only that she has exhibited qualities that do not conform to society's "appropriate sex-role," but that she has actively pursued this non-appropriate behavior in what was an exclusively male territory.

Felshin[1] would say that this conflict, anxiety and cognitive dissonance, exists for the female athlete because of the apologetic attitude society has forced her to embrace. In order to maintain femininity, apologetic-oriented behavior appears in order to reduce the unacceptability of the female's participation in sport. Participation in sport in a serious way is inconsistent with society's view of femininity. Therefore, athletes reduce or deny the importance of their athletic prowess and/or exhibit many qualities to support their femininity.

One way to quantify the apologetic attitude of women athletes is to measure their view of the women's role in society. For sportswomen to reconcile feelings about their own femininity and still participate intensely in sport, they may hold onto a traditional or what we may call a conservative view of the women's role in society. In a sense this conservative view would substantiate that sportswomen are "real" women. Moreover, athletes in sports that have traditionally been accepted for women, i.e., sports that conform to acceptable female behavior, figure skating, dance, tennis, gymnastics, swimming, may be freer to have a more liberal view of the women's role. Conversely, sportswomen in many team sport activities which require overt aggression, strength, and even physical contact, i.e., basketball, softball, ice hockey, football, may apologize by espousing a traditional view of the women's role. In the present study tennis players and swimmers were compared to basketball and softball athletes in their view of the women's role. It was hypothesized that the tennis players and swimmers would collectively express a more liberal view of the women's role because they would be experiencing less dissonance and therefore be compelled to express less apologetics.

METHOD

Subjects

The subjects used in the study were 102 female varsity team members from three senior college branches of City University of New York. The varsity teams were tennis, swimming, basketball and softball. Brooklyn College, however, did not have a swimming team.

Apparatus

The Attitude Toward Women Scale (AWS) developed by Spence and Helmreich[8] was the instrument employed. It is a 55-item scale each with four response alternatives (agree strongly to disagree strongly) including the vocational, educational, intellectual roles of women. It includes areas of freedom and independence, dating, courtship, etiquette, sexual behavior, marital relationships and obligations. Normative data are available on approximately 1600 college students.

Design and Procedure

Two factorial designs were employed. A 2 × 3 factorial was employed with the following independent variables: sports conforming to stereotypic sex-role behavior (tennis/swimming as those sports which approximate female sex-role behavior and basketball/softball as those sports that do not) × school in attendance (Queens, Brooklyn and Lehman). The second factorial design was a 4 × 3 with each sport representing four levels of the first independent variable and the three colleges representing three levels of the second independent variable. The score in both designs was the score achieved in the administration of the AWS. All subjects were administered the instrument with all members of their respective team at the college in attendance.

RESULTS

Two analyses of variance (ANOV) were calculated. The results for the first ANOV indicated that the main effect of the first factor (sports conforming to the stereotypic female role) did not reach the critical level of probability, $F (1, 96) = 2.89$, $.05 > p < .08$. However, there was a tendency ($p < .08$) for women participating in sports which do not conform to the stereotypic view of the female role (basketball/softball) to espouse more of a traditional view of the women's role than swimmers/tennis players. Mean scores for basketball/softball was 117.64, for swimmers/tennis players 124.81. High scores reflect a more liberal attitude. The F values for the main effect of college in attendance and the two-day interaction were non-significant, $F (2, 96) = 1.41$ and .72, $p > .05$.

The second 4 × 3 ANOV was computed for the four teams individually and the three colleges. The F values for the main effect of schools and the two-day interaction were significant, F (2, 90) = 3.80, $p<.05$, F (6, 90) = 4.78, $p<.05$. The main effect of teams, however, was non-significant, F (3, 90) = 1.99, $p>.05$. All individual comparisons were computed using Tukey's Honestly Significant Difference. The difference between colleges occurred between Lehman ($\bar{x}$ = 125.34) and Brooklyn ($\bar{x}$ = 111.00). Queens College had an overall mean of 117.47. For the interaction the results at Queens and Brooklyn indicated that both tennis teams were different from all three other teams: swimming, basketball and softball. The tennis teams were most liberal. So that when observing individual teams at two colleges the hypothesis was supported. The tennis team at two colleges in conforming to appropriate sex-role behavior demonstrated less apologetics than either the basketball, softball or swimming teams did.

DISCUSSION

Kennicke[7] reported that athletes are not really different from one another, but that they are perceived as being different. She compared athletes in creative, socially-acceptable sports, dance and synchronized swimming, and athletes in structured team sports. Although the athletes did not see themselves as being different from others in either a social or athletic situation, they perceived one another as being quite different. In the present study it seemed that the athletes were perceived as being the same but in fact were quite different. That is, the combination of tennis and swimming did not support the hypothesis when viewed collectively. Rather, at two colleges swimmers were more like basketball and softball players than they were like tennis players. It was the tennis teams at these two colleges (Queens and Brooklyn) that were different from all the other athletes. Compared to basketball and softball those tennis teams had a substantially more liberal attitude toward the women's role. It is understandable that tennis players would experience less cognitive dissonance and therefore not be compelled to embrace apologetics for their behavior. Playing tennis is viewed as acceptable today and for these subjects did not create conflict. Compared to norms derived by Spence and Helmreich[8] from undergraduate students at the University of Texas at Austin, the tennis players scored at the 90th percentile for women. The most traditional score observed (Brooklyn College's basketball team) was at the 70th percentile.

It should be noted that the phenomenon of apologetics in women's athletics is limited in time. It exists only as long as society continues to support the stereotyped view of acceptable female behavior which is in conflict with the requirements for sport participation. Hopefully we will see the demise of apologetics as stereotypic behavior loses support.

REFERENCES

1. Felshin, J.: The triple option . . . for women in sport. *Quest, 21,* 36, 1974.
2. ————: The social view. In E. Gerber, J. Felshin, P. Berlin, and W. Wyrick, (Eds.), *The American Woman in Sport,* Reading, Massachusetts, Addison-Wesley Publishing Co., 1974.
3. Griffin, A.: What is a nice girl like you doing in a profession like this? *Quest,* 19, 96, 1973.
4. Harris, D. V.: Psychosocial consideration, *JOPER, 46,* 32, 1975.
5. Horner, M.: A bright woman is caught in a double bind. In Wendy Martin, (Ed.), *The American Sisterhood,* New York, Harper & Row, 1972.
6. Kane, J. E.: Psychosocial aspects of sport with special reference to the female. In D. V. Harris (Ed.), *Women and Sport: A National Research Conference,* University Park, Pennsylvania, College of Health, Physical Education, and Recreation, 1972.
7. Kennicke, L.: Masks of Identity. In D. V. Harris (Ed.), *Women and Sport: A National Research Conference,* University Park, Pennsylvania, College of Health, Physical Education, and Recreation, 1972.
8. Spence, J. T. and R. Helmreich: *The Attitude Toward Women Scale,* American Psychological Association, Journal Supplement Abstract Service, Catalog of Selected Documents in Psychology, 2, 66, 1972.

Section 3

SOCIETY, SPORT INVOLVEMENT, AND SPORT ACHIEVEMENT

Greendorfer presents a review of a massive amount of literature in the area of socialization through and into sport. A visual outline of the material which follows may be helpful.

Introduction
Socialization
    Sport and socialization
    Female sport socialization
Social learning paradigm
    Personal attributes
        Sex role development
        Female sport socialization
    Socializing agents
        Sex role development
        Sport socialization
        Female sport socialization
        Role models
        Role models and women in sport
    Socializing situation (opportunity set)
        Sport involvement
        Female sport involvement
    Social structure
        Socialization
        Sex-role development
        Sport involvement
        Female sport involvement
Conclusions

Greendorfer's data lead her to several important conclusions which seem rich in meaning for the sport feminist.

We find that for girls the school has not functioned as the initial agent of sport involvement as it has for boys. The school has not functioned as the continuing support for female sport involvement as it has for males. We can hope that Title IX effects and the impact of the AIAW-NAGWS programs will change the picture soon.

Greendorfer indicates that high reference group support was significantly related to initial sport involvement for girls. The encouragement of parents and friends was needed to neutralize other negative social influences. After initial involvement, Greendorfer indicates that opportunity set was significantly related to continuing involvement. This means that women who are fine athletes today had opportunities for sport open to them when they were youngsters. The implication is clear that expanding the opportunity base will expand the pool of women who are skilled performers.

A third finding of special impact is that males, at all life cycle stages, functioned as significant role models for women in Greendorfer's studies. We can be happy that the role models were there. There might be few "women in sport" to talk and write about if they were not there. The female role model at all levels of sport must become more prominent, however. The availability of same sex *and* cross sex role models can only contribute to the expansion of the pool of women choosing active sport involvement.

C.A.O.

Chapter 7
SOCIALIZATION INTO SPORT

Susan L. Greendorfer

Women in sport has been a topic virtually ignored by most scholars and, thus, female sport socialization has been a relatively undeveloped area of research. Sex-role stereotyping, male research bias, and the reward structure of society have contributed to this neglect. However, the furor created by the Equal Rights Amendment, Title IX, and the growing consciousness pertaining to the role of women have evoked a sensitivity and concern for the female athlete as well as the recognition of the significance of her sport participation. Currently, sport for women represents a fast growing, changing element in American culture, and recent trends have sparked a need for knowledge about the female sport participant.

Who is she? How and where did she acquire her disposition, interest, and early experiences in sport activities? What were her childhood and adolescent sport participation patterns? Who were the significant others influencing her participation? Were there positive sanctions and rewards for such participation? What circumstances and environmental opportunities predisposed her toward sport participation? The search for answers to these questions involves a study of the process of sport socialization. Moreover, the answers will provide important descriptive information which can be inserted into theoretical models; these models can facilitate understanding by providing knowledgeable explanations.

Therefore, this chapter examines the process of female socialization into sport. Female sport participation will be examined from the perspective of sport roles.[70,71] It is assumed that women possess the cognitive and motor capacity for sport role occupancy; that enactment of such sport roles depends on several factors, namely those related to the process of socialization. The chapter has been divided into three segments: (1) an overview of the process of socialization; (2) the social learning paradigm, including personal attributes, socializing agents, and social structure; and (3) conclusions.

SOCIALIZATION

Historically, the process of socialization has been systematically examined by three fields: psychology, sociology, and anthropology, each of which has developed specific concepts and offered distinctive theoretical frameworks. Regardless of approach, however, socialization theory has been concerned with discovering how individuals learn to participate effectively in social interaction. Consequently, socialization in its broadest sense can be defined as the process whereby persons become participants in their society; it is the means by which social and cultural continuity is attained. Thus, the socialization process is a means by which society communicates to an individual the kind of person he or she is *expected* to be.

Whereas we have introduced the process of socialization from quite a broad perspective, there is need to further delimit socialization concepts. To accomplish this purpose we are going to focus on three recent developments in socialization theory: (1) utilization of a social learning approach for identifying social variables;[4,16–18,23,25] (2) consideration of the process as continuous throughout the life cycle;[17,24,57,133] and (3) the incorporation of role theory into socialization concepts.[40,133] Hence, socialization has been defined as the process whereby individuals learn to play various social roles necessary for effective participation in society. According to Goslin,[40] the process involves the acquisition of knowledge, skills, and dispositions which enable a person to perform in accordance with the expectations of others as she moves from position to position in the social order through the life cycle. Thus, the process encompasses learning of motives and feelings as well as skills and cognitive sets. From this perspective we can focus on limited aspects of the socialization process, namely, specific behaviors and dispositions. (For example, we can view sport participation as a sport role and examine the means by which women acquire the skills necessary for role enactment.)

Since the socialization process involves notions of expected behaviors, it follows that there is appropriate and inappropriate behavior, and that there are norms and sanctions which direct individuals along various dimensions of behavior. Consequently, one of the most important aspects of the process of socialization is the development of sex roles and the notion of sex-typed behaviors, ". . . those which typically elicit different rewards for one sex than for another, whereby the consequences vary according to the sex of the performer."[113] Viewed in this context such behaviors would be the result of social learning, whereby individuals acquire appropriate sex-role behaviors through the processes of discrimination, generalization, and observation.

Sport and Socialization

There are two orientations relating sport to the process of socialization. The first focuses on sport as a medium or vehicle for social learning, and the influence of sport on childhood and adolescent socialization is examined. The research of Helanko,[54,55] Roberts and Sutton-Smith,[127] Kenyon,[67] Webb,[160,161] Snyder,[144] and Loy and Ingham[89] are examples. From this perspective sport is treated as an independent variable and sport socialization is related to other social phenomena.

The second orientation concerned with socialization *into* sport, is pertinent to this chapter. In this context sport is considered a dependent variable. Several empirical investigations have attempted to identify the variables that best contribute to the acquisition of sport roles, while also providing a theoretical basis from which sport involvement can be explained.[64,66,68,71-73,97,101-104] Despite the fact the focus has been on male athletes who represented a rather homogeneous group relative to skill level and degree of involvement (i.e., Olympic performers, varsity team members), research modelled after the above studies can provide valuable data on female participants and at the same time contribute to theory. Theoretical perspectives are sexless; consequently, research on male sport socialization should not be ignored.

Female Sport Socialization

Few studies have considered the impact of differences according to sex in socialization *via* game or sport experience. Stoll, Inbar, and Fennessey[147] found that game types have a differential impact by sex; that is, sport participation is related to the expression of achievement values for males but not for females.

In contrast several studies relating to play behavior offer insight into female socialization *into* play activities. Lewis[84] found sex differences in play behavior at 1 year of age quite reminiscent of sex role differences found in older children and adults. He suggested that sex role appropriate play is already established by that early age. In a study of play choices Sutton-Smith, Rosenberg and Morgan[154] demonstrated the existence of sex preferences at the ages of 8 to 9 years. They also discovered that from puberty onwards playing games was a predominantly masculine phenomenon in this culture. Games and sports were positively associated with the male sex role but negatively associated with the female sex role.

However, in an earlier study examining sex differences in play choices over a period of time, Sutton-Smith and Rosenberg[152] concluded that the sexes have become increasingly similar in game preference over the last 60 years and that the increasing similarity in game preference was primarily due to shifts in female preference. This phenomenon of a wider choice of games by pre-pubertal girls has also been demonstrated by Brown[19] and Ward.[158] In a discussion

5

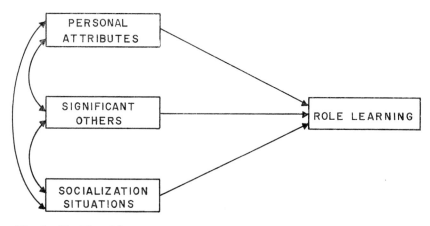

Fig. 4.   The Three Elements of The Social Learning Paradigm.

of femininity and achievement in sport Zoble[172,173] considered such findings to be a consequence of a more generally prescribed sex role for females prior to puberty, hence a wide range of play choices. Zoble felt such choices would narrow after puberty when society offers a more definite stereotyped female sex role.

As observed, most literature pertaining to female sport socialization discusses the process from a broad behavioral and dispositional basis. Female behavior in sport and games has been viewed as a microcosm of norms and behavioral expectations of society in general.

THE SOCIAL LEARNING PARADIGM

Although there are many approaches available to study the process of socialization, one fruitful method is through a social learning paradigm. This paradigm has been utilized in effort to identify social variables which mediate the socialization process. Generally speaking, three classes of variables have been identified: the *personal attributes* of the socializee, *socializing agents* (significant others), and the *social structure*. The social learning approach places greater emphasis on the latter two factors, since it is believed that cultural content and social context interact with an individual's personal attributes.[25] Nevertheless, some aspects of the first variable warrant attention.

Personal Attributes

Sex-Role Development

Facets of the personal attributes element can be found in the psychoanalytic[110] and cognitive approaches.[36,77,78] The importance of certain attributes has also been suggested by Brim and Wheeler[17] and

Inkeles.[57] They proposed that personality characteristics, values, and attitudes learned early in the life cycle will influence the socialization at later stages.

Kohlberg[77] best exemplifies the viewpoint that sex roles are the result of cognition and emerge independently of specific training and learning experiences. In contrast to social learning theorists, Kohlberg argued that basic patterning of sex-role concepts is found in the universal aspect of the child's cognitive organization of his social world; thus, gender identity is derived from basic cognitive judgments made early in life.

Sport Socialization of Women

Most of the research pertaining to women in sport has considered topics which would be classified as personal attributes variables. Although the literature is replete with studies relative to: (1) *attitudes;*[50,98,99,114,136,159] (2) *femininity, self-image and self-concept;*[2,20,48,51,80,117,132,141,142,146,150] and (3) *personality,*[3,12,60–62,94,95,118,164] the majority of this research was not based on a theoretical framework. Furthermore, the process of socialization has been ignored in these investigations. Recently, however, criticism has been levelled at the atheoretical approach.[2,11] Allen[2] has discussed the definition and dimensionality of self-concept as a narrow aspect of personality and has presented a summary of various empirical findings relative to the female sport participant. Similarly, Berlin[11] considered various approaches to the concept of personality and motivation relative to the female athlete. To date, she has offered the most inclusive summary of personal attributes factors.

Although few in number, there have been some attempts to examine female sport involvement from a theoretical framework. For example, Richardson and Hall[126] used a model similar to the social learning paradigm in their attempt to analyze determinants of female sport involvement. They concluded that attitudes and motivational dispositions played a minimal role in determining the degree of primary involvement; situational determinants were by far the most important.

It appears that the empirical data relative to personal attributes have not been systematically applied to an analysis of how women become involved in sports. Thus, the findings relative to personality, attitude, and self-image represent isolated fragments and provide little theoretical insight into female sport socialization. A more penetrating examination of dispositional factors[49,126] would be fruitful. In addition, the cognitive dimension, which pertains to sport knowledge and expertise, has been shown to be theoretically and empirically viable in the study of sport socialization.[68,72,103] However, little attention has been given to this dimension in the case of women.

Socializing Agents

Socializing agents substantially influence the outcome of the socialization process. These agents become important variables because of their prestige and power to distribute love, rewards, and punishments—mechanisms for instilling and confirming values, normative behavior, and sanctions. Two important aspects of socializing agents are significant others and reference groups.

Significant others refers to the singularity and particular identification of individuals who by word or example exercise a major influence over the attitudes of the socializee.[166] *Reference groups* refers to the plurality or the group as it influences the socialization process. Many investigators have examined the type and amount of influence of these agents on attitude formation, attitude change, and social behavior.[30,107,166] However, one of the problems in utilizing the significant other-reference group concept is determining how and why they are selected by the socializees.[24,79] Regardless of the difficulty posed by this problem, the three types of reference groups identified by Kemper[65] have been utilized in socialization research (e.g., the normative group, the comparison group, and the audience group).

According to Inkeles[56] socializing agents have a concept of what a child is to become. Therefore, early in the process values, attitudes, and need dispositions are acquired as well as other social attributes necessary for the next stage of development. The first agents of socialization, the nuclear family, impose expectations for behavior. Other social units that impose expectations are the peer group, school personnel, neighbors, family friends, the mass media, and formal agencies such as political parties or bureaucratic organizations.[56]

Sex-Role Development

The role of significant others and reference groups is also discussed in the sex-typing literature. In a review of fundamental antecedents and underlying mechanisms of sex-typing, Mussen[116] mentioned that the family, peers, teachers, members of the community and experiences of later childhood and adolescence influence the process. Mussen also noted that sex-typing occurs early in life, and, if social learning theory is applicable, there must have been rewards present for sex-type behavior. However, some investigators have found little evidence that infant boys and girls receive any significant differential treatment by either or both parents.[8,137] Recently, this observation has been challenged, as many researchers have presented evidence to the contrary.[59,84] Goldberg and Lewis[38] reported that, indeed, there are sex differences in the way a mother treats a child at the age of 6 months.

Further evidence has indicated that differential expectations and pressures from parents do exist, according to sex of the children.[1,53,131] Inkeles[56] reported that boys are trained to attain different objectives than are girls. Tasch's data[155] demonstrated that certain types of motor abilities are instilled by fathers in sons in contrast to other types of abilities instilled in daughters. These differences in activities occurred after the pre-school period.

Sport Socialization

Several sport-oriented investigations have discussed the general elements of socialization, particularly with reference to significant others and reference groups.[64,66,71,72,97,101-104] Pudelkiewicz[123,124] indicated that the initial stimulus to become interested in sport is received from a home environment which considers sport to be an important facet of life and, to a lesser degree, from peers. Snyder and Spreitzer[145] analyzed family influence as a predictor of sport involvement by operationalizing involvement into behavioral, affective, and cognitive dimensions. Viewing the family as the most potent of socialization institutions, they attempted to extend previous research on family influence variables. Apparently, sports involvement begins in childhood, is reinforced by parental encouragement, continues into middle age, and diminishes only in the last stages of the life cycle.[145]

Kenyon and McPherson[73] utilized a path analysis technique to explain the factors precipitating primary sport involvement. A male with a high level of sport aptitude living in a large city which has adequate facilities and instructors and who received encouragement from significant others within and outside the school has a greater likelihood of being socialized into a primary involvement sport role. In a theoretical and methodological discussion of sport socialization Wohl and Pudelkiewicz[167] cited basic requirements for active sport involvement: preliminary knowledge as well as certain abilities; acquisition of sport roles (usually through the school); association with groups that possess an interest in sport (usually neighborhood groups); situational factors; parental approval; sufficient margin of leisure; industrialization and urbanization (as indirect factors).

Additional research relevant to significant other influence on sport socialization indicated that socialization was situationally influenced by significant others within specific social settings.[73] Specifically, peers were important agents stimulating interest in most sports, while teachers and coaches appeared to be more influential than peers in stimulating an interest in track and field (among Olympic aspirants in track and field and gymnastics). Family influence was noticed in generating interest in traditional spectator sports. Roethlisberger[128] investigated the socialization patterns of gymnasts who were Olympic

Team aspirants. Initial involvement in gymnastics occurred between the sixth and tenth grades, with fathers and coaches serving as the most influential significant others. Also, the subjects were raised in an upper-middle class environment.

McPherson's study[101] on Canadian ice hockey and tennis players focused on factors which accounted for becoming involved in sport. Ninety-six per cent were interested in sport by the age of 10, and specialization in one or two sports occurred during high school. Mothers were more influential agents for tennis players than for hockey players; moreover, interest in sport was initially aroused within the family, mainly by the father. During high school years family influence decreased, while peers, coaches, and physical education teachers became more important.

The empirical research on males can be summarized as follows: (1) primary involvement begins during childhood; (2) the learning of the sport role of active participant is situationally influenced by significant others who teach and reinforce the specific role behaviors within specific social settings (e.g., the school is the major socialization agency, and coaches and peers are the most important significant others); (3) the influence of significant others appears to be sport specific; (4) since influence is differential over time, a temporal factor may be involved in the nature of significant other influence.

Female Sport Socialization

Information specific to the role of significant other influence relative to female sport participation comes from relatively few studies. For example, Malumphy[94] indicated that the age of first participation differed according to sport type, and the girls received complete approval from their significant others. In a second study Malumphy[95] reported that family influence was a major factor in college women's competing in sport. Not only did the typical female athlete have family approval for her participation and competition, but there was also a history of family participation in sports. Furthermore, the athlete was encouraged by at least 50 per cent of her significant others.

Greendorfer[42] provided descriptive information relative to age of first sport involvement, type of first sport and significant other influence responsible for initial sport involvement (N = 585). Approximately 70 per cent of the women were participating in some form of sport by the age of 8. Furthermore, the entire sample were actively involved by the age of 14. Relative to agents responsible for first sport involvement, 39.5 per cent indicated the family stimulated initial interest; whereas 31.1 per cent learned through the neighborhood, 23.6 per cent through the school, 3.4 per cent through the community, and only 1.7 per cent became involved through private clubs. In contrast to data on male participants, the school was not the initial agent for sport involvement for at least three-fourths of the women. In a second study of initial agents Greendorfer[44] found similar patterns (N = 86). The family was reported as the initial socializing agent by 46.5 per cent of the respondents, while 21 per cent indicated that the school was the initial agent. Although these data demonstrate a slight shift from the earlier study, this slight increase was not viewed as a trend; moreover there is a great similarity in the findings from both studies.

More conspicuous than the dearth of descriptive data pertaining to females is the insufficient number of empirical studies based on a theoretical framework. Although some recent attempts have altered this situation slightly, the conceptual approaches used have been quite broad. For example, the theoretical basis incorporated in the research of Hall,[49] Richardson,[125] Richardson and Hall[126] considered attitudinal, dispositional, and situational determinants as well as socialization determinants. Thus, specific findings relative to socialization variables were rather limited.

Unfortunately, data pertinent to differential influence of sport socialization agents emanate from a single investigation. In a study of female sport socialization, this author[42] examined whether differences existed between three systems of socializing agents—family, peers, and school—during three life cycle stages. Generally speaking, the findings concurred with previous research on male athletes. During childhood the female participants were more likely to have been influenced by peers and family, respectively, than by teachers and coaches. At the adolescent stage the influence of family was not significant, while peers and teachers-coaches, respectively, served as significant agents. During young adulthood the most influential predictor of sport involvement was the peer group, accompanied by a significant decreased influence exerted by the family. Teachers and coaches were not significant socializing agents at this stage. Thus, the data suggest that the family, as a social system, decreases in importance, while other social systems diminish its effect. A further result of this analysis demonstrated a decreasing ability of the theoretical model to explain sport involvement as the life cycle progressed. These implications will be discussed in a later section.

Role Models

A more specific aspect of socializing agents incorporates the concept of role models—individuals (actual and symbolic) whose attitudes, values, and social responses are exemplified behaviorally.

Clausen[25] discussed models as an important element in childhood acquisition of roles. However, he included other factors, such as the position of the child in the family and the introduction of additional agents into the process during adolescence. In his discussion of social structure Inkeles[56] also considered socializing agents in terms of role theory and modelling. Models were defined as a means of continuity of the social order, whereas absence of role models was noted by increased importance placed on sanctions.

Several investigators' treatment of sex differences falls under the theoretical conceptualization of role theory and role models.[19,28,31] Mischel[113] suggested that the acquisition of sex-typed behaviors occurs through live and symbolic models until a person finally performs appropriate sex-typed behavior. He stressed the importance of the agent's power and willingness to reward as determinants of effectiveness as a model. Also, the more powerful model is usually the more influential, regardless of sex.

The mechanisms of reward and power have been utilized to explain why some studies indicate that young girls express greater preference for the masculine role in American society.

Germane to the issue of role models and also affecting sex-role preference is the sex of siblings. Cross-sex traits have been found in boys with an older sister[76,129,153] as well as girls with older brothers.[15]

Role Models and Women in Sport

The literature pertaining to women's sport's participation has virtually ignored role theory. Hence, role models have been considered to only a slight extent. When this concept has been included in discussions, it has usually been limited to the context of the peer group or to sibling constellations.

Ziegler[170] argued that girls' social structure oriented them away from the sports world, and unless girls were under the influence of older brothers or male gang counterparts (role models), they would grow into the socially preconceived feminine model. In addition she cited the fear of success syndrome as a barrier between women and athletic success. Data pertinent to these issues were absent, however. Zoble[172,173] was concerned with achievement orientation among women. Female non-achievement in sport was examined as a part of stereotyped female incompetence. Factors fostering non-achievement training and decreased sport participation were: differential treatment by the father of female and male children, the greater prestige associated with the masculine role, society's negative feeling toward aggressive behavior for girls, and competitiveness as a male trait. She concluded that interests and activities were things one has been conditioned for because one is masculine or feminine, not because the activity is inherently masculine or feminine.

Ordinal position and sex of siblings have also been considered as significant factors in female sport participation and may influence role model selection.[81,82,122] Since siblings are close in age and often interact in play groups throughout the socialization years, they represent an important structural variable. However, results from empirical research conflict; therefore, each of the four explanatory hypotheses has been used to explain results—sibling similarity, sibling opposite, structural balance, and conformity theory. For example, Landers[81,82] found women with younger and older brothers over-represented among physical education majors and women athletes, thus supporting the sibling similarity hypothesis. However, this hypothesis received strong support only when the sex of the siblings was considered (not birth order); moreover, Landers mentioned other empirical results which supported the conformity hypothesis. Furthermore, when male sport participation was considered, Landers[82] suggested that sibling opposite hypothesis might provide the most valid explanation. In her discussion of female participation in sport Portz[122] utilized the sibling similarity hypothesis. She also incorporated sibling opposite and structural balance, however, to explain participation. Unfortunately, no empirical data were presented.

Kenyon and McPherson's[74] theoretical consideration of the process of sport socialization is relevant to the discussion pertaining to sex of siblings and the influence of role models. Utilizing a social role-social system approach they cast several propositions. Adhering to theoretical notions that: (1) siblings serve as powerful role models, and (2) sibling opposite hypothesis, they proposed that the propensity for sport involvement would increase as the number of male siblings increases and the number of female siblings decreases. Two recent investigations of female sport participation cast doubt on the acceptability of the Kenyon-McPherson proposition. Both studies revealed that female sport participants were just as likely to have older sisters as older brothers; moreover, the number of male versus female siblings was not substantially different.[42] Thus, more empirical data are needed to accompany theoretical discussions relating to ordinal position and sex of siblings. Currently, the data are most confusing, if not purely spurious, to say the least.

Despite numerous discussions and speculation, little is known about the influence of the sex of role models relative to the process of socialization of females into sport. Based on the belief that males occupied a greater number of sport roles (e.g., participants, spectators, entrepreneurs), Greendorfer[42] hypothesized that within a social learning context the most influential role models for women participating in sport would be male. When the proposition was examined for three life cycle periods, a changing pattern of significance was found. More specifically, males were the dominant role models during childhood; both sex models were significant predictors of sport involvement during adolescence; and female role models were more significant at the adult stage. Such findings were reflective of the fact that there is a tendency for male contact in sport activities to decrease as the female advances in age.[42] Furthermore, during adolescence separation of sports programs according to sex is a common practice. Despite the shift toward female role models during this stage, however, male role models were slightly more predictive of sport involvement. Most noticeable in this finding is the fact that males never ceased to be significant role models at any stage.

A more narrow interpretation of role models, namely that of athletes only, was also examined in the same study.[42] Subsequent analyses compared the influence of male athletes with that of female athletes. Results indicated that male athletes were the predominant role model through each life cycle stage, while female athletes *never* represented a significant factor.

Socializing Situation (Opportunity Set)

Sport Involvement

The most general form of the social learning model (Fig. 4) consists of three classes or sets of independent variables: personal attributes, significant others, and socializing situations—each of which contributes to the dependent variable of sport involvement. This same theoretical framework, cast as a causal model has been utilized by several investigators.[72,97,101,103,143] Kelly[64] proposed that sport involvement could be explained by variation of the environment and agents of socialization who operate in that environment. The importance of the socializing situation has been emphasized elsewhere.[44] More specifically, the home, neighborhood, school, role models and exposure to the mass media have been identified as influential agencies in the process of sport socialization. Moreover, the importance of socializing situation varied by sport, along with the influence of significant others and role models.

Recently Kenyon and McPherson[73,74] argued for separate treatment of each social system (e.g., family, peers, school, church) as a potential role learning situation because of the nature, complexity and pervasiveness of sport roles. Their "modular" concept of model building represented a strategy for identifying influential variables considered sport relevant in each social system. Situational facilities and opportunity set (socializing setting) were both implicit and explicit components of system-level factors.

Female Sport Involvement

The notion of opportunity set (socializing situation) has been virtually unexplored in reference to women in sport. Consequently, little is known relative to the function of significant others within the context of differing opportunity sets. On the other hand, research pertaining to male sport socialization has revealed that the potency of significant other influence and the strength of opportunity set have contributed substantially to the enactment of sport roles.[68,71,103] Therefore, it can be assumed that similar factors would explain female sport role enactment.

Greendorfer[42] examined the association between the degree of opportunity set and age of first sport involvement; a second analysis attempted to find an association between level of reference group influence and age of first sport involvement. Whereas reference group influence was significantly related to age of first involvement, opportunity set was not. Thus, high reference group support influenced early sport involvement, while a strong opportunity set was unrelated to age of early involvement.

Since such findings were unexpected in light of the social learning model, Greendorfer[42] suggested that the two independent variables could be sequential rather than concurrent. For instance, reference groups could be the original stimulus for involvement, thereby facilitating sport participation at younger ages; *then* opportunity set would serve as an intervening variable for reinforcing participation. Thus, a temporal component is introduced to the theoretical model, suggesting antecedent as well as facilitating independent variables.

The previous discussion of the role of socializing situation may have cast doubt on the feasibility of the social learning paradigm. Therefore, the applicability of the model was analyzed.[42] Results indicated that both opportunity set and significant others were significant predictors of sport participation during childhood; similarly, the model explained a substantial proportion of the variance at this stage ($R^2 = 22$ per cent). However, as the life cycle progressed through adolescence and adulthood, the model decreased in effectiveness, although the independent variables continued to be significant predictors of female sport involvement ($R^2 = 12$ per cent, $R^2 = 3.6$ per cent, respectively). These results demonstrate the applicability of the model; however, they further suggest that some "new" conceptualizations regarding continued sport involvement are in order. Logically, the model which explains initial socialization into sport may be inappropriate for explaining reinforcement of involvement, especially when one variable, opportunity set, becomes increasingly more significant as the life cycle progresses.[42]

While the previous discussion considered the importance of the socializing situation, some attention should be given to the role of opportunity set in the presence of, or as a context for, other independent variables. For example, research from Kenyon and

McPherson,[73,74] Wohl and Pudelkiewicz[167] has indicated that: (1) the learning of the sport role of active participant is situationally influenced by significant others who teach and reinforce the specific role behaviors within specific social settings; and (2) situational factors as well as interest groups are basic requirements for active sport involvement. Therefore, the nature of interplay (if any) between opportunity set and reference groups was examined relative to female participants.[42]

Essentially, it was predicted that: (1) in the case of a low opportunity set the correlation between reference group and sport involvement would be high; (2) when a medium opportunity set was available, a moderate relationship between these variables would exist; and (3) with a high opportunity set no relationship between reference group influence and active sport involvement would be observed. This hypothesis considered opportunity set to be a more critical or influential variable than reference group influence. Despite some tendency toward the interplay between these variables, a significant relationship was not found.

Social Structure

Socialization

Parsons and Bales[119] emphasized the importance of considering the socialization process in relation to the present or future social structure in which the individual will find himself. The child is never socialized only for and into his family of orientation, but rather into the structures which extend beyond his family (i.e., school, peer, and work group). To Clausen[25] the original social matrix of family, social class, and ethnic background provides initial orientations. The child is confronted by different constellations of values, beliefs, people, and opportunities depending upon family location in social, geographical, and temporal terms. Supporting this stance, Goslin[40] indicated that a number of structural characteristics affect the availability of information to individuals within a social system, thereby altering socialization settings. Thus, a person's location within the social structure determines which facets of the culture he will (and will not) have access to, and, therefore, which facets of culture he transmits to his children.[16,26] Inkeles[56,57] also noted the influence of social structure in the socialization process when he described a four-dimensional paradigm which influenced the network of social relations in which the individual lives. Thus, differences in geographical location, birth order, or social class could result in differential socialization outcomes.

Sex-Role Development

A specific aspect of social structure which is influential in sex-role development is social class or socio-economic status. Minuchin[112] examined the relationship of sex-role concepts and sex-typing with differences in attitudes and models offered by school and home. She found sex-typing to occur in some segments of the population but not in others (i.e., the lower classes); in addition different philosophies of child rearing and education were influential in the formation of sex-role attitudes and actions. Bardwick[7] also indicated that sex-typing is more rigorous in the lower classes. Moreover, she agreed with Kagan and Moss[58] that the higher the education level of the family the less likely the adherence to orthodox sex-role traits.

Sport Involvement

There is an extensive literature in which social structure variables are related to sport participation; particular attention has been focused on social class relationships. Davis and Havighurst[29] indicated that social class has a definite bearing upon selection of physical activity for adolescents due to differing attitudes toward certain activities among classes. Wightman[165] concluded that selection of recreative activities as a leisure pursuit is directly affected by accessibility and proximity of facilities in the immediate environment. Therefore, a low income may be prohibitive since it restricts the choice of activity to one involving little or no cost, whereas a higher income affords a greater range of activities. Kelly[64] found that socialization of males into sport is a function of social situations and age, social class background, family size, and affiliation with sport agencies. Furthermore, lower class boys participated more in team sports than did higher class boys.

McPherson,[105] Stueber,[151] Lundberg,[90] Wrightstone,[168] Loy,[87] Luschen,[91] and Webb[161] have also examined differential participation in types of sport according to social class. Level of education, amount of income, influence of peers and parents have been suggested as explanatory variables. Sport as a function of ethnic group background has also been discussed.[22,121,130,162] McPherson[102,104] hypothesized that involvement in sport by members of minority groups can be attributed to differential socialization experiences early in life. This notion has been empirically supported by Castine and Roberts.[21]

Female Sport Involvement

Relative to women in sport, few investigators have considered social structure variables or specifically focused on social class influence. Hall[47] did include such variables in her theoretical conceptualization of differential sport involvement; however, social structural variables were an incidential aspect of her proposal. In her discussion of women who participated in intercollegiate competition Malumphy[94,95] noted certain socio-economic relationships. Team sport participants had more fathers in skilled labor fields than did the individual sports group. Also, she noted the differences between sport groups in the perception of the femininity image, which may have been a function of social class as well as personality. Greendorfer[42] found a relationship between father's level of education and type of sport participation. A second measure of socio-economic status, namely occupation, also revealed a similar relationship to type of sport. Specifically, the lower the father's educational and occupational status, the more likely the girl was a team sport participant; while the higher educational and occupational levels were associated with individual and dual sport participation. Such findings are in strong agreement with empirical evidence pertaining to males.[64,68,87,101,128,148]

Although a relationship between social class and specific sport types has been theoretically postulated, explanations for such a relationship have not been empirically tested. Perhaps the influence of specific reference groups is a reflection of social structure variables (i.e., socio-economic status) and, hence, accounts for socialization into various kinds of sports. Basis for such an assumption can be found in the stratification literature. For example, Gans[35] and Inkeles[56,57] have suggested that, depending upon socio-economic status, certain reference groups might be more relevant than others in the socialization process. These notions suggest an examination of social class variables and sport type relative to reference group influence. Data from a recent study[42] indicated that, according to sport type, no difference in influence could be determined when peer group was compared to family. (The specific proposition hypothesized that team sport participants were more influenced by peers, while individual and dual sport participants were more influenced by family.)

CONCLUSIONS

Current interest in female sport involvement notwithstanding, there are many unexplored topics which merit attention. One important consideration lies in the very definition of sport. Although the term is quite familiar to most, sport as defined by Loy[86] may not be applicable to females, particularly during childhood. The difficulty with the term rests in the *degree of institutionalization* of games and competition available to girls and women. Prior to Title IX and decisions by Little League, except for a select few, "sport" was virtually a non-existent phenomenon for girls during childhood. Related to definition is the concept *degree of involvement* in sport. For example, does degree of involvement differ between women intercollegiate competitors and Olympic contenders? Is the degree of involvement of the first group similar to that exhibited by male varsity team members?

Secondly, alternative research designs which pertain to female sport involvement should be utilized. Specifically, comparative studies between female participants and nonparticipants are necessary. Research on female sport *participants* as well as on *accomplished performers* is warranted. Also, female athletic involvement can be compared with male athletic involvement; thus, a broad perspective of participation and a greater understanding of factors which predispose women to enact sport roles would be provided.

Most noticeable in this chapter is the absence of data pertinent to the black female in sport. Of the few studies available attention has focused on personality[76] and "selected" involvement patterns.[100] Therefore, there is need to incorporate black participants in theoretical-empirical considerations. Information pertaining to opportunity, significant others, norms, and sanctions, as they apply to black women, is vital to any research concerning women in sport.

Another critical consideration is the need for *theoretically based* investigations and the development of research instruments *specifically designed for the research problem at hand*. Refinement of research tools, expansion and improvement of measures, theoretically defined research problems, specific formulation and definition of concepts, and explicit hypotheses to be tested will extend research beyond mere description. Data will be more meaningful, while explanations and predictions could be based on empirical data rather than belief or opinion.

In reference to the social learning model which served as the framework for this chapter, a more dynamic conceptualization of variables is essential. Temporal factors as well as sequential effects should be incorporated into a *revised* paradigm. Perhaps a separate model which explains reinforcement of sport socialization should be formulated.

This chapter has provided an overview of the socialization of women into sport, with particular attention given to social learning theory, sex-typing, and empirical results from research on female sport involvement. Briefly, we can conclude the following:

(1) The female participant begins sport early. Her involvement is influenced by family and peers, with peers serving as the more significant factor. Strength of opportunity set is not a factor influencing early age of participation, whereas level of reference group influence is.

(2) Peers, family and teachers-coaches represent three social systems influencing female socialization into sport. Peers and family are significant childhood socialization agents; peers and teacher-coaches are influential during adolescence;

and peers are the strongest positive agent during young adulthood.

(3) Male role models are more important agents during childhood; however, female role models increase in importance as the life cycle progresses. Male athletes are more important role models than are other female athletes during every life cycle stage.

(4) Although opportunity set increases in importance as a factor in female sport socialization, it is not a more significant variable than reference group influence.

(5) Female sport participation is a function of socio-economic status. More specifically, team sport participants come from a lower social class background, whereas individual and dual sport participants come from higher social class backgrounds. Socialization into various sport types is not a function of specific reference group influence.

(6) The social learning paradigm is an effective theoretical model for explaining initial involvement of women into sport. However, the model decreases in effectiveness over the life cycle.

(7) Although data pertaining to ordinal position and sex of siblings are confusing, it appears that the female athlete is just as likely to have older sisters as older brothers. Also, she appears to be the middle or youngest child in the family rather than first born or only child.

REFERENCES

1. Aberle, David F. and Kaspar Naegele: Middle-Class Fathers' Occupational Role and Attitudes toward Children. *Amer. J. Orthopsychiatry, 22,* 366, 1952.
2. Allen, Dorothy: Self-Concept and The Female Participant. In D. Harris (Ed.), *Women and Sport: A National Research Conference.* Penn State HPER Series No. 2, 1973, Pp. 35–52.
3. Balazs, Eva: Psycho-Social Study of Outstanding Female Athletes. *Res. Quart., 46,* 267, 1975.
4. Bandura, Albert: Social Learning through Imitation. In M. R. Jones (Ed.), *Nebraska Symposium on Motivation.* Lincoln, University of Nebraska Press, 1962, Pp. 211–269.
5. —————: Social-Learning Theory of Identificatory Process. In D. A. Goslin (Ed.), *Handbook of Socialization Theory and Research.* Chicago, Rand McNally and Co., 1969, Pp. 213–262.
6. Bandura, Albert and Richard Walters: *Social Learning and Personality Development.* New York, Holt, Rinehart & Winston, Inc., 1963.
7. Bardwick, Judith: *Psychology of Women: A Study of Bio-Cultural Conflicts.* New York, Harper & Row, 1971.
8. Barry, H. III, Margaret K. Bacon, and I. I. Child: A Cross-Cultural Survey of Some Sex Differences in Socialization. *J. Abnormal Social Psychol., 55,* 327, 1957.

9. Becker, H. S., et al.: *Boys in White: Student Culture in Medical School.* Chicago, University of Chicago Press, 1961.
10. Berger, Peter L.: *Invitation to Sociology: A Humanistic Perspective.* Garden City, New York, Anchor Books, 1963.
11. Berlin, Pearl: The Woman Athlete. In E. Gerber, J. Felshin, P. Berlin, and W. Wyrick, *The American Woman in Sport.* Reading, Massachusetts, Addison-Wesley Publishing Co., 1974, Pp. 283–400.
12. Bird, Evelyn: Personality Structure of Canadian Intercollegiate Women Ice Hockey Players. In G. Kenyon (Ed.), *Contemporary Psychology of Sport.* Chicago, Athletic Institute, 1970, Pp. 149–156.
13. Blyth, Myrna: Girl Athletes: What Makes Them Skate, Fence, Swim, Jump, Run? *Cosmopolitan*, 110–114, October 1969.
14. Brim, Orville G., Jr.: The Parent-Child Relation as a Social System: I. Parent and Child Roles. *Child Development, 28*, 344, 1957.
15. ——————: Family Structure and Sex Role Learning by Children: A Further Analysis of Helen Koch's Data. *Sociometry, 21*, 1, 1958.
16. ——————: Personality Development as Role Learning. In I. Iscoe and H. Stevenson (Eds.), *Personality Development in Children.* Austin, University of Texas Press, 1960, Pp. 127–160.
17. ——————: Socialization through the Life Cycle. In O. G. Brim and S. Wheeler (Eds.), *Socialization after Childhood: Two Essays.* New York, John Wiley & Sons, Inc., 1966.
18. ——————: Adult Socialization. In J. A. Clausen (Ed.), *Socialization and Society.* Boston, Little, Brown & Co., 1968, Pp. 184–222.
19. Brown, Daniel: Sex-Role Development in a Changing Culture, *Psychological Bulletin, 55*, 232, 1958.
20. Brown, Ruth: A Use of the Semantic Differential to Study the Feminine Image of Girls. Unpublished Doctor's Dissertation, Florida State University, 1965.
21. Castine, Sandra and Glyn Roberts: Modeling in The Socialization Process of The Black Athlete. *International Review of Sport Sociol., 3–4*, 59, 1974.
22. Charnofsky, H.: The Major League Baseball Player's Self-Conception Versus the Popular Image. *International Review of Sport Sociol., 3*, 39, 1968.
23. Clausen, J. A.: Research on Socialization and Personality Development in the United States and France: Remarks on the paper by Professor Chombard de Lauwe. *Amer. Sociological Review*, 31, 248, 1966.
24. ——————: Socialization as a Concept and as a Field of Study. In J. A. Clausen (Ed.), *Socialization and Society.* Boston, Little, Brown & Co., 1968, Pp. 2–17.
25. ——————: Perspectives on Child Socialization. In J. A. Clausen (Ed.), *Socialization and Society.* Boston, Little, Brown & Co., 1968, Pp. 132–177.
26. Cohen, Yehudi: *Social Structure and Personality.* New York, Holt, Rinehart & Winston, 1961.
27. Coleman, James S.: *The Adolescent Society.* New York, The Free Press, 1961.
28. D'Andrade, Roy: Sex Differences and Cultural Institutions. In E. E. Maccoby (Ed.), *The Development of Sex Differences.* Stanford, California, Stanford University Press, 1966, Pp. 174–203.
29. Davis, W. Allison and Robert J. Havighurst: *Father of the Man: How Your Child Gets His Personality.* Boston, Houghton Mifflin Company, 1947.
30. Denzin, N. K.: The Significant Others of A College Population. *Sociological Quart., 7*, 298, 1966.
31. Dornbusch, Sanford: Afterword. In E. E. Maccoby (Ed.), *The Development of Sex Differences.* Stanford, California. Stanford University Press, 1966, Pp. 205–219.
32. Duncan, Otis Dudley: A Socioeconomic Index for All Occupations. In A. J. Reiss (Ed.), *Occupation and Social Status.* New York, Free Press, 1961, Pp. 109–138.

33. ————: Properties and Characteristics of the Socioeconomic Index.: In A. J. Reiss (Ed.), *Occupation and Social Status.* New York, Free Press, 1961, Pp. 139–161.
34. Elder, G. and C. E. Bowerman: Family Structure and Child Rearing Patterns: The Effect of Family Size and Sex Composition. *Amer. Sociological Review, 28,* 891, 1963.
35. Gans, Herbert J.: *The Urban Villagers.* New York, The Free Press, 1962.
36. Gewirtz, J. L.: Mechanisms of Social Learning: Some Roles of Stimulation and Behavior in Early Human Development. In D. A. Goslin (Ed.), *Handbook of Socialization Theory and Research.* Chicago, Rand McNally & Co., 1969, Pp. 57–212.
37. Goffman, Erving: *Asylums: Essays on the Social Situation of Mental Patients and Other Inmates.* Garden City, New York, Doubleday and Co., Inc., 1961.
38. Goldberg, Susan and Michael Lewis: Play Behavior in the Year-Old Infant: Early Sex Differences. *Child Development, 40,* 21, 1969.
39. Goode, W. J. and P. K. Hatt: *Methods in Social Research.* New York, McGraw-Hill Book Co., Inc., 1952, Chapter 12.
40. Goslin, D. A. (Ed.), Introduction. In D. A. Goslin (Ed.), *Handbook of Socialization Theory and Research.* Chicago, Rand McNally & Co., 1969, Pp. 1–19.
41. Gould, Julius and William Kolb (Eds.): Reference Groups, *Dictionary of the Social Sciences.* Compiled under the auspices of the United Nations Educational, Scientific and Cultural Organization, New York, Free Press, 1964.
42. Greendorfer, Susan: The Nature of Female Socialization into Sport: A Study of Selected College Women's Sport Participation. Unpublished Doctor's Dissertation, University of Wisconsin, August, 1974.
43. ————: Female Sport Participation Patterns. *NAGWS Research Reports: Women in Sport, 3,* 1977.
44. ————: A Social Learning Approach to Female Sport Involvement. Paper presented at American Psychological Association Convention, Washington, D.C., September, 1976.
45. Griffin, Patricia: Perceptions of Women's Roles and Female Sport Involvement among a Selected Sample of College Students. Unpublished Master's Thesis, University of Massachusetts, 1972.
46. Hage, Jerald: *Techniques and Problems of Theory Construction in Sociology.* New York, John Wiley & Sons, 1972.
47. Hall, M. Ann: Women and Physical Recreation: A Cross-Cultural Analysis of Two Societies. Lecture given at Coventry College of Education, March 22, 1972.
48. ————: A 'Feminine Woman' and An 'Athletic Woman' As Viewed by Female Participants and Non-Participants in Sport, *Brit. J. Physical Education, 3,* 14, 1972.
49. ————: Women and Physical Recreation, A Causal Analysis. Unpublished Doctor's Dissertation. University of Birmingham, England, 1974.
50. Harres, Bea: Comparison of Attitudes toward Intensive Competition for High School Girls. *Res. Quart., 39,* 278, 1968.
51. Harris, Dorothy: The Social Self and Competitive Self of The Female Athlete. Paper presented at Third International Symposium on Sociology of Sport, Waterloo, Ontario, Canada, August, 1971.
52. Hart, M. Marie: On Being Female in Sport. In M. Marie Hart (Ed.), *Sport in the Socio-Cultural Process.* Dubuque, Wm. C. Brown Co , 1972.
53. Hartley, Ruth: Children's Concepts of Male and Female Roles. *Merrill-Palmer Quart.,* Winter, 83, 1959.
54. Helanko, R.: Sports and Socialization. *Acta Sociologica, 8,* 229, 1960.
55. ————: The Yard Community and Its Play Activities. *International Review Sport Sociol., 4,* 177, 1969.
56. Inkeles, Alex: Society, Social Structure and Child Socialization. In J. A.

Clausen (Ed.), *Socialization and Society.* Boston, Little, Brown & Co., 1968, Pp. 75–129.

57. ————: Social Structure and Socialization. In D. A. Goslin (Ed.), *Handbook of Socialization Theory and Research.* Chicago, Rand McNally & Co., 1969, Pp. 615–632.

58. Kagan, Jerome and H. Moss: *Birth to Maturity.* New York, John Wiley & Sons, Inc., 1962.

59. Kagan, Jerome and M. Lewis: Studies of Attention in the Human Infant. *Merrill-Palmer Quart., 11,* 95, 1965.

60. Kane, John and J. Callaghan: Personality Traits of Tennis Players. *Brit. Lawn Tennis,* 1965.

61. Kane, John: Personality and Physical Ability. In Kato (Ed.), *Proceedings Sports Science Conference,* Tokyo, 1966.

62. Kane, John: Personality and Physical Ability. In G. Kenyon (Ed.), *Contemporary Psychology of Sport.* Chicago, Athletic Institute, 1970, Pp. 131–141.

63. ————: Psychology of Sport with Special Reference to The Female Athlete. In D. Harris (Ed.), *Woman and Sport: A National Research Conference.* Penn State HPER Series No. 2, 1973, Pp. 19–34.

64. Kelly, Colin: Socialization into Sport among Male Adolescents from Canada, England and the United States. Unpublished Master's thesis, University of Wisconsin, 1970.

65. Kemper, Theodore: Reference Groups, Socialization and Achievement. *Amer. Sociological Review, 33,* 31, 1968.

66. Kenyon, G. S.: The Significance of Physical Activity as a Function of Age, Sex, and Socio-Economic Status of Northern U. S. Adults. *International Review of Sport Sociology, 1,* 41, 1966.

67. ————: Fact and Fancy: Sociological Considerations. *J. Health, Physical Education and Recreation, 39,* 31, 1968.

68. ————: Socialization into the Role of Olympic Track and Field Athlete. Unpublished study, University of Wisconsin, 1968.

69. ————: *Values Held for Physical Activity by Selected Urban Secondary School Students in Canada, Australia, England, and the United States.* Report of U.S. Office of Education Contract S-276. Washington: Educational Resources Information Center, 1968.

70. ————: Sport Involvement: A Conceptual Go and Some Consequences Thereof. In G. S. Kenyon (Ed.), *Aspects of Contemporary Sport Sociology,* Chicago, The Athletic Institute, 1969, Pp. 77–84.

71. ————: Explaining Sport Involvement. Paper presented at Fall Conference of Eastern Association of Physical Education for College Women, Lake Placid, N.Y., October 8, 1969.

72. ————: The Use of Path Analysis in Sport Sociology with Special Reference to Involvement Socialization. *International Review Sport Sociol., 5,* 191, 1970.

73. Kenyon, G. S. and Barry McPherson: An Approach to the Study of Sport Socialization. Paper presented at the Seventh World Congress of the International Sociological Association, Varna, Bulgaria, September, 1970.

74. ————: Becoming Involved in Physical Activity and Sport: A Process of Socialization. In G. L. Rarick (Ed.), *Physical Activity: Human Growth and Development.* New York, Academic Press, 1973.

75. Kerlinger, Fred: *Foundations of Behavioral Research.* New York, Holt, Rinehart & Winston, Inc., 1964.

76. Koch, Helen: Sissiness and Tomboyishness in Relation to Sibling Characteristics. *J. Genetic Psychol., 88,* 231, 1956.

77. Kohlberg, Lawrence: A Cognitive-Developmental Analysis of Children's Sex-Role Concepts and Attitudes. In E. E. Maccoby (Ed.), *The Development of Sex Differences.* Stanford, California, Stanford University Press, 1966, Pp. 82–173.

78. ————: Stage and Sequence: The Cognitive-Developmental Approach to Socialization. In D. A. Goslin (Ed.), *Handbook of Socialization Theory and Research.* Chicago, Rand McNally and Co., 1969, Pp. 347–380.
79. Kuhn, Manford: The Reference Group Reconsidered. *Sociological Quart., 5, 5,* 1964.
80. Landers, Daniel: Psychological Femininity and The Prospective Female Physical Educator. *Research Quarterly, 41,* 164, 1970.
81. ————: Sibling Sex-Status and Ordinal Position Effects on Females' Sport Participation and Interests. *J. Social Psychol., 80, 247,* 1970.
82. ————: Sibling-Sex and Ordinal Position as Factors in Sport Participation. Paper presented at Third International Symposium on Sociology of Sport, Waterloo, Ontario, Canada, August, 1971.
83. Levine, R. A.: Culture, Personality and Socialization: An Evolutionary View. In D. A. Goslin (Ed.), *Handbook of Socialization Theory and Research.* Chicago, Rand McNally and Co., 1969, Pp. 503–541.
84. Lewis, Michael: Sex Differences in Play Behavior of the Very Young. *J. Health, Physical Education and Recreation, 43,* 38, 1972.
85. Lippit, R.: Improving the Socialization Process. In J. A. Clausen (Ed.), *Socialization and Society.* Boston, Little, Brown & Co., 1968, Pp. 322–373.
86. Loy, John W. Jr.: The Nature of Sport: A Definitional Effort, *Quest, 10,* 1, 1968.
87. ————: The Study of Sport and Social Mobility. In G. S. Kenyon (Ed.), *Aspects of Contemporary Sport Sociology.* Chicago, The Athletic Institute, 1969, Pp. 101–119.
88. Loy, John W. Jr. and J. F. McElvogue: Racial Segregation in American Sport. *International Review Sport Sociol., 5,* 5, 1970.
89. Loy, John W. Jr. and A. G. Ingham: Play, Games and Sport in the Psycho-Sociological Development of Children and Youth. In G. L. Rarick (Ed.), *Physical Activity: Human Growth and Development.* New York, Academic Press, Inc., 1973.
90. Lundberg, George, et al.: The Amount and Uses of Leisure. In E. Larrabee and R. Myersohn (Ed.), *Mass Leisure.* Glencoe, Illinois, The Free Press, 1958.
91. Luschen, Gunther: Social Stratification and Social Mobility among Young Sportsmen. In J. W. Loy and G. S. Kenyon (Ed.), *Sport, Culture and Society.* London, The Macmillan Co., 1969, Pp. 258–276.
92. Lynd, Robert S. and Helen M. Lynd: *Middletown.* New York, Harcourt, Brace & World, Inc., 1937.
93. Maccoby, E. E.: The Choice of Variables in the Study of Socialization. *Sociometry, 24,* 357, 1961.
94. Malumphy, Theresa: Personality of Women Athletes in Intercollegiate Competition. *Res. Quart., 39,* 610, 1968.
95. ————: The College Woman Athlete—Questions and Tentative Answers. *Quest, 14,* 18, 1970.
96. Martin, Carolyn: The Personality Characteristics of Black Female High School Athletes. Paper presented at Research Section, AAHPER National Convention, Atlantic City, New Jersey, March, 1975.
97. Martindale, Colin: Sport Involvement as a Function of Social Class and Ethnic Group Background. Unpublished Master's thesis, University of Wisconsin, 1971.
98. McCue, Betty: Constructing An Instrument for Evaluating Attitudes towards Intensive Competition in Team Games. *Res. Quart., 24,* 205, 1953.
99. McGee, Rosemary: Comparisons of Attitudes toward Intensive Competition for High School Girls. *Res. Quart., 27,* 60, 1956.
100. McLeod, Juliette: The Black Female Athlete: Patterns, Attitudes, and Social Factors of Her Participation. Unpublished Master's Thesis, University of Illinois, 1973.
101. McPherson, Barry D.: Psychosocial Factors Accounting for Learning the

Role of Tennis and Hockey Player. Unpublished study, University of Wisconsin, 1968.

102. ————: Minority Group Socialization: An Alternative Explanation for the Segregation by Playing Position Hypothesis. Paper presented at the Third International Symposium on the Sociology of Sport, Waterloo, Ontario, Canada, August 22–28, 1971.

103. ————: Socialization into the Role of Sport Consumer: The Construction and Testing of a Theory and Causal Model. Unpublished Doctor's dissertation, University of Wisconsin, 1972.

104. ————: Minority Group Involvement in Sport: The Black Athlete. In J. Wilmore (Ed.), *Exercise and Sport Sciences Reviews*, Vol. 2, New York, Academic Press, Inc., 1974, Pp. 71–101.

105. McPherson, Orpha: *Summer Vacation Activities of 100 Farm Boys and Girls in a Selected Area.* New York, New York Teachers College, Columbia University, 1939.

106. Mead, Margaret: Socialization and Enculturation. *Current Anthropology,* 4, 184, 1963.

107. Merton, Robert K.: *Social Theory and Social Structure.* New York, The Free Press, 1957.

108. Metheney, E.: On Women and Sport, *Connotations of Movement in Sport and Dance.* Dubuque, Iowa, Wm. C. Brown & Co., 1965.

109. Miller, D. M. and K. Russel: Sport and Women, *Sport: A Contemporary View.* Philadelphia, Lea & Febiger, 1971.

110. Miller, D. R.: Psychoanalytic Theory of Development: A Re-Evaluation. In D. A. Goslin (Ed.), *Handbook of Socialization Theory and Research.* Chicago, Rand McNally & Co., 1969, Pp. 481–502.

111. Miller, N. B. and J. Dollard: *Social Learning and Imitation.* New Haven, Connecticut, Yale University Press, 1941.

112. Minuchin, Patricia: Sex-Role Concepts and Sex Typing in Childhood as a Function of School and Home Environments. *Child Development, 36,* 1033, 1965.

113. Mischel, Walter: A Social Learning View of Sex Differences in Behavior. In E. E. Maccoby (Ed.), *The Development of Sex Differences.* Stanford, California, Stanford University Press, 1966, Pp. 56–81.

114. Moore, Beverly: The Attitudes of College Women toward Physical Activity as a Means of Recreation. *Res. Quart., 12,* 720, 1941.

115. Mowrer, O. H.: *Learning Theory and the Symbolic Process.* New York, John Wiley & Sons, 1960.

116. Mussen, Paul H.: Early Sex-Role Developmnet. In D. A. Goslin (Ed.), *Handbook of Socialization Theory and Research.* Chicago, Rand McNally & Co., 1969, Pp. 707–730.

117. Ogilvie, Bruce: The Unanswered Question: Competition, Its Effect Upon Femininity. Paper presented to the Olympic Development Committee, Santa Barbara, California, June, 1967.

118. ————: Psychological Consistencies within The Personality of High-Level Competitors. *J.A.M.A., 205,* 780, 1968.

119. Parsons, T. and R. F. Bales: *Family, Socialization and Interaction Process.* Glencoe, Illinois, The Free Press, 1955.

120. Parten, Mildred: *Surveys, Polls and Samples—Practical Procedures.* New York, Harper & Brothers, 1950.

121. Pascal, A. H. and L. A. Rapping: Economics of Racial Discrimination in Organized Baseball. In A. H. Pascal (Ed.), *Racial Discrimination in Economic Life.* Lexington, Massachusetts, Heath, 1972, Pp. 119–156.

122. Portz, Eileen: Influence of Birth Order, Sibling Sex on Sports Participation. In D. Harris (Ed.), *Women and Sport: A National Research Conference.* Penn State HPER Series No. 2, 1973, Pp. 225–234.

123. Pudelkiewicz, Eugeniusz: Sociological Problems of Sports in Housing Estates. *International Review Sport Sociol., 5,* 73, 1970.

124. ――――: Sport Consciousness As An Essential Component of Involvement in Sport and Socialization. Paper presented at the Third International Symposium on the Sociology of Sport, Waterloo, Ontario, Canada, August 22–28, 1971.

125. Richardson, D. A.: Women and Physical Activity: A Socio-Cultural Investigation of Primary Involvement. Unpublished Doctor's Dissertation, University of Georgia, 1974.

126. Richardson, D. A. and M. A. Hall: Women and Physical Activity: A Cross National Perspective. Paper presented at the Canadian Association of Sport Sciences Meetings, Edmonton, Alberta, Canada, Sep. 3–Oct. 2, 1974.

127. Roberts, J. and B. Sutton-Smith: Child Training and Involvement, Ethnology, 1, 166, 1962.

128. Roethlisberger, F. A.: Socialization of the Elite Gymnast. Unpublished Master's thesis, University of Wisconsin, 1970.

129. Rosenberg, B. G. and B. Sutton-Smith: Ordinal Position and Sex-Role Identification. Genetic Psychology Monographs, 70, 297, 1964.

130. Rosenblatt, A.: Negroes in Baseball: The Failure of Success, Transaction, 5, 51, 1967.

131. Rothbart, Mary and E. E. Maccoby: Parent's Differential Reactions to Sons and Daughters. J. Personality and Social Psychol., 4, 237, 1966.

132. Sakers, A.: The Relationship between A Selected Measure of Motor Ability and The Actual-Ideal Self Concept, Body Image and Movement Concept of The Adolescent Girl. Unpublished Master's Thesis, University of Maryland, 1968.

133. Sarbin, T. R. and V. L. Allen: Role Theory. In G. Lindzey and E. Aronson (Eds.), Handbook of Social Psychology, Vol. 1. Reading, Mass., Addison-Wesley Publishing Co., 1968, Pp. 488–567.

134. Schafer, Walter: Some Social Sources and Consequences of Interscholastic Athletics: The Case of Participation and Delinquency. In G. S. Kenyon (Ed.), Aspects of Contemporary Sport Sociology. Chicago, The Athletic Institute, 1969, Pp. 29–44.

135. ――――: Sport And Male Sex-Role Socialization. Sport Sociology Bulletin, 4, 47, 1975.

136. Scott, Phoebe M.: Attitudes toward Athletic Competition in Elementary Schools. Res. Quart., 24, 352, 1953.

137. Sears, R. R., E. E. Maccoby and H. Levin: Patterns of Child Rearing. Evanston, Ill., Row, Peterson, 1957.

138. Sewell, William H.: Some Recent Developments in Socialization Theory and Research. Ann. Amer. Acad. Political Science, 349, 163, 1963.

139. Sewell, William H. and V. P. Shah: Socioeconomic Status, Intelligence and the Attainment of Higher Education. Sociol. of Education, 40, 1, 1967.

140. Sewell, William H., A. O. Haller and A. Portes: The Educational and Early Occupational Attainment Process. Amer. Sociological Review, 34, 82, 1969.

141. Smith, Hope and M. Clifton: Sex Differences in Expressed Self Concepts Concerning The Performance of Selected Motor Skills. Perceptual and Motor Skills, 14, 71, 1962.

142. ――――: A Comparison of The Expressed Self Concepts of Athletes and Non-Athletes in Their Performance of Movement Patterns. Perceptual and Motor Skills, 16, 199, 1963.

143. Smith, Michael: Social and Psychological Determinants of Assaultive Behavior in Young Hockey Players. Unpublished Doctor's dissertation, University of Wisconsin, 1972.

144. Snyder, Eldon: Aspects of Socialization in Sports and Physical Education. Quest, 14, 1, 1970.

145. Snyder, Eldon and Elmer Spreitzer: Family Influence and Involvement in Sports. Res. Quart., 44, 249, 1973.

146. Snyder, Eldon and Joseph Kivlin: Women Athletes and Aspects of Psychological Well Being and Body Image. Res. Quart., 46, 191, 1975.

147. Stoll, C., M. Inbar and J. J. Fennessey: Socialization and Games: An Exploratory Study of Sex Differences, Report No. 30. Baltimore: The Center for the Study of Social Organization of Schools. The Johns Hopkins University, 1968.

148. Stone, Gregory: Some Meanings of American Sport. *Proceedings National College Physical Education Association for Men, 60, 6, 1957.*

149. ————: Some Meanings of American Sport: An Extended View. In G. S. Kenyon (Ed.), *Aspects of Contemporary Sport Sociology.* Chicago, The Athletic Institute, 1969, Pp. 5–16.

150. Strati, Joan: Body Image and Performance. In D. Harris (Ed.), *Women and Sport: A National Research Conference.* Penn State HPER Series No. 2, 1973, Pp. 61–70.

151. Stueber, Ralph: A Study of Some Leisure Time Activities Participated in by Boys and Girls in Grades 7 through 12 in Wausau, Wisconsin. Unpublished Master's thesis, University of Wisconsin, 1955.

152. Sutton-Smith, B. and B. G. Rosenberg: Sixty Years of Historical Change in the Game Preferences of American Children. *J. Amer. Folklore, 74, 17, 1961.*

153. ————: Age Changes in Effects of Ordinal Position on Sex-Role Identification. *J. Genetic Psychol., 107, 61, 1965.*

154. Sutton-Smith, B., B. G. Rosenberg and E. E. Morgan: The Development of Sex Differences in Play Choices during Pre-Adolescence. *Child Development, 34, 119, 1963.*

155. Tasch, R. G.: The Role of the Father in the Family. *J. Experimental Education, 20, 319, 1952.*

156. Unpublished study, University of Wisconsin (1969), (Class Project for P.E. 500).

157. Unpublished study, University of Wisconsin (1970), (Class Project for P.E. 500).

158. Ward, William D.: Variance of Sex-Role Preference among Boys and Girls. *Psychological Reports, 23, 467, 1968.*

159. Wear, Carlos: The Evaluation of Attitudes toward Physical Education as an Activity Course. *Res. Quart., 22, 114, 1951.*

160. Webb, Harry: Professionalization of Attitudes toward Play among Adolescents. In G. S. Kenyon (Ed.), *Aspects of Contemporary Sport Sociology.* Chicago, The Athletic Institute, 1969, Pp. 161–180.

161. ————: Reaction to Loy Paper. In G. S. Kenyon (Ed.), *Aspects of Contemporary Sport Sociology.* Chicago, The Athletic Institute, 1969, Pp. 120–131.

162. Weinberg, S. K. and H. Arond: The Occupational Culture of the Boxer. *Amer. J. Sociology, 57, 460, 1952.*

163. Wheeler, Stanton: The Structure of Formally Organized Socialization Settings. In O. G. Brim and S. Wheeler (Eds.), *Socialization after Childhood.* New York, John Wiley & Sons, Inc., 1966, Pp. 53–116.

164. Widdop, James and Valerie Widdop: Comparison of The Personality Traits of Female Teacher Education and Physical Education Students. *Res. Quart., 46, 274, 1975.*

165. Wightman, Brian J.: Extra-Curricular Physical Activity of Entering University Freshmen during Their High School Senior Year as a Function of Social Class, Residence Location, and High School Graduating Class. Unpublished Master's thesis, University of Wisconsin, 1965.

166. Woelfel, J. and A. O. Haller: Significant Others, the Self-Reflexive Act and the Attitude Formation Process. *Amer. Sociological Review, 36, 74, 1971.*

167. Wohl, Andrzej and E. Pudelkiewicz: Theoretical and Methodological Assumptions of Research on the Processes of Involvement in Sport and Sport Socialization. *International Review Sport Sociology, 7, 69, 1972.*

168. Wrightstone, Wayne: Social Effectiveness of Education. *Encyclopedia of Educational Research, 3rd Ed.* New York, The Macmillan Co., 1960, P. 1291.

169. Zetterberg, H.: *On Theory Verification in Sociology.* Totowa, New Jersey, Bedminister Press, 1965.
170. Ziegler, Susan: Self-Perception of Athletes and Coaches. In D. Harris (Ed.), *Women and Sport: A National Research Conference.* Penn State HPER Series No. 2, 1973, Pp. 293–305.
171. Zigler, E. and I. L. Child: Socialization. In G. Lindzey and E. Aronson (Eds.), *The Handbook of Social Psychology,* Vol. 3. Reading, Massachusetts, Addison-Wesley Publishing Co., 1969, Pp. 450–589.
172. Zoble, Judith: Femininity and Achievement in Sports. In D. Harris (Ed.), *Women and Sport: A National Research Conference.* Penn State HPER Series No. 2, 1973, 203–223.
173. ————: Femininity, Achievement, and Sports. *DGWS Research Reports: Women in Sports, Vol II.* Washington, D. C., AAHPER Press, 1973, Pp. 34–48.

Chapter 8

ACHIEVEMENT RELATED MOTIVES AND THE WOMAN ATHLETE

Susan Birrell

We have seen that socialization considerations help us to better understand the women involved and uninvolved in sport. Susan Birrell's insightful study of achievement related motives advances understanding through another perspective. We view the dilemma of sport participation by women intensified by contradictory feelings toward achievement itself. Birrell's chapter is rich with summations of previous work in psychology and sport science, innovative research hypotheses, and direct recommendations for teaching and coaching women. Her section on the development of achievement related motives provides a review of some of Greendorfer's chapter. Her section on the resultant achievement motivation model foreshadows the next chapter on causal attribution. The chapter is a courageous work which should be "mined for gold" for a long time.

C.A.O.

Chapter 8

ACHIEVEMENT RELATED MOTIVES AND THE WOMAN ATHLETE

Susan Birrell

Charles Schulz knows a lot about the image of women athletes in American society. In *Peanuts*, Schulz offers the public three varieties of female sport involvement. At one extreme is Peppermint Patty, tomboy and serious athlete, who is not above trading her friends to strengthen her baseball team and who is often referred to as "Sir" in deference to her unfeminine interest. At the other extreme is Marci, straight-haired, buck-toothed, bespectacled, neophyte intellectual, a restricted character with no redeeming athletic qualities. In between is Lucy Van Pelt, everywoman-in-training, whose lack of athletic skill and total unconcern for the outcome of the game cause her no visible distress or embarrassment. Lucy knows she has side bets: "I'm too feminine for this game," she proclaims after her efforts to kick a football prove an utter failure.

Although only a caricature, Lucy's comic-strip character is informed by the most traditional myths about the American girl: she doesn't care about sports, she isn't any good at sports, and her failure in sports is inconsequential and excusable because she's a girl. Doing well in sports is just not that important for girls.

The myth of women as unaspiring underachievers has long permeated American culture on many levels and is by no means restricted to the ballpark where small children play out their sex roles. Are women guilty as charged? Do women have less desire to achieve than men? Until recently, psychological research designed to explore the achievement motive, or the need to achieve, failed to address the question directly. In experimental situations, the achievement behavior of male subjects with high needs to achieve was fairly predictable; however, the achievement behavior of female subjects was inconsistent with their levels of achievement motivation. The confusion over sex differences in the achievement motive was so profound that most psychologists skirted the issue by restricting their research to male subjects. Perhaps nothing sums up the attitude of puzzlement and frustration among early researchers as concisely as Atkinson's treatment of the problem. After compiling an impressive volume of the latest empirical findings and theoretical concerns of research on the achievement motive, Atkinson[6] dealt with the achievement drives of women in a single footnote in which he referred to them as "the most persistent unresolved problem."

Today the confusion over sex differences in the achievement motive persists, but attempts to deal with the problem have become more sophisticated. The most substantial and exciting contribution to the awakening interest in that research area was Horner's[45] dissertation on sex differences in achievement motivation, which was guided by Atkinson. Horner's research reconceptualized an old concept (fear of success) and added a new energy to the field.

Horner's solution to the problem, the postulation of a motive with power to explain sex differences in achievement behaviors, is only one alternative. One might also begin with the criticism that reported sex differences are the result of a research tradition flawed by some myths of its own. As any review of achievement motivation research will indicate, the research is beset with sex-specific measures which have generated sex-specific propositions which have been incorporated into sex-specific theories having a limited and sex-specific generalizability. And of course the specific sex in achievement motivation research is male. An underlying contention of this review is that a theory which explains the behavior of only half the population is not a theory at all but merely a call for further research.

To accuse psychologists investigating the achievement motive of deliberate sexism in their research, however, is unfair. Rather they are guilty of an androcentric, or male centered, conceptualization of achievement behavior which defines achievement in task-oriented terms more appropriate to traditional male sex role behavior than to female sex roles. As this review attempts to point out, this limited conceptualization of a multifaceted concept has retarded the development of knowledge about achievement motives and behaviors of women. Given the time at which the research began (i.e., the early 1950s) such an oversight is hardly surprising. And it is appropriate that the major breakthrough in research on the achievement motive in women should occur in the late 1960s.

In the pages which follow, a critical assessment of research on achievement related motives such as need to achieve and fear of success is undertaken in order to furnish a research-based perspective of the achievement behaviors of women involved in sport. In general, the review examines two of the more widespread myths concerning women and achievement. The first is that women do not have a high need to achieve. The second is that achievement orientations are developed solely as the result of early child training practices and that level of achievement motivation is therefore irreversibly fixed in an individual at an early age.

The review is divided into three major sections. *First,* a general review of achievement related motives is presented and the general research evaluated. Of specific importance in this section are sex differences in achievement patterns. The *resultant achievement motivation* model of Atkinson and Feather[7] is presented with some comments on that model's applicability to both sexes. A factor analytic approach to achievement motivation is discussed and implications for sport are presented.

Second, sport studies utilizing concepts from achievement motivation research are reviewed. *Third,* the development of achievement related motives is discussed. Research on sex differences in early socialization of the achievement motive is reviewed and an attempt is made to integrate that review into a model of greater scope and more direct applicability to sport: the *conflict-enculturation* model of Roberts and Sutton-Smith.[89] Finally successful efforts by McClelland and Winter[62] to raise the achievement motive of individuals in an "underachieving" culture are reviewed and the implications for women are discussed.

ACHIEVEMENT RELATED MOTIVES

The Need to Achieve

Three motives related to achievement behavior have been identified by social scientists: the *need to achieve* (or hope of success), the *fear of failure,* and the *fear of success.* Need to achieve was the first construct to be examined experimentally, and most of the early research was the product of David McClelland, John Atkinson, and their colleagues. As Atkinson's statement implies, these early researchers were seeking

. . . . to account for the expression of selectivity, preference, or direction in behavior that is governed in some way by the relationship of particular actions to an objectively definable consequence, end, or goal, and for the tendency, of action, once initiated, to persist until the end, or goal, is attained.[5]

Both Atkinson and McClelland conceive of need to achieve as "a relatively stable disposition to strive for achievement or success."[4]

Since need to achieve, like any need, is difficult to assess directly, McClelland et al.[61] adopted the Thematic Apperception Test (TAT), a projective test originally devised by Murray.[73,74] Since the theory upon which the TAT is based states that needs must be aroused in order to be observable, the testing situation typically begins with statements intended to arouse the achievement motives in the subjects by informing them that the test they are about to take is capable of assessing their intelligence, skill in organizing material, and leadership.[61] Subjects are then presented with a series of stimulus pictures and told to write a short story about each one describing what is happening, what has happened, what is likely to follow, and what are the reactions and responses of the figures in the picture. The resulting stories are then content analyzed for achievement imagery. Scores on the TAT have been shown to correlate highly with subjects' scores on puzzle-like tests intended to measure achievement behavior, which are presented in the same testing situation.

Behavioral correlates of need to achieve have been fairly consistent when only male subjects are used. For example, a high need to achieve has repeatedly been shown to be related to tendencies to seek out achievement situations,[7] to set realistic goals,[7,8,60] to persist in tasks,[28,32] and to succeed.[30,61,95]

Two of these correlates are especially pertinent for they are most characteristeric of the individual with a high need to achieve. The first is the tendency to seek out achievement situations—a tendency here labeled the *approach tendency*. The second is the tendency to perform well or succeed—here labeled the *success tendency*. As is explained more thoroughly below, the inter-relating valence of these two tendencies provides a means for discriminating between achievement related motives.

Sex Differences in the Achievement Motive

In testing situations, the achievement behavior of women whose TAT scores indicated that they had a high need to achieve was unpredictable and inconsistent. Soon women were eliminated as subjects in most such studies, but a few interested researchers continued to explore the problem.

Almost from the beginning it was noted that women had achievement motives equal to or greater than men when in an unaroused testing situation,[3,63] but attempts to arouse the need further by emphasizing intellectual and leadership qualities resulted in a decrease in need to achieve females and an increase for males.[94] However, Field (reported in McClelland et al.[61]) found an increase in achievement motive in women following the arousal of concern about social acceptance, and Sears (cited in Hoffman[39]) discovered that at an earlier age, girls' achievement behavior was related to a desire for social approval. Hoffman[39] has proposed that the greater affiliative needs of girls may be an important factor in explaining sex differences in achievement. She cites several other researchers[19,21,35] whose research led them to conclude that affiliative motives were incentives for achievement for girls, while strivings for mastery explained the achievement behavior of boys.

One obvious criticism of the research tradition, then, is that from the start the experimental setting was more conducive to the display of achievement motives for men than for women. Another criticism reveals the same sex-limited design of the research: Lesser et al.[53] found need to achieve could be aroused in females by the use of stimulus pictures with female rather than male cue figures. Thus the activities in the cue situations were inadvertently designated as male activities, and the possibility that women saw such territory as out of bounds and wrote stories accordingly must not be overlooked. Further proof of this is the fact that the achievement motive has been found to have its greatest validity in the everyday world in the prediction of entrepreneurial success—traditionally a male bastion of achievement.

The very concept of achievement has been defined in male terms, and it is small wonder that women do not respond enthusiastically to the challenge. In order to make a fairer assessment of the different levels of the achievement motive in men and women, a broader interpretation of the need to achieve must be accepted. The expansion of the achievement motive to include both a positive and a negative factor and the development of a model incorporating both motives represents one interpretation.

Hope of Success, Fear of Failure, and Resultant Achievement Motivation

Investigators quickly realized that the achievement motive was a more complex concept than they had originally believed. In 1966, Atkinson and Feather[7] reconceptualized the motivation process as the interaction of two motives, a positive motive which they termed *hope of success* (a direct conceptual descendent of *the* achievement motive) and a negative motive termed *fear of failure*. These concepts were not conceived as polar concepts but were thought to interact, producing what Atkinson and Feather termed *resultant achievement motivation*.

Fear of Failure

An individual characterized by a high fear of failure is one to whom the possibility of failure in an achievement situation is so threatening that avoidance of failure at almost any cost becomes the primary concern. Generally, this avoidance takes one of three forms: (1) avoidance of participation in achievement situations, (2) attempts to restructure the situation as a non-competitive one so that success or failure cannot be directly assessed (i.e., by becoming ill, by not trying as hard as one could, or by setting goals so unrealistic that no one could be expected to succeed), or (3) when all else fails, by striving for success.[14]

Research by Birney et al.[14] revealed that individuals characterized by fear of failure responded to a projective test with images of hostile press, a mild persecution-like anxiety. The more common means of operationalizing fear of failure, however, is through scores on a state anxiety test such as the Mandler-Sarason Test Anxiety Questionnaire (TAQ).

An interesting aspect of individuals characterized by fear of failure is that they often succeed: *success tendency* does not distinguish between those characterized by a high need to achieve and those with a high fear of failure. The factor which does discriminate is the *approach tendency*. Therefore, while an individual characterized by hope of success has a positive approach tendency and a positive success tendency, the individual characterized by a fear of failure has a negative approach tendency and a positive success tendency.

The Resultant Achievement Motivation Model

Taking hope of success and fear of failure into consideration, Atkinson and Feather[7] developed a model for the prediction of the approach tendency in a given achievement situation. The model explains resultant achievement motivation (RAM) as a function of the interaction and relative strength of two motives: hope of success, or the tendency to approach success (T_s), and fear of failure, or the tendency to avoid failure (T_{-f}):

$$RAM = T_s - T_{-f}$$

However, both the tendency to approach success and the tendency to avoid failure are determined by the relative strength of three factors: expectancy (or subjective probability), incentive, and motive. According to Atkinson "an expectancy is a cognitive anticipation, usually aroused by cues in a situation, that performance of some act will be followed by a particular consequence."[4] Incentive "represents the relative attractiveness of a specific goal that is offered in a situation, or the relative unattractiveness of an event that might occur as a consequence of some act."[4] And, finally, "a motive is conceived as a disposition to strive for a certain kind of satisfaction."[4]

As the model indicates, the tendency to approach success (T_s) is a function of an individual's motive to succeed (M_s), the expectancy or probability of success (P_s), and the incentive to succeed (I_s). Tendency to avoid failure is a function of the motive to avoid failure (M_{-f}), the probability of failure (P_f), and the incentive to fail, or lack of incentive to succeed (I_f):

$$T_s = M_s \times P_s \times I_s$$
$$T_{-f} = M_{-f} \times P_f \times I_f$$

Finally, resultant achievement motivation is seen as the result of the relative weighting of T_s and T_{-f}:

$$RAM = (M_s \times P_s \times I_s) - (M_{-f} \times P_f \times I_f) \text{ or}$$
$$RAM = T_s - T_{-f}$$

The model's greatest contribution to an understanding of achievement behavior is the integration of purely intrinsic factors (the motives) with factors modified by the specific achievement situation (probability and incentive). Resultant achievement motivation is not a general, latent disposition similar to the *motives* hope of success and fear of failure but is a situation-specific, situationally aroused tendency to act, or a *motivation*. The differences between the motive and the motivation have important implications for sex differences in achievement behavior. Research has shown that women have an achievement *motive* as strong as men's but that the cues which arouse such a motive, translating it to a motivation, differ by sex. Therefore it is likely that the evaluation of goals differs by sex as well.

According to the formula, motive determines only a third of the outcome. Equally weighted are the probability factor and the incentive factor. Mathematically, a strong lack of incentive or a low estimate of the probability of success will depress the effects of the achievement motive.

Several researchers have suggested that women's subjective assessment of probability of success is lower than men's.[33,36] Another recent line of research related to attribution theory has shown that women attribute success to luck and failure to lack of ability, while men reverse the process and attribute success to ability and failure to poor luck.[27]

Although less research has investigated the incentive factor, evidence indicates that for many women the incentive to achieve, particularly in male domains, is negative rather than positive, and is the result of pressures for sex role conformity. Moreover, Horner's[45] research on fear of success provides further evidence that women's success in male domains stimulates grave feelings of apprehension, in short: negative incentive. The following section reviews that research more thoroughly.

Fear of Success

The gravest obstruction to a deeper understanding of achievement motives in women is the lack of clarification of the concept *fear of success.* Since Horner[45] popularized the construct, investigations by other researchers have produced results so deviant from Horner's that the reliability and validity of the concept are in serious doubt. Horner substituted sentence cues for the picture cues of the TAT. In response to cues describing individuals of the same sex who had succeeded in a task ("After mid-term exams, Anne (John) finds she (he) is at the top of her (his) medical school class"), 65 per cent of a sample of college women wrote stories about Anne which contained images of negative consequences resulting from success. Less than 10 per cent of the male subjects responded with such imagery about John.

Horner identified this tendency as a fear of success and defined it as the tendency to avoid success because of its negative consequences.[44] Following the projective test, subjects were given tasks, such as anagrams tests, to do in one of three competitive situations: alone, in the presence of another subject of the same sex, and in the presence of another subject of the opposite sex. Horner found those who had scored high in fear of success performed better alone (i.e., in the noncompetitive situation), while those low in fear of success performed better in the presence of another subject (i.e., in the competitive situation).

In light of subsequent research, it appears that Horner's contribution has been overshadowed by an enthusiastic misinterpretation of the data. It seems logical that fear of success does exist. Freud discussed a "success phobia," as do Ogilvie and Tutko.[78] However, in those studies fear of success was conceptualized as a pathological disorder not restricted by sex. In order to conceptualize fear of success as a motive comparable to hope or success and fear of failure, it is necessary to define it in terms of approach tendency and success tendency. Using those criteria, fear of success can be defined as an achievement related motive characterized by a negative approach tendency and a negative success tendency. The next section elaborates on this point.

Replications of Horner's work have failed to substantiate the assumption that fear of success is a sex-linked motive. When Horner's projective cues are given to subjects in a cross-sex manner (i.e., when both males and females write about John and Anne), both males and females write more stories which contain negative consequences for Anne than for John.[23,29,38,40,49,54,68,71,105] This finding strongly suggests that the behavioral response termed fear of success is not the motive that Horner had conceived as a stable, enduring personality characteristic[44] but a situation- or cue-specific tendency better labeled "fear of inappropriate sex role behavior"[90] or even sex stereotyping.

Two other methodological flaws further mar the research. The cues used in the fear of success study differ from those used in achievement motivation studies in one critical aspect. The TAT used to assess the achievement motive presents situations in which success or failure are problematic: the subject is scored in part by whether he or she projects success or failure into the story. Horner's sentence cues presented achievement as a *fait accompli*. Thus subjects did not project feelings of success or failure but rather responded to a more future event—the consequences of success. This response is more consistent with a reaction to the incentive factor in the RAM model than to the motive factor.

A second problem is revealed by Maccoby and Jacklin.[63] In their summary of research findings related to the psychology of sex differences they note

> . . . the tendency for young women of college age to lack confidence in their ability to do well on a new task, and their sense that they have less control over their own fates than men do. These trends are not seen among older or younger women. Age 18–22 is the period of their lives when many young adults are marrying or forming some other kind of relatively enduring sexual liaison. In the dating and mating game, women traditionally are expected to take less initiative than men. Perhaps it is at this period of their life more than any other that individuals define themselves in terms of their "masculinity" and "femininity" and when greater sex differences may therefore appear than at earlier or later ages, with respect to any attribute considered central to this definition.

Thus an unanticipated age factor may have contaminated the results. Conclusions based on data restricted to the age group 18 to 22 must be strengthened by a sampling from other age groups. It is a further irony that the easily accessible college population may have been distorting research conclusions regarding sex differences for years.

Nevertheless, Horner's contribution to the research is a positive one. Put into the context of the Atkinson and Feather model, the behaviors labeled as fear of success could be reconceptualized as the interaction between motive and incentive. The negative incentive offered to women for achievement in predominantly male domains, such as sport, hardly needs documentation. With further research on the topic, the possibility of integrating sex differences into a model previously regarded as sex-specific becomes a real and exciting one.

A Paradigm of Achievement Related Motives: Is There a Need to Fail?

Need to achieve, fear of failure, and fear of success have been discussed above in terms of their relationship to two primary components of achievement behavior: the approach tendency and the success tendency. When properly conceptualized in this manner, achievement related motives can be distinguished from one another

Approach Tendency

	Approach	Avoidance
Success	Need to Achieve	Fear of Failure
Failure		Fear of Success

Success Tendency (row label)

Fig. 5. A Paradigm of Achievement Related Motives.

by the inter-relating valence of these two factors. Figure 5 shows these relationships.

The interaction of these two variables results in four possible combinations. Three have been identified. The fourth possible motivational tendency has never been conceptually linked to these other three. That fourth motive, identified as the *need to fail,* or hope of failure, might be defined as a tendency to approach achievement situations so that one might fail.

Empirical support for such a position, while not conclusive, is highly suggestive. Some traits on psychological inventories, such as the need for abasement on the Edwards Personal Preference Schedule, have some conceptual similarity. Studies of perennial losers, compulsive gamblers,[12] martyrs, suicides, and other self-destructive personality tendencies provide some empirical support. Some popular journalists have interpreted former President Nixon's last year in the White House as demonstrating his need to fail.[34] Moreover, the presence in the resultant achievement motivation model of the factor designated (I_f), the incentive to fail or lack of incentive to succeed, further supports the possibility that such a motive is within the realm of the conceptual model. Finally, Winter[99] has suggested the plausibility of the existence of a need to fail although basing his suggestion upon a different rationale.

The tendency of women to prefer situations in which luck and not their own efforts and ability determine the outcome[26,27] indicates a denial of positive self-action and reflects a lack of desire for control over one's own destiny. Extensive research must be done to substantiate the claim that a need to fail does in fact exist. However, the logical necessity for positing the existence of such a motive seems undeniable. While speculations as to sex differences may seem premature, the rationale underlying the models based on the above review indicates that such a motive, like the fear of success, is best conceptualized as a general and not a sex-specific motive. Moreover, the effects of such a motive upon behavior in sport situations remains to be clarified.

A Factor Analysis of the Achievement Motive

The resultant achievement motivation model represents one way in which to expand upon the limited concept of the need to achieve. The factor analysis of Veroff et al.[93] offers another. Veroff et al. have recently expressed grave reservations about the specificity of the achievement motive, claiming that social comparison is inherent in the concept as it has been researched. They claim "clear evidence that the measure reflects a highly internal self-directed competence-based orientation to success is lacking."

This critique runs somewhat counter to one presented by Martens[65] in his theory of competition. Martens questioned the utility of the achievement motive in sport related research because "achievement motivation is a broad system of goal direction and does not imply any particular mode in which achievement may be directed." Instead, Martens suggested the explication of the concept "competitiveness" because it "implies a motive to achieve or succeed, and also implies that the achievement will be sought through objective, competitive situations." Although the criticisms of Veroff et al. and Martens originate from opposite viewpoints, the factor analysis by Veroff et al. supports both their critiques.

Through a factor analysis of responses to an instrument including projective and objective measures of the achievement motive borrowed from a variety of sources, Veroff et al. discovered that the achievement motive could be broken down analytically to six component factors. These factors are described as follows. Two affective factors emerged:

Factor 6: hope of success—defined as a gratification for meeting standards of excellence; this factor is closest to the traditional definition of achievement motivation.

Factor 3: fear of failure—a negative motive to avoid possible failure; this factor is also familiar from previous research.

One time factor was evident:

Factor 5: future achievement orientation—fantasy projection of future achievement settings; although fear of success did not emerge as an independent factor, Veroff et al. suggest that fear of success is the antithesis of future achievement orientation, an interpretation wholly consistent with the argument presented above.

Finally, three factors refer to different styles of structuring successful accomplishment:

Factor 2: task competence motivation—a motivation to achieve the demands of the task.

Factor 1: assertive competence motivation—a motivation strongly related to autonomy and power needs and inversely related to needs to affiliate; this motive represents a positive interest in competence. The reference group need not be present but may be distant, such as competition against some standard of excellence.

Factor 4: social comparison motivation—seeking to compare one's performance wth others'; this factor is the closest to a competitive motive.

Based on scores for each factor, women differed significantly from men on three of the six factors.[63] They scored significantly higher on Factor 6 and lower on Factor 3 and Factor 1. Veroff et al. were unable to explain satisfactorily the contradiction between these findings and the bulk of achievement motivation research; however, they suggested that their instrument had succeeded in eliminating the socially desirable responses which confounded earlier research. They also suggested that those involved in research should explore the different varieties of achievement display uncovered by this research. One cannot help but agree, for the findings hint directly at new directions for research in sport and sex differences in achievement behavior.

ACHIEVEMENT RELATED MOTIVES AND SPORT

Because the athlete with the highest skill level and the team that looks best on paper are often not the winners in athletic contests, those concerned with athletic excellence speak of the need for "getting up for the game," "mental preparation," and "psyching oneself up." Despite this popular interest, physical educators and sport scientists have provided little insight into the process.

As it has been used in most physical education research, "motivation" is an imprecise concept. A review of research reported in the professional journals purporting to deal with achievement motivation uncovers almost as many definitions as articles: motivation is variously conceived of as "drive," "desire," "pluck," and the like. With some exceptions, physical educators have ignored the body of research on achievement motivation. Likewise, psychologists have ignored the fact that sport situations might present an in vivo laboratory for the development of their own research. Sport conforms to all three of McClelland's[59] criteria for achievement situations:

1. the outcome is challenging and uncertain
2. behavior is evaluated by a definite standard of excellence, and
3. the individual perceives that the outcome is determined by his skill and not by chance factors.

Although it seems logical to assume that sport presents such a situation, one *caveat* must be sounded: the situation must be perceived by the individual as a relevant achievement situation. Research has shown that participants differ in both their reasons for participation in sport[50,55] and their style of participation,[55,96] and that the differences are most often sex-linked. Therefore, one may hypothesize that to the degree that an individual perceives sport as a viable setting for the display of achievement behavior, to that degree achievement motivation is a significant factor in predicting attitudes toward and behaviors in sport situations.

While many researchers realize the importance of assessing motivation in order to understand variations in sport performance, only a few have made efforts to integrate the available body of literature on achievement motives to research in sport settings.[2,92,98] In a more comprehensive attempt, Maehr[64] criticized McClelland's research as culture-bound and suggested several alternative models.

A variety of measures have been used in sport studies to assess need to achieve. Among those measures used were the TAT,[1,13,37,97] Costello's Two Scales of Achievement Motivation,[18,91] Worrell's measure of consistent aspirations,[51] Lynn's achievement motivation scale,[15,16] the French Test of Insight,[86] Edwards Personal Preference Schedule,[25,75,77] and the Achievement Scale for Females.[102] Several researchers developed their own measures.[1,24,79] Perhaps due to this inconsistency in measurement, the achievement motive has been unreliable in predicting either participation (the approach tendency) or achievement (the success tendency) in sport situations for either males or females.

Descriptive Research on Need to Achieve and Fear of Failure in Sport

The Approach Tendency

Since individuals with a high need to achieve are drawn to situations in which the outcome is under their own control, then if sport is considered a viable situation, those engaged in competitive sport should have a higher achievement motive (hope of success) than non-participants. However, the research is too contradictory to support this hypothesis. Ogilvie's work with his Athletic Motivation Index[77] led him to conclude that male athletes possess a higher degree of need to achieve than the general male population. However, Gorsuch[37] and Plummer[79] found no significant differences in need to achieve between male athletes and non-athletes in college samples, and Birrell[16] reported similar findings in a high school sample. In a sample of high school and college males, Birrell[15] found that the configuration of hope of success and fear of failure was highly correlated with participation in both competitive and non-competitive sports.

In three different samples of women athletes,[25,75,79] levels of achievement motivation were higher than those of the general female population, but the differences were not statistically significant. Birrell[15] found neither the need to achieve nor the fear of failure nor a combination of the two was related to the competitive or non-competitive sport involvement patterns of high school or college women.

The Success Tendency

More research has concentrated upon using level of achievement motivation or an interrelationship of hope of success and fear of failure motives to predict achievement. Used alone, a general measure of need to achieve (hope of success) has not been a valid indication of achievement level in sport for either males,[1,13,91,97] or females,[18,24,102] although a sport specific measure was significantly related to achievement in studies by Albinson[1] and Daugert.[24]

When the interrelationship of hope of success and fear of failure is assessed, results are somewhat more consistent with general achievement motivation research. Ryan and Lakie[86] used both a need to achieve and a fear of failure measure to predict achievement of male subjects. Those with a high hope of success and low fear of failure did better in a competitive motor skill, while those with low hope of success and high fear of failure did better in non-competitive situations. Albinson[1] reported contrary results: those high in hope of success and a high in fear of failure performed better in a physical task (shooting basketball lay-ups) than did individuals with any other motive configurations. Bethe[13] and Willis[97] found that the configuration high hope of success and low fear of failure was the best predictor of sport achievement, although the relationships were not significant.

Descriptive Research on Fear of Success in Sport

Ogilvie[76] and Ogilvie and Tutko[78] were the first sport psychologists to explore the fear of success among athletes. Their treatment of the concept, however, was based upon case studies rather than experimental research. Their observations were limited to male athletes, and they clearly regarded fear of success as a pathological tendency. Ogilvie identified what he termed "causal factors" of fear of success in athletes:

1. a growing sense of social and emotional isolation
2. guilt over self-assertion or overt aggression

3. the habitual use of rationalization to protect the athlete from having to face the reality of his true physical potential
4. unconscious feelings of resentment as a reaction to exaggerated external demands for excellence (usually by a parent)
5. an unconscious fear of old traditions or old idols; an unconscious fear with regard to supporting success or being a record holder.

Two recent studies have attempted to measure fear of success in both male and female athletes. Wittig[101] presented sentence cues about successful female (tennis) and male (golf) athletes to male and female college students. The results of the content analysis of their stories revealed a negative reaction to the female athlete from both males and females. Wittig concluded that his subjects were responding to stereotypical roles. In a follow-up study in which the cue was a female swimmer on an all-male team, Wittig[101] analyzed the stories for positive and negative attitudes toward the cue figures and found the opposite results. The response to the woman swimmer was a positive one, particularly from the women students. Wittig admitted his bewilderment over such confusing findings, but he suggested that a possible "sensitizing" process had taken place during the elapsed time between studies.

In a similar study using a sample of male and female high school and college students, Birrell[15] attempted to relate need to achieve, fear of failure, and fear of success to patterns of sport involvement. An instrument designed to measure fear of success was constructed using six sentence cues representing women in a variety of successful situations (Table 11). The cues included a balance of three sport situations (represented by Anne, Carole, and Linda) and three non-sport situations, and a balance of three traditional and three non-traditional models of achievement (represented by Ellen, Anne, and Linda). Below each cue was a list of ten personality dimensions arranged in a differential semantic format. Most of the dimensions

---

Table 11. Fear of Success Cues

MARY's boss has just given her a big raise because he thinks she's the best secretary he's ever had.

Jim has just asked SALLY to marry him.

As she nears the end of the mile run, LINDA looks back and sees she is way ahead of all the men in the race.

CAROLE has just received a 9.5 score for her gymnastics routine.

At the end of mid-term exams, ELLEN finds she is at the top of her med school class.

ANNE is the center for the women's basketball team and is averaging 20 points a game.

---

were suggested by the themes of social rejection, lack of femininity, and general unhappiness which Horner found in the responses to her study.

T-tests were computed to determine significant sex differences in the responses to the cues. Of the 60 possibilities (6 cues with 10 dimensions each), only 3 significant sex differences were found. Although the results are limited by the fact that both sexes responded to female cue figures, the study provides further support for the conclusion that such studies are not tapping a deep-seated motive such as fear of success but rather responses to appropriate and inappropriate sex-role behavior.

As would be predicted by sex stereotypes, the women in nontraditional success roles were judged more harshly than those in traditional roles. Both males and females found Linda less popular, less attractive, more aggressive, and sadder than the other girls. Anne and Ellen were next in general misfortune. Mary and Sally, whose successes were most traditional, and Carole, whose athletic success occurred in a sex-appropriate sphere (Metheny[67]) received more positive ratings.

The Power Motive

Although the incomplete work on achievement motivations *per se* provides ample research opportunities for those interested in women in sport, two other areas of contingent interest should be mentioned briefly in order to round out the discussion. The first of these is the power motive.

Power is "the capacity to produce effects (consciously or unconsciously intended) on the behavior or feelings of another person."[99] A person with a high need for power is "concerned about his impact, about establishing, maintaining or restoring prestige or power."[99] McClelland's[57] research on the motive has succeeded in discriminating four styles of power motivation which are concurrent with Freud's and Erikson's theory of psycho-social development. Although McClelland's conclusions are sometimes more sweeping than his data truly justify, several suggestions from the research are of interest to sport scholars, particularly in light of the relevance of this line of research to that of Veroff et al.[93] The need for power seems to answer Veroff's call for further research on the components of the achievement motive, in this case Factor 1: assertive competence motivation.

Power motivation of the Stage I variety is characterized by feelings of dependency, drawing strength from others, and/or serving powerful others. Power oriented reading (*Playboy* and *Sports Illustrated* are suggested by McClelland) is characteristic of individuals at Stage I.

Stage II is characterized by autonomy and the desire for self-control. Prestige possessions often characterize individuals at this stage.

Stage III individuals are assertive and competitive. It is not surprising therefore to find individuals at this stage drawn to sports. However, not any sport will do: individuals at Stage III are interested in sport characterized by man-to-man (sic) competition such as football, baseball, basketball, and tennis. Sports such as track, swimming, and golf were not significantly related to Stage II power motivation.[17,99]

The final stage is characterized by altruism, and the individual sees himself or herself as an instrument of higher authority. Creative scientists fit within this stage. Taken to an extreme, Stage IV can result in the Messianic complex.

Two aspects of this research have direct relevance to sport. The distinction in Stage III behavior between sports which serve as an area for the power motive and those which do not indicates differential motivation for different categories of sports. Perhaps this is one reason why research on the achievement motive and sport is equivocal. Varieties of sport experiences are as great as are varieties of achievement motives. Perhaps a better match between the two would provide a motivation-based explanation for the differential appeal of certain sports to certain individuals.

Closely linked to this implication is the possibility of sex differences in styles of power. Although unable to document them fully, McClelland has hypothesized such a difference. Generally, women are characterized by Stage I and Stage II styles of power, where they serve as a power resource rather than actively asserting their influence over others. Stage III, and the associated preference for power oriented sports, is more congenial to the male role. Although still in a rough form, the expansion of this line of research holds some obvious potential for understanding achievement related motives and sport.

Group Achievement Motivation

Another area of promise is Zander's[103,104] research on *group achievement motivation*. Although developed independently from Atkinson and Feather's[7] model of resultant achievement motivation, Zander's model of group achievement motivation closely resembles that model. The disposition *desire for group success* is balanced by a *desire to avoid group failure*, and both are influenced by probability and incentive factors. However, as Zander points out, person- and group-oriented motives are separate and often unrelated variables.

Zander[103] himself has noted the possible application of several of his findings to sport. In a paper presented at the 1975 meetings of the North American Society for the Psychology of Sport and Physical Activity, he cited evidence indicating the relevance of such aspects of group achievement motivation as the setting of moderate and challenging goals, the positive function of "chatter" among group member, and the emergence of leaders from positions of task centrality. This last point reflects the concern of one of the more prominent research traditions in sport sociology: the tendency for team leaders to emerge from positions of centrality in sports, i.e., the catcher, the quarterback, the middle linebacker.[56] Klein and Christiansen[51] have furnished further support for the contention that group achievement motivation is a reliable predictor of team success.

Since women have greater affiliative needs than men, one might argue that group-oriented achievement situations are more appealing to them than individual-oriented achievement situations. However, since Zander's research has been conducted solely on male subjects, the effect of group achievement motivation on women's achievement behaviors remains an open question.

The theoretical implications of research on achievement related motives for the understanding of women's sport involvement may be summarized briefly. The value of achievement motives in assessing either approach tendencies or success tendencies in athletes remains to be proven. Perhaps it is comforting to note that no less is known about the achievement related motives of women in sport than is known about those of men.

New research in the area of achievement related motives and women athletes might expand upon the Atkinson and Feather model of resultant achievement motivation or upon the factor analytic research of Veroff et al. Additional insights may be furnished by research on the power motive and on group achievement motivation.

The bulk of the research reviewed indicates that while there are sex differences in the display of achievement behavior, the belief that women have a lower need to achieve than do men is groundless, based in part on a research tradition flawed by an inherent sex bias. The second myth with which this review is concerned is the belief that the achievement motive is a trait developed at an early age and thereafter remains unaffected by later experience.

THE DEVELOPMENT OF ACHIEVEMENT RELATED MOTIVES

From the beginning, need to achieve has been considered a stable personality disposition, i.e., a motive, and research on the development of achievement motivation in males supports such an assumption. Research has shown that the achievement motive can be observed in the male perhaps as early as the age of 3.[47] Evidence also points to the conclusion that the need to achieve is a socialized trait, developed as the result of child-rearing practices and often associated with early independence training.[11,100] Rosen and D'Andrade[83] found that parents of boys characterized by high achievement motivation were competitive and involved in and concerned about their sons' performance. They had higher aspirations for their sons, set higher standards, expected better performances from them, and rewarded success with warmth and approval and failure with disappointment. Parental indulgence and carelessness with sons resulted in a low need to achieve.[61,83]

Sex of the parent has a differential effect upon a boy's achievement orientation. Rosen and D'Andrade[83] found that while a strong and demanding father impaired the development of a high need to achieve, a strong and demanding mother was less harmful. They theorized that the male child does not perceive the mother to be as threatening as he does the father. Since only male children were included in this sample, one may only speculate on the relative effects of mother and father on the development of the achievement motive in the female child.

Other research has confirmed the significant role of the mother in developing achievement motives.[22,82] Winterbottom[100] concluded that mothers play a key role in the development of need to achieve in their sons, and that boys with a high regard to achieve have mothers who are more demanding, more rewarding, and who evaluate their son's accomplishments more highly. To age 7, these mothers tend to make more demands on their sons; between ages 7 to 10, they impose more restrictions.

Little research has assessed the early environment of the young girl with a high need to achieve. Crandall et al.[21] found that mothers of achievement oriented girls were less affectionate and less nurturant. Kagan and Moss[47] found that maternal over-protectiveness in the first 3 years of life was negatively related to adult achievement behaviors for girls. Thus, consistent with the general trends of achievement motivation research, less is known about the early achievement socialization of girls than boys.

However, a substantial amount of research has been compiled to document sex differences in other child-rearing practices in the United States and cross-culturally. For example, based on cross-cultural data, Barry et al.[10] concluded that males receive a higher degree of achievement and self-reliance training, while females receive higher obedience and nurturance training. Using this model as a basis, Sutton-Smith and his colleagues[80,81,84,85,89] investigated game involvement across several cultures. One finding of particular significance was the preference of males for games whose outcomes were determined by physical skill (sport) and the preference of females for games of chance or strategy. These results have a certain degree of power for describing historical under-representation of females in athletics in America.

Despite the differential stress placed on early independence training for boys and girls, one must remember that women's unaroused motive to succeed is higher than men's aroused motive to succeed. To account for the inconsistency of the display of achievement behavior, one must review the different patterns of achievement for the two sexes by age.

As the girl grows older she is subjected to confusing expectations. Exactly when the conflict between sex-role expectations and achievement striving reaches its height remains a matter of controversy. Kohlberg's[52] developmental scheme fixes the period at which values are placed on sex appropriate behavior at the ages 6 to 8. At this age, children demonstrate a preference for unfamiliar toys labeled by others as appropriate for their own sex. Other researchers identify the grade school years (ages 5 to 11) as those during which females develop a growing awareness of the social distaste for the feminine role. Morgan et al.[69,70] found that during this period, females show an increasing amount of anxiety over their own achievement.

Margaret Mead[66] has ably summarized the dilemma:

> Throughout her education and her development of vocational expectancy, the girl is faced with the dilemma that she must display enough of her abilities to be considered successful, but not too successful; enough ability to get and keep a job, but without the sort of commitment that will make her too successful or unwilling to give up the job entirely for marriage and motherhood.

Perhaps the conflict has been resolved for most in favor of sex appropriate behavior by the junior and senior high school years. Evidence shows that a girl's academic performance levels off during those years while a boy's increases.[46,48,72] However, summarizing their review of the development of sex role identity, Maccoby and Jacklin[63] identified the college years (18 to 22) as those during which a woman's confidence in her abilities is at is lowest point, and they stated

> Perhaps it is at this period of their life more than any other that individuals define themselves in terms of their "masculinity" and "feminity," and when greater sex differences may therefore appear than at earlier or later ages.

Prior to the recent surge in interest in sports for women, the dropout rate for girls in school or community sport programs corresponded with this chronology. One interesting way to summarize the findings on the development of achievement motivation, the conflict between achievement and sex appropriate behavior for women, and the relevance to sport is through the *conflict-enculturation* model of Roberts and Sutton-Smith.

The Conflict-Enculturation Model

In order to integrate differences in child rearing practices with the choices of games, Roberts and Sutton-Smith formulated the *conflict-enculturation model* depicted in Table 12. Although some parts of the model remain untested, Roberts, Sutton-Smith and their colleagues[69,71,81,89] have offered much evidence in support of the different hypotheses which comprise it.

The conflict-enculturation model can be summed up as follows. Any social system or society has "cultural maintenance problems" which must be solved in order for the system to continue as an ongoing entity. As one solution, the system utilizes "socialization practices" as a means of easing individuals into necessary roles or perspectives. If the process is a successful one, the result is "enculturation" or the reproduction of cultural values within the individual. However, Roberts and Sutton-Smith[89] contend that socialization practices engender "conflict and/or anxiety" over one's ability to fulfill role prescriptions. Because a direct confrontation with preferred patterns is often too stressful for the individual, he or she learns to handle the problem through model situations, often through "expressive models" such as sport. If successful, the model situation eases the individual into a satisfactory confrontation with the real situation

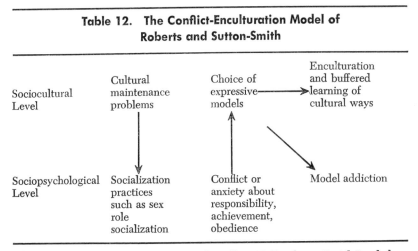

Table 12. The Conflict-Enculturation Model of Roberts and Sutton-Smith

Sociocultural Level	Cultural maintenance problems	Choice of expressive models	Enculturation and buffered learning of cultural ways
Sociopsychological Level	Socialization practices such as sex role socialization	Conflict or anxiety about responsibility, achievement, obedience	Model addiction

Adapted from Lambert, William W. and Wallace E. Lambert: *Social Psychology.* Englewood Cliffs, Prentice-Hall, Inc., 1964.

and provides "buffered learning of cultural ways." If unsuccessful, i.e., if the individual resists enculturation into proper culture maintaining roles, he or she may become "model addicted" and display an unwillingness to leave the security of the model situation. The model offers one explanation for the differential appeal of sport to boys and girls in American society. Societies have a vested interest in the perpetuation of established sex roles and therefore establish practices to ensure proper sex role socialization. For boys, socialization generally entails independence training for the development of achievement orientations; for girls, training is more likely to include responsibility and obedience training. Quite naturally, the expressive models chosen by boys and girls reflect their concern with learning and enacting proper roles: boys choose games of physical skill, which are achievement models, while girls choose games of chance or strategy, models of responsibility and obedience.[26,81]

As it has traditionally been interpreted, however, the model offers little insight into the dilemma of the girl caught between achievement strivings and pressures for sex-role conformity. Accordingly, a compensatory interpretation of the conflict-enculturation model is suggested here for purely speculative purposes.

Anxiety is especially high for those young girls whose achievement strivings are highest, for they must continually choose between conflicting strivings. In such cases, a girl's choice of expressive model may be significant for her psychological well-being. Perhaps she reads books about Amelia Earhart and Eleanor Roosevelt; perhaps she learns to cook and sew; perhaps she chooses sport. Her choice will have repercussions, for some choices are perceived as more appropriate channels for feminine achievement than others. Some choices, most notably sport, serve to extend the conflict of achievement and sex role expectations and perhaps serve as a compromise between these two forces in the eyes of both the individual and society. In such cases, since deviant *model* behavior is more acceptable than deviant behavior in "real" situations, expressive models can become addictive, and enculturation into the proper role becomes blocked. Such an analysis leads one to the inevitable conclusion that women who continue their athletic careers beyond the adolescent years are addicted to models of inappropriate achievement strivings. Although untested, this interpretation offers one framework for understanding both the psychological and social reactions to athletic participation for women.

Achievement Motivation Can Be Developed

Despite the motive-like conceptualization of need to achieve, McClelland[58,61,62] has long believed that the development of achievement motives is not limited solely to appropriate training during childhood. In the 1960's McClelland and Winter[62] instituted a 3-year project in India under the auspices of the Small Industries Extension Training Institute, in which native businessmen underwent intensive training aimed at increasing their levels of achievement motivation. In brief, the development program included inputs of four types:

1. the achievement syndrome—individuals were taught behaviors characteristic of individuals with high needs to achieve, such as producing achievement fantasy in response to the TAT.
2. self-study—individuals confronted the significance of achievement motivation as it related to their own lives, their careers, their goals and values.
3. goal setting—individuals were coached in the precise goals they should set and encouraged to measure their progress toward them.
4. interpersonal supports—the instructors and other participants cooperated in providing an atmosphere of warmth and mutual support.

Each type of input was based upon three propositions, and some of the resulting twelve propositions have direct relevance to the development of achievement motives in women:

Self-Study Proposition S-1. The more an individual perceives that developing a motive is required by the demands of his career and life situation, the more educational attempts designed to develop that motive are likely to succeed.

Self-Study Proposition S-2. The more an individual can perceive and experience the newly conceptualized motive as consistent with the ideal self-image, the more the motive is likely to influence his future thoughts and actions.

Self-Study Proposition S–3. The more an individual can perceive and experience the newly conceptualized motive as consistent with prevailing cultural values and norms, the more the motive is likely to influence his future thoughts and actions.

Goal Setting Proposition G-1. The more reasons an individual has to believe that he can, will or should develop a motive, the more educational attempts designed to develop that motive are likely to succeed.

Interpersonal Support Proposition I-1. Changes in motives are more likely to occur in an interpersonal atmosphere in which the individual feels warmly but honestly supported and respected by others as a person capable of guiding and directing his own future behavior.

Interpersonal Support Proposition I-3. Changes in motives are more likely to occur and persist if the new motive is a sign of membership in a new and continuing reference group.

These propositions serve as an excellent summary for the review presented here for they restore to the research perspective a social factor which has been too long overlooked. Likewise, they indicate a restructuring of incentives for success which has been noted above as an ignored aspect of the resultant achievement motivation model. Most of all, however, they indicate the possibilities for myth breaking. If Indian businessmen, raised in a culture in which social incentives for success are low, can develop a need to achieve and then go on to achieve, then American women, raised in an atmosphere of similarly low incentives, can surely do the same. The propositions spelled out by McClelland and Winter provide a programmatic statement which clearly points to the steps which must be taken to elevate the incentives for the display of achievement motivations by women. The myth of the unaspiring underachieving female can be dispelled.

CONCLUSIONS

Those interested in combating the myth of the underachieving woman would do well to familiarize themselves with the findings of these researchers, and to set out on their own replications and extensions. Perhaps a synthesis of findings from such related research traditions as those outlined above will provide a more comprehensive framework for the study of achievement related motives in women athletes. With the trend toward acceptance of women in positions of high achievement in worlds of business, politics, broadcasting, and athletics, perhaps one may look forward to the day when Lucy Van Pelt replaces Schroeder in her team's position of centrality, adjusts her cap, pounds her catcher's mitt, and yells out to the pitcher's mound, "C'mon Charlie Brown, pitch it to me, baby."

REFERENCES

1. Albinson, John G.: The Relationship of Need Achievement and Test Anxiety to Performance of Physical Tasks. Paper presented at the Canadian Association of Sport Science, Quebec, 1970.
2. Alderman, Richard B.: Achievement in Sport, Chapter 9, *Psychological Behavior in Sport.* Philadelphia, W. B. Saunders Co., 1974, Pp. 203–224.
3. Alper, T. G. and E. Greenberger: Relationship of Picture Structure to Achievement Motivation in College Women. *J. Personality and Social Psychology, 7,* 362, 1967.
4. Atkinson, John W.: Motivational Determinants of Risk Taking Behavior, in *A Theory of Achievement Motivation,* John W. Atkinson and Norman T. Feather (Eds.). New York, John Wiley & Sons, Inc., 1966, Pp. 11–29.
5. ————: Some General Implications of Conceptual Developments in the Study of Achievement-Oriented Behavior. *Human Motivation: A Symposium.* Lincoln, University of Nebraska Press, 1965, Pp. 3–31.
6. ————(Ed.): *Motives in Fantasy, Action and Society: A Method of Assessment and Study.* Princeton, Van Nostrand, 1958.
7. Atkinson, John W. and Norman T. Feather, (Eds.): *A Theory of Achievement Motivation.* New York, John Wiley & Sons, Inc., 1966.
8. Atkinson, John W. and George H. Litwin: Achievement Motive and Test Anxiety Conceived as Motive to Approach Success and Motive to Avoid Failure, in *A Theory of Achievement Motivation,* John W. Atkinson and Norman Feather (Eds.). New York, John Wiley & Sons, Inc., 1966.
9. Atkinson, John W. and Joel Raynor (Eds.): *Motivation and Achievement.* New York, Halsted, 1974.
10. Barry, H., M. K. Bacon, and I. L. Child: A Cross-Cultural Survey of Some Sex Differences in Socialization. *J. Abnormal and Social Psychol., 55,* 327, 1957.
11. Baumrind, D. and A. E. Black: Socialization Practices Associated with

Dimensions of Competence in Pre-school Boys and Girls. *Child Development, 38*, 291, 1967.
12. Begler, Edmund: *The Psychology of Gambling.* New York, International Universities Press, 1958.
13. Bethe, Donald R.: Success in Beginning Handball as a Function of the Theory of Achievement Motivation. PhD. dissertation, Ohio State, 1968.
14. Birney, R. C., H. Burdick, and R. C. Teevan: *Fear of Failure.* Princeton, Van Nostrand, 1969.
15. Birrell, Susan: Achievement Related Motives and Sport Participation in High School and College, Paper presented at Women and Sport Conference, Philadelphia, 1976.
16. ————: An Analysis of the Inter-relationships among Achievement Motivation, Athletic Participation, Academic Achievement, and Educational Aspirations. International J. Sport Psychol., forthcoming 1977.
17. Boyatzis, R. E.: Drinking as a Manifestation of Power Concerns. Paper presented at the Ninth Congress on Anthropological and Ethnological Sciences. Boston, McBer & Co., 1973.
18. Burton, Elsie Carter: State and Trait Anxiety, Achievement Motivation and Skill Attainment in College Women. *Res. Quart., 42*, 139, 1971.
19. Crandall, Vaughan J.: Achievement, in *Child Psychology: the Sixty-Second Yearbook of the National Society for the Study of Education.* H. W. Stevenson (Ed.). Chicago, University of Chicago Press, 1963, Pp. 416–459.
20. Crandall, Virginia C.: Achievement Behavior in Young Children, in *Achievement in American Society.* B. C. Rosen, H. J. Crockett, Jr. and Clyde Z. Nunn (Eds.). Cambridge, Schenkman, 1969, Pp. 95–111.
21. Crandall, V., Rachel Dewey, W. Katkovsky, and Anne Preston: Parents' Attitudes and Behaviors and Grade School Children's Academic Achievements. *J. Genetic Psychol., 104*, 53, 1964.
22. Crandall, Vaughan J., Anne Preston, and Alice Rabson: Maternal Reactions and the Development of Individualism and Achievement Behavior in Young Children. *Child Development, 31*, 243, 1960.
23. Curtis, Rebecca, Mark Zanna, and Woodrow Campbell: Fear of Success, Sex, and the Perceptions and Performance of Law School Students. Paper presented at the Eastern Psychological Association Meetings, Washington, D.C., 1973.
24. Daugert, Patricia Joan: Relationship of Anxiety and nAch to Learning of Swimming. PhD. dissertation, University of Michigan, 1966.
25. Dayries, John L. and Ronald L. Grimm: Personality Traits of Women Athletes as Measured by the Edwards Personal Preference Schedule. *Perceptual and Motor Skills, 30*, 229, 1970.
26. Deaux, Kay, Leonard White, and Elizabeth Farris: Skill versus Luck: Field and Laboratory Studies of Male and Female Preferences. *J. Personality and Social Psychol., 32*, 629, 1975.
27. Deaux, Kay and Tim Emswiller: Explanations of Successful Performance on Sex Linked Tasks: What is Skill for the Male is Luck for the Female. *J. Personality and Social Psychol., 29*, 80, 1974.
28. Feather, Norman T.: The Relationship of Persistence at a Task to Experience of Success and Achievement Related Values. *J. Abnormal and Social Psychol., 63*, 552, 1961.
29. Feather, Norman T. and Alfred C. Raphelson: Fear of Success in Australian and American Student Groups: Motive or Sex Role Stereotype? *J. Personality, 42*, 190, 1974.
30. French, Elizabeth: Some Characteristics of Achievement Motivation, in *Motives in Fantasy, Action and Society.* John W. Atkinson (Ed.). Princeton, Van Nostrand, 1958, Pp. 270–277.
31. French, Elizabeth and Gerald S. Lesser: Some Characteristics of the Achievement Motive in Women. *J. Abnormal and Social Psychol., 68*, 119, 1964.

32. French, Elizabeth and F. H. Thomas: The Relationship of Achievement Motivation to Problem Solving Effectiveness. *J. Abnormal and Social Psychol., 56,* 46, 1958.

33. Frieze, Irene Hanson: Women's Expectations for and Causal Attributions of Success and Failure, in *Women and Achievement: Social and Motivational Analyses.* M. T. S. Mednick, S. S. Tangri and L. W. Hoffman (Eds.). New York, Wiley, 1975, Pp. 158–171.

34. Fox, Frank and Stephen Parker: Why Nixon Did Himself In: A Behavioral Examination of His Need to Fail. *New York, 7,* 26, 1974.

35. Garai, J. E. and A. Scheinfeld: Sex Differences in Mental and Behavioral Traits. *Genetic Psychology Monographs, 77,* 169, 1968.

36. Gjesme, T.: Achievement Related Motives and School Performance for Girls. *J. Personality and Social Psychol., 26,* 131, 1973.

37. Gorsuch, Harvey Ray: The Competitive Athlete and the Achievement Motive as Measured by a Projective Test. MS thesis, School of Physical Education, Pennsylvania State University, 1968.

38. Heilbrun, Alfred B. Jr., Carol Kleemeier, and Gary Piccola: Developmental and Situational Correlates of Achievement Behavior in College Females. *J. Personality, 42,* 420, 1974.

39. Hoffman, Lois Wladis: Early Childhood Experiences and Women's Achievement Motives, in *Women and Achievement: Social and Motivational Analyses.* M. T. S. Mednick, S. S. Tangri, and L. W. Hoffman (Eds.). New York, John Wiley & Sons, Inc., 1975, Pp. 129–150.

40. —————: Fear of Success in Males and Females, 1965–1971. *J. Consulting and Clinical Psychol., 42,* 353, 1974.

41. Horner, Matina S.: The Measurement and Behavioral Implications of Fear of Success in Women, in *Motivation and Achievement.* J. W. Atkinson and Joel Raynor (Eds.). New York, Halsted, 1974.

42. Horner, Matina S.: Toward an Understanding of Achievement Related Conflicts in Women. *J. Social Issues, 28,* 157, 1972.

43. —————: The Motive to Avoid Success and Changing Aspirations of College Women, in *Readings on the Psychology of Women.* J. M. Bardwick (Ed.). New York, Harper & Row, 1972, Pp. 62–67.

44. —————: Femininity and Successful Achievement: A Basic Inconsistency, in *Roles Women Play: Readings Toward Women's Liberation.* Michele Hoffnug Garskof (Ed.). Belmont, California, Brooks/Cole Publishing Co., 1971, Pp. 97–122.

45. —————: Sex Differences in Achievement Motivation and Performance in Competitive and Non-Competitive Situations. PhD. dissertation, Department of Psychology, University of Michigan, 1968.

46. Horrocks, J. E.: *The Psychology of Adolescence: Behavior and Development. Boston,* Houghton Mifflin, 1969.

47. Kagan, Jerome and H. A. Moss: *Birth to Maturity.* New York, John Wiley & Sons, Inc., 1962.

48. —————: The Stability of Passive and Dependent Behavior from Childhood through Adulthood. *Child Development, 31,* 577, 1960.

49. Katz, Marlaine L.: Female Motive to Avoid Success: A Psychological Barrier or a Response to Deviancy. Unpublished paper, Stanford University, 1972.

50. Kenyon, Gerald S.: A Conceptual Model for Characterizing Physical Activity, in *Sport, Culture and Society.* John W. Loy and Gerald S. Kenyon (Eds.). New York, The Macmillan Co., 1969, Pp. 71–81.

51. Klein, Michael and Gerd Christiansen: Group Composition, Group Structure and Group Effectiveness of Basketball Teams, in *Sport, Culture and Society.* John W. Loy and Gerald S. Kenyon (Eds.). New York, The Macmillan Co., 1969, Pp. 397–408.

52. Kohlberg, Lawrence: A Cognitive-Developmental Analysis of Children's Sex-Role Concepts and Attitudes, in the Development of Sex Differences.

Eleanor Maccoby (Ed.). Stanford, Stanford University Press, 1966, Pp. 86–173.
53. Lesser, G. S., R. N. Krawitz, and R. Packard: Experimental Arousal of Achievement Motivation in Adolescent Girls. *J. Abnormal and Social Psychol., 66,* 59, 1963.
54. Levine, Adeline and Janice Cumrine: Women and Fear of Success: A Problem in Replication. *Amer. J. Sociology, 80,* 964, 1975.
55. Loy, John W. with Susan Birrell and David Rose: The Professionalization of Attitudes toward Play as a Function of Selected Social Identities and Level of Sport Participation. Paper presented at the International Seminar on Play in Physical Education and Sport, Wingate Institute, Tel Aviv, Israel, 1975.
56. Loy, John W. and Joseph McElvogue: Racial Segregation in American Sport. *International Review of Sport Sociology, 5,* 5, 1970.
57. McClelland, David C.: *Power: The Inner Experience.* New York, Irvington Press, 1975.
58. ———: Achievement Motivation Can Be Developed. *Harvard Business Review, 6,* 6, 178, 1965.
59. ———: *The Achieving Society.* New York, Free Press, 1961.
60. ———: Risk Taking in Children with High and Low Need for Achievement, in *Motives in Fantasy, Action and Society,* John W. Atkinson (Ed.). Princeton, Van Nostrand, 1958, Pp. 306–321.
61. McClelland, David C., John W. Atkinson, Russell A. Clark, and Edgar L. Lowell: *The Achievement Motive.* New York, Appleton-Century-Crofts, 1953.
62. McClelland, David C. and David G. Winter: *Motivating Economic Achievement.* New York, Free Press, 1969.
63. Maccoby, Eleanor Emmons and Carol Nagy Jacklin: *The Psychology of Sex Differences.* Stanford, Stanford University Press, 1975.
64. Maehr, Martin L.: Toward a Framework for the Cross-Cultural Study of Achievement Motivation: McClelland Reconsidered and Redirected. Paper presented at the Annual Conference of the North American Society for the Psychology of Sport and Physical Activity, 1973.
65. Martens, Rainer: The Process of Competition, Chapter 5, *Social Psychology and Physical Activity.* New York, Harper & Row, 1975, Pp. 66–86.
66. Mead, Margaret: *Male and Female: A Study of Sex in a Changing World.* New York, Dell, 1968.
67. Metheny, Eleanor: Symbolic Forms of Movement: The Feminine Image in Sports, in *Sport and American Society,* 2nd ed., George H. Sage (Ed.). Reading, Massachusetts, Addison Wesley Publishing Co., 1974, Pp. 289–301.
68. Monahan, L., D. Kuhn and P. Shaver: Intrapsychic versus Cultural Explantations of 'Fear of Success' Motive. *J. Personality and Social Psychol., 29,* 60, 1974.
69. Morgan, E., B. Rosenberg, and B. Sutton-Smith: Anxiety as a Function of Change in Sex Role. Paper presented at the Midwest Psychological Association meetings, Chicago, 1961.
70. Morgan, E., B. Sutton-Smith, and B. G. Rosenberg: Age Change in the Relation Between Anxiety and Achievement. *Child Development, 31,* 515, 1960.
71. Morgan, S. W. and Bernard Mausner: Behavioral and Fantasied Indicators of Avoidance of Success in Men and Women. Unpublished paper, Department of Psychology, Beaver College, 1971.
72. Moss, H. A. and J. Kagan: Stability of Achievement and Recognition Seeking Behaviors from Early Childhood through Adulthood. *J. Abnormal and Social Psychol., 62,* 504, 1961.
73. Murray, Henry A.: *Manual of Thematic Apperception Test.* Cambridge, Massachusetts, Harvard University Press, 1943.

74. ————: *Explorations in Personality.* New York, Oxford University Press, 1938.
75. Neal, P.: Personality Traits of U.S. Women Athletes Who Participated in the 1959 Pan American Games. MS thesis, University of Utah, 1959.
76. Ogilvie, Bruce C.: The Unconscious Fear of Success. *Quest, 10,* 35, 1968.
77. Ogilvie, Bruce C. and Keith W. Johnsgard: The Personality of the Male Athlete. Paper presented at the American Academy of Physical Education, Las Vegas, Nevada, 1967.
78. Ogilvie, Bruce C. and Thomas A. Tutko: *Problem Athletes and How to Handle Them.* London, Pelham Books, Ltd., 1966.
79. Plummer, Peter J.: A Q-Sort Study of the Achievement Motivation of Selected Athletes. MS thesis, University of Massachusetts, 1969.
80. Roberts, John M., Malcolm J. Arth, and Robert R. Bush: Games in Culture. *American Anthropologist, 61,* 597, 1959.
81. Roberts, John M. and Brian Sutton-Smith: Child Training and Game Involvement. *Ethnology, 1,* 166, 1962.
82. Rosen, B. C.: Family Structure and Value Transmission. *Merrill-Palmer Quarterly, 10,* 59, 1964.
83. Rosen, B. C. and Roy G. D'Andrade: The Psychosocial Origins of Achievement Motivation, in *Achievement in American Society,* B. C. Rosen, H. J. Crockett, Jr., and Clyde Z. Nunn (Eds.). Cambridge, Schenkman, 1969, Pp. 55–84.
84. Rosenberg, B. G. and Brian Sutton-Smith: A Revised Conception of Masculine-Feminine Differences in Play Activities. *J. Genetic Psychol., 96,* 165, 1960.
85. ————: The Measurement of Masculinity and Femininity in Children. *Child Development, 30,* 373, 1959.
86. Ryan, E. Dean and W. L. Lakie: Competitive and Non-competitive Performance in Relation to Achievement Motive and Manifest Anxiety. *J. Personality and Social Psychol., 1,* 342, 1965.
87. Sherif, Carolyn Wood: Females in the Competitive Process, in *Women and Sport: A National Research Conference,* Dorothy Harris (Ed.). Pennsylvania State University, HPER Series No. 2, 1972, Pp. 115–139.
88. Stein, Althea Huston and Margaret H. Bailey: The Socialization of Achievement Orientation in Females. *Psychological Bulletin, 80,* 345, 1973.
89. Sutton-Smith, Brian, John M. Roberts, and Robert M. Kozelka: Game Involvement in Adults. *J. Social Psychol., 60,* 15, 1963.
90. Tresemer, David: Fear of Success: Popular but Unproven. *Psychology Today, 7,* 82, 1974.
91. Usher, Peter M.: Achievement Motivation and Levels of Sport Performance, *Mouvement 7, Proceedings of the Seventh Canadian Psycho-Motor and Sport Psychology Symposium,* Quebec, 1975, Pp. 349–353.
92. Vanek, Miroslav and V. Hosek: Need for Achievement in Sport Activity. *International J. Sport Psychol., 1,* 83, 1970.
93. Veroff, Joseph, Lou McClelland, and David Ruhland: Varieties of Achievement Motivation, in *Women and Achievement: Social and Motivational Analyses,* M. T. S. Mednick, S. S. Tangri and L. W. Hoffman (Ed.). New York, John Wiley & Sons, Inc., 1975, Pp. 172–205.
94. Veroff, Joseph, Sue Wilcox, and John W. Atkinson: The Achievement Motive in High School and College Age Women. *J. Abnormal and Social Psychol., 48,* 108, 1953.
95. Warner, W. Lloyd and James C. Abegglin: *Big Business Leaders in America.* New York, Harper, 1955.
96. Webb, Harry: Professionalization of Attitudes Toward Play among Adolescents, in *Aspects of Contemporary Sport Sociology: Proceedings of C.I.C. Symposium on the Sociology of Sport,* G. S. Kenyon (Ed.). Chicago, Athletic Institute, 1968, Pp. 161–178.

97. Willis, Joe Don: Achievement Motivation, Success, and Competitiveness in College Wrestling. PhD. dissertation, Ohio State University, 1968.
98. Willis, Joe D. and D. R. Bethe: Achievement Motivation: Implications for Physical Activity. *Quest,* XIII, 18, 1970.
99. Winter, David G.: *The Power Motive.* New York, Free Press, 1973.
100. Winterbottom, Marian R.: The Relation of Need for Achievement to Learning Experiences in Independence and Mastery, in *Motives in Fantasy, Action, and Society.* J. W. Atkinson (Ed.). Princeton, Van Nostrand, 1958, Pp. 453–478.
101. Wittig, Arno F.: Attitudes Towards Females in Sport. *Proceedings of the North American Society for Psychology of Sport and Physical Activity* meetings, Pennsylvania State University, 1975.
102. Yeary, Sheryl: A Comparison of Achievement Motive and Anxiety Level in College Women Athletes in Selected Sports. MS thesis, School of Physical Education, University of Massachusetts, 1971.
103. Zander, Alvin: Motivation and Performance of Sport Groups. *Proceedings of the North American Society for Psychology of Sport and Physical Activity* meetings, Daniel M. Landers (Ed.). Pennsylvania State University, 1975.
104. ————: *Motives and Goals in Groups.* New York, Academic Press, 1971.
105. Zuckerman, Miron and Ladd Wheeler: To Dispel Fantasies about the Fantasy-Based Measure of Fear of Success. *Psychological Bulletin, 82,* 932, 1975.

McHugh, Duquin, and Frieze present an excellent summary of attribution theory and apply it creatively in analyzing the sport environment as it exists for women. The authors paint another view of Felshin's apologetic. This one presents the female athlete continuing to report that she plays "just for fun" and that she wins by luck. A new explanation for the apologetic is offered, however, in that the female athlete attributes the causes of her successes to factors *external* to herself.

The authors suggest that women are better able to handle failure in a psychologically healthy manner than men. At this point, a sport feminist may be tempted to indulge in some dark humor concerning the many occasions in which women have had opportunities to deal with failure. As the sport world turns around for her, however, it would be desirable if the sportswoman could develop attitudes yielding more personal pride in her victories yet maintaining her point of view toward defeat.

Of special note are the authors' concluding remarks about the debilitating effects on female athletes when coaches hold sexist biases. The implication is strong that by whatever means quality control is maintained in coaching (i.e., job descriptions and hiring procedures, certification requirements), the disqualification of those who persist in sexist beliefs is imperative.

Chapter 9

BELIEFS ABOUT SUCCESS AND FAILURE: ATTRIBUTION AND THE FEMALE ATHLETE

Maureen C. McHugh, Mary E. Duquin

and Irene Hanson Frieze

People speculate about the possible causes of wins and losses at all levels of sports participation. The sports commentator is paid to tell her viewers why the local teams are winning or losing. College students hold the team's coach responsible for a recent series of losses. Fans express delight with their athletic heroes' "will to win" and disgust for the "bad calls" given them by referees. The winner of a major golf tournament attributes the win to long hours of practice. The amateur bowler feels her recent losses are due to a streak of bad luck. The Little League pitcher is confident that natural ability explains recent successes. Thus, the question "Why"? is prevalent in sports situations, and is asked and answered by athletes, coaches, fans, commentators, and the common observer.

The causal explanations given for everyday events have been investigated within a body of research known as attribution theory. Attribution theory is considered a form of "naive psychology" meaning that it deals with the psychology of everyday events, and with the way the nonpsychologist views his/her environment. Specifically, attribution theory deals with causal explanation, how people answer questions beginning with "why"?[26] Questions about why events occurred are asked and answered daily in all aspects of everyday life; they are especially important in sports situations because of the competitive component, the winning-losing aspect of games. Attribution theory focuses on both the process of making causal inferences, and the implications of making one or another attribution. The attribution one makes is seen as having behavioral and emotional consequences. Causal attributions affect expectancies for the future, an individual's choice of future performance, the pride or shame one experiences, and one's subsequent performance levels.[47] For example, assume that a runner feels that she lost the race because she had a bad start. She feels shame in her failure, but also feels that she could win a subsequent race. She may spend extra time practicing or exert more effort in training to insure a better performance in the next race. Attribution theory is a common sense analysis of such daily situations; however, it is also a systematized and scientific investigation of cognitive processes.

Although much of the research relating to attribution theory has focused on academic success and failure, the basic principles and concepts appear to be applicable in a wide variety of settings.[5,9] One setting in which the evaluating of causes of success and failure has special relevance is that of sports. Wankel[46] has suggested that attribution theory should serve as the theoretical basis of future research in sport psychology. And although few existing studies have focused directly on attributions made for sports events, we agree that attribution theory has important implications for understanding sports participation of women and men.

ATTRIBUTING THE CAUSES OF SUCCESS AND FAILURE

Weiner and his associates[47,49] have done extensive research demonstrating the importance of attributions or beliefs about why success or failure occurs in understanding achievement-oriented behavior. Most of this research concerns the attributions made by an individual about his or her own successes and failures and how these attributions influence emotional reactions, future expectancies and subsequent achievement strivings. It is assumed that people will be more likely to attempt tasks where they feel they have a high expectancy of doing well and that they will desire to maximize positive feelings about success and minimize negative feelings about failure. Both affect and expectancy are determined by the type of causal attribution made about why a particular event was a success or failure.

A modified diagram of the attributional process as conceptualized by Frieze et al.[17] is shown in Figure 6. This process begins with a particular win or loss. After the outcome is established, the athlete utilizes available information, such as his or her expectancy for success at this task, past history of successes and knowledge of how well other people did, to determine the cause of the outcome. People have well-established patterns of making causal attributions in familiar situations so that extensive information processing is not necessary.[16] Thus, for example, a highly competent male may see his high abilities as responsible for his achievement successes without having to consider the particular circumstances of any one event.[16] Such patterns may well exist in athletic events but they have not been empirically demonstrated.

For any situation there are many possible reasons why a particular success or failure might occur and, therefore, many causal attributions

The Attribution Process

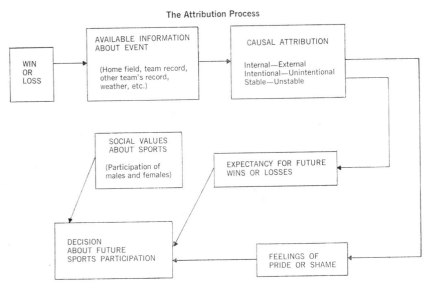

Fig. 6.   The Attribution Process.

which can be made. The four most studied causes of achievement outcomes are ability, effort, luck and task ease or difficulty.[49] Thus a person may succeed at an exam because of his or her ability, trying hard, good luck and/or the fact that the task was relatively easy. Failure may result from low ability, not trying sufficiently hard, bad luck and/or task difficulty. More recent work[9,15] has indicated that other causal factors are frequently employed to explain the successes and failures of others as well as for oneself. These include stable effort or a consistent pattern of diligence or laziness, other people who may aid or interfere with performance, mood and fatigue or sickness, having a good or poor personality and physical appearance.[9] In athletic situations, athletes most often attribute their wins to their own or the team effort, training hard, being up for the game or meet, wanting to win, good coaching, the team's ability, the encouragement of teammates and the support of the crowd in attendance at the game or meet. Failures are most attributed to not trying, not being up for the game, not training enough, not wanting to win enough or having a poor team.[18]

DIMENSIONS OF CAUSAL ATTRIBUTIONS

Causal attributions in achievement settings can be classified along three dimensions: internal-external; stable-unstable; and intentional-unintentional.[9] Ability, effort, mood, personality and knowledge are causes originating within or internal to the individual, while task difficulty, other people's help or hurt and luck are causes within the environment or external to the individual. This internal versus external dimension of causality (the I-E dimension) has been widely investigated, especially in terms of individual differences in stable tendencies to make either internal or external attributions.[38,42] This dimension has been shown to be particularly important for affect. More pride or satisfaction is reported by people who attribute their successes internally than if the attribution is made to an external cause.[48,50] These same studies have shown that internally attributed failures lead to more shame or dissatisfaction after failure. We expect that apparently internal attributions such as training, trying hard at a game, having a good team or being a good athlete or being up for the game will affect pride in a similar way as compared to more external causal categories such as luck, the coach, the other team or the referees. Table 13 shows our hypothesized classification system.

A general finding of attribution research has been that success is attributed more to internal causes, while failure is attributed more to external causes.[47] This tendency has also been demonstrated in sports situations. Mann[30] found that fans of losing football teams tended to attribute outcomes more to external causes such as luck and biased

Table 13.   A Dimensional Analysis of Sports Attribution Based on the Dimensional Analysis of Elig and Frieze[9]

INTENTIONAL

	STABLE	UNSTABLE
INTERNAL	training practice continuing desire to win	trying hard unfair play desire to win a particular event
EXTERNAL	coaching continuing teammate support opponent's training	fan support teammate support during event opponent's effort official's bias

UNINTENTIONAL

	STABLE	UNSTABLE
INTERNAL	natural ability characteristics that make a good competitor	fatigue nervousness mood or being psyched up
EXTERNAL	opponent's ability task difficulty	home court advantage luck officiating errors situational factors opponent's mood

officiating, while fans of winning teams attributed game outcomes more to the ability of the team. Roberts[35] reports that Little League players rated effort and ability higher when winning, and luck higher when losing. And in a study by Iso-Ahola[25] internal attributions were given for both clear-win and bare-win baseball games; however, clear losses were attributed to task difficulty (external) and effort (internal).

A second dimension along which the various causes may be differentiated is in their stability. Ability, training, or the coach, are relatively stable causes, while trying hard at a particular game, mood and luck may be highly changeable over time. If success at a particular type of sport was due to a person's high ability, one would anticipate continued success for that person in the same sport. Similarly, if a failure was due to a stable cause, continued failure would be anticipated. Conversely, unstable causes lead to acknowledging the possibility of change. Failures attributed to bad luck or lack of trying may result in expectations for eventual success since bad luck might finally change or trying harder might lead to future success.

In achievement settings, the stability of the causal attributions has been found to relate to expectancies for the future.[32,45,50] Stable attributions lead to expectancies for continued success or failure. Unstable attributions lead to expectations of changes in outcomes. Genov[20] also discusses the fact that confidence or uncertainty concerning the attainment of personal goals results from the self-assessment of the sports participant.

The importance of such confidence, expectancies, or subjective probability of success in determining performance has been emphasized by Diggory.[7] Hammer[24] mentions that an athlete's beliefs about future successes may become self-fulfilling prophecies, and suggests that nurturing positive expectations can improve performance. In a related study, Smith[41] found that members of a university football squad that had low expectations were less successful and more likely to quit the team. Thus, a stable attribution after success will lead to an expectation of future success, and improved performance and persistence, while an unstable attribution for failure should increase the subjective probability of success.

Roberts[35] suggests that previous experience in the sport interacts with current outcomes to produce attributions that differ on the stability dimension. In a study of Little League players, members of previously unsuccessful teams were more likely to attribute an immediate success to unstable causes such as luck and effort; and previously successful players encountering a loss also attributed it to unstable factors. Similarly, generally unsuccessful teams that suffered another loss attributed it to low ability, while successful teams that lost the current game rated their ability as high as winning successful teams did.

This hypothesis that subjects on teams with consistent and repeated past success or failure attribute their team outcomes to stable factors was partially supported in the Iso-Ahola study.[25] In cases of continuous success, effort and ability were assigned as prime factors for winning, while effort and task difficulty were seen as responsible for repeated failure. It should be pointed out in explanation of these results that effort may be viewed as a stable trait (training) or as an unstable trait.[9]

The two dimensions of internality and stability were first conceptualized by Weiner et al.[49] Rosenbaum[36] suggested that a third dimension, intentionality, might be added to the two-dimensional system to differentiate between effort and mood as well as to more fully understand all the various causal attributions. An attribution is considered to be intentional to the degree that the person is perceived to have control over his or her actions. Thus, ability and mood are factors within the person over which that person has little control, and events attributed to these would be unintentional. However, the athlete is perceived to have control over the effort he or she exerts so that attributions to effort are intentional (as well as being internal). The intentionality dimension appears to be related to reward and punishment, with most reward and punishment given for performances attributed to internal, intentional causes, although further research is needed to clarify these relationships, especially in sports situations. It would appear that successes attributed to really wanting to win and trying hard (intentional) would result in pride, and reward or reinforcement from the coach and others.

INDIVIDUAL AND TEAM ATTRIBUTIONS

Most of the attributional studies done up to this point have investigated situations in which subjects experience success or failure individually. Attributions for sports outcomes may be different since the individual often experiences success and failure together with teammates. Only a few studies have addressed this question of how group and self attributions differ, and to what extent group outcomes are attributed to individual factors, and individual outcomes to group factors. Shaw and Breed[39] report that when members are accused by others for group failure, they tend to underevaluate group abilities. Dustin[8] also found that team members reacted to the team's poor performances in a manner that prevented declines in their own ego levels. Other studies have demonstrated a tendency on the part of group members to overevaluate group products,[4] and that this overevaluation is increased with competition and increased importance of the situation.[13]

In a study utilizing both team and individual attributions for game wins and losses, Roberts[35] found few differences for team versus individual causal attribution choices. However, there was a significant interaction between individual and team effort attributions and outcome indicating that when the team lost, players considered the team effort lower than when winning; however, individuals considered that they tried just as hard when the team lost as when the team won. This may be viewed as a self enhancing type of attribution, or may be seen as resulting from direct knowledge of one's own effort, while other's effort is inferred.

Iso-Ahola[25] also found that team and individual attributions were used in similar ways. In this study, players relied on team outcome to assess personal ability and effort, rather than basing these self attributions on estimates of their own performance. That is, attributions about one's *own* ability or effort were based on whether the *team* won or lost. Neither objective or subjective estimates of individual performance significantly affected the attributions of the players.

Both of these studies were conducted with all male Little League players. Thus, it is not clear if female athletes would make differential use of team and individual attributions. However, a study by Zander, Fuller, and Armstrong[54] suggests that males and females react to group performance differently in an achievement setting. Subjects were given information about the group outcome, and group effort and ability, but were not given estimates of their individual contributions. Group members were then requested to indicate how much pride and shame they felt in both self and group. Male subjects indicated more pride in the group when the group had succeeded and had high ability, and more shame in the group when the group failed and had low ability. Females, on the other hand, expressed more shame in self when the group failed and had expended low effort. In this study then, males attended to ability cues more than females, while females attended more to effort cues. And for the males, group ability affected group pride and shame, but for the females, group effort affected personal or self pride and shame.

Since team and group attributions have not been extensively investigated, the implications of such attributions are unclear. Attribution theory would predict that internal team attributions for success such as team-effort and team-ability would result in greater pride in the team than external attributions such as luck and poor competition. However, the relationship of team attributions to self pride and shame are less clear. Does a team success that is attributed to team ability mediate feelings of pride in oneself, or is self pride only associated with positive self evaluation? Similarly, does the individual athlete feel shame when a team loss is attributed to low ability or not trying hard enough, or is personal affect mediated by estimates of one's own effort and ability? These questions should be investigated in future research by measuring affect and expectancies as well as attributions for success and failure within a team sport situation.

IMPLICATIONS OF ATTRIBUTIONS

The implications of individual attributions have been clarified by the attributional framework and research of Weiner and his associates.[19,47,49–52] According to the model, maximum security in success is derived from ability attributions, an internal stable factor. The athlete who feels that she succeeded because of natural ability has both pride in success, and high expectations of future successes. Maximum pride is associated with a win resulting from trying hard, but the athlete that makes this attribution can only expect continued success with continued effort. When success is attributed to external factors such as good coaching or the other team, the individual participant would feel less pride, although future expectancies would not necessarily be low. Unstable external factors and luck attributions for success result in less pride and low or uncertain expectancies of future success. Such attributions, external unstable factors and luck, might be responsible for the superstitious behavior observed in some athletes. To the extent that individuals rely on a rabbit's foot, wearing a certain number, eating a designated breakfast and other ritualized behaviors to produce success, they are undermining the pride that they feel with winning, and the certainty of future success.

An opposite pattern of attributions occurs with failure attributions. Athletes attributing losses to not trying hard enough, poor training, and/or lack of ability would feel maximum shame. When lack of ability (internal stable) is perceived to be the cause of failure, the shame persists, and the individual would probably eventually quit the team or the event, since she will believe that there will be no way in which the failure can be avoided, except for occasional instances of good luck. Lack of effort, although leading to shame, would be changeable and, therefore would result in higher hopes of future success than lack of ability attributions. Failures attributed to bad luck or task difficulty would produce less shame. And when bad luck, poor referees, or the ability of the opponent is viewed as responsible for the loss, future successes might be anticipated as these variables change.

It is hypothesized that in many cases people have well-established patterns of making causal attributions. Maximum self-esteem and confidence would theoretically be associated with a tendency to make internal (especially if stable) attributions for success and external or unstable attributions for failure. Fitch[14] verified these hypotheses with achievement situations by showing that high self-esteem males attributed success more to internal causes. Although these patterns of perceiving success and failure may lead to great confidence, other data suggest that maximum achievement striving is associated with slightly different patterns. Kukla[28] demonstrated that high achievement motivated men tend to attribute their successes to both high ability and effort, while they perceive their failures as due to lack of effort. The attribution of failure to lack of effort would lead to greater subsequent trying. This attribution pattern explains the motivating effects of failure for high achievement motivated males reported by Atkinson[2] and Weiner.[51] Also, high achievement motivation is generally associated with higher estimates of personal ability.[3,28] Low achievement motivated male subjects are less likely to see their successes as due to internal causes, but see failures as caused by their low ability.[51,52]

Athletes should show analogous attribution patterns since they are the "high achievers" in sports. If the successful athlete attributes her success to her natural sports ability and training, she will be confident of future successes and feel proud of her wins. If she believes her losses are the result of not trying hard enough, she'll be motivated to train harder and try harder at her next event.

SEX DIFFERENCES IN ATTRIBUTIONS

Within the existing literature, certain sex differences in attributions have been predicted and investigated. In general women and girls have low beliefs in their own ability, and lower expectations of success

Initial Expectancy	Performance Level	Causal Attribution	Final Expectancy
HIGH[1] ——→	HIGH ——→	Ability, or other stable internal factors	——→ HIGHER
HIGH ——→	LOW ——→	Bad luck, or lack of effort or other unstable factors	——→ HIGH
LOW[2] ——→	HIGH ——→	Good luck, or special effort, or other unstable factors	——→ LOW
LOW ——→	LOW ——→	Lack of ability, or other stable internal factors	——→ LOWER

[1]Associated with males.
[2]Associated with females.

Fig. 7. Self Fulfilling Prophecies for Expectations. (From Valle and Frieze.[45])

7

than males.[17] Attributional patterns of women have been predicted given these low expectancies of women in general.[10,19] According to the attributional model, if a women expects to do poorly, but succeeds, she is likely to attribute the outcome to an unstable cause such as luck. She then would not increase her expectancies for success, and would feel little pride in her success (Fig. 7). When a female with low expectancies fails on a task, she tends to attribute it to lack of ability resulting in a high degree of shame and low expectancies for future success. Thus, low expectancies may be self perpetuating when they lead to attributions which maintain their accuracy. Studies conducted within the achievement framework have demonstrated this predicted pattern. McMahan[33] found that women are more likely than men to attribute failure to lack of ability. In another study grade school girls attributed failure to lack of ability to a greater extent than they attributed success to high ability.[17]

A more frequently found attribution pattern for women is one of externality.[17] This pattern is characterized by attributions to external factors such as luck and task difficulty regardless of outcome. For example, some studies found that females rate tasks easier than do males in both success and failure conditions.[3,32] By rating the tasks as easier after either success or failure, females reduced the value of their successes, and increased the negative implications of their failures. These task ease attributions are similar in substance to the luck-low ability pattern discussed above, in that these patterns are self derogatory and would serve to perpetuate low expectancies.

A number of studies have found that females make greater use of luck attributions than males for both success and failure.[3,11,33,40,53] This pattern is also characterized by a general externality, but has different implications from task ease attributions. The pattern of luck attributions implies that, at least within traditionally masculine areas, women take less responsibility for and feel less pride in their successes and less shame about their failures. Thus, women employing this attributional pattern would experience relatively little affect and would not be confident of future successes.

ATTRIBUTIONS OF FEMALE ATHLETES

Attribution theory may be useful in understanding and optimizing the motivations of female athletes. As in the case of achievement related situations, sex differences in attributions for sports successes and failures can be predicted and investigated.

A pattern parallel to the one predicted for women in general may be predicted for women athletes. Based on women's internalization of beliefs in their own physical inferiority,[34] female athletes may attribute success to external factors such as luck, and failure to low ability. However, the female that consistently attributes her failure in sport to her own inability would probably discontinue her sports participation in favor of some more rewarding activity. And a female athlete that attributes her success in sports to luck would probably not develop the internal confidence needed for higher levels of sports experience.[34] Thus, this pattern may be found in young girl athletes or women in general, but the female that makes this type of attributions would probably not be found in advanced athletic programs.

Alternatively, the societal attitudes that allude to females' natural inability in sports[1,44] may produce a pattern of external attributions. The combination of the attitudes that females must overcome physical handicaps in order to succeed, and the idea of sport as demanding but dangerous, may result in females emphasizing task difficulty in their attributions. When they do succeed, the task must have been easier than most sports events, perhaps because of equally unskilled competition. And when girls are led to believe that sport is too rough and tough an activity for them, then female failure in sports becomes understandable and acceptable because the task is viewed as too difficult for them. Thus, like women in other "masculine" areas, the female athlete may have a tendency to make more external attributions than male participants. External attributions like task difficulty and luck decrease the responsibility one admits for outcomes. Women are discouraged from seriously pursuing sports excellence[21] and serious participation in competitive sport is viewed as unfeminine. Thus, the female athlete that reports playing just for fun, and winning by luck or task ease conforms more to society's view of femininity than the female who admittedly tries hard.

A third prediction of female athletes' attributional patterns could be made based on the fact that female athletes have been found to be generally self confident, autonomous, persevering, and achievement oriented.[22,44] The prediction based on these studies might be that the attributions of the female athlete would reflect the attributional patterns of the achievement oriented women in general. Preliminary studies have suggested that highly motivated women employ more effort attributions for both success and failure than low achievement oriented women.[12] Bar-Tal and Frieze[3] also found that high achievement motivation was related to higher estimates of ability for both male and female subjects, but that the finding was stronger for men. Greater use of effort attributions by female athletes might also be expected on the basis of the additional barriers to participation that they must hurdle in addition to the standard demands of athletic endeavors. Neal and Tutko[34] discuss the way in which women athletes do not receive positive reinforcement by way of social approval and encouragement in the pursuit of physical excellence, receive inferior and less training, lack equipment and adequate facilities, and receive less financial aid and backing. Thus it seems likely that successful participation does require more effort on the part of women. Neal and Tutko[34] also suggest that beliefs about female unsuitability present a psychological barrier to physical performance for women. They suggest that women have no concept of their own abilities since they have been indoctrinated with a view of themselves as having limited potential. These factors may undermine the ability attributions of female athletes, causing them to rely on effort as an explanation of their successes and failures.

In a study of female and male athletes,[18] both males and females rated "trying very hard" as the factor most important in causing success. However, there were also several significant sex differences in attributions for success. Females rated the encouragement of their teammates and the hard training of the team higher than males did. This finding may be related to earlier findings that female athletes have a strong affiliative motive for sports participation.[22] Males saw their wins as more influenced by their having high ability and training hard than did females. These are two internal attributions that should result in pride and high expectations for the males. The greater use of ability attributions by males is not surprising in view of the previous discussion of societal attitudes, and the fact that this result has commonly been found in other areas of achievement. However, males also rated "the other team played poorly," "your team was lucky," and "the crowd was on your side," higher than females. These attributional factors are external and unstable, and have often been predicted as a female pattern because of their implications for low future expectancies. A possible explanation of these external attributions of males for success may be that in teaching male athletes to make defensive external attributions for failure,[34] coaches may be inadvertently undermining the males' assumption of responsibility for success.

Following failure there was a trend for males to make more defensive types of attributions including the "other team had the home court advantage," "the crowd was on the other team's side," "you were unlucky," and "there are few good players on your team." Neal and Tutko[34] suggest that because females are not inhibited in their expression of emotion, they can handle failure better than males. Defensive attributions such as blaming the coach, other players, or the referees result from unexpressed sorrow and frustration at losing. They also suggest that the male coach often serves to perpetuate defenses against defeat by training athletes to respond in this way which may be damaging psychologically.

The Frieze et al. study[18] supports the prediction that female athletes attribute their outcomes differently than male athletes. However, there is little evidence that supports the prediction that attributions of female athletes mediate low expectancies or undermine their pride in success. Contrary to some predictions, these female athletes appeared to make slightly more internal attributions than male athletes for both success and failure, although females rated ability attributions lower. The demonstrated pattern, of female attributions then, is most similar to that of the achievement motivated female with effort being the most important causal factor. This pattern is viewed as more desirable in terms of its implications for pride and shame and future expectancies than the external attributions demonstrated by the male athletes.

OTHERS' EXPECTATIONS AND ATTRIBUTIONS

Up to this point the chapter has focused on internal cognitions of females and males. However, the cognitions of others concerning women may be as important, or more important, than the women's internal cognitions. First, the expectations for and attributions concerning women's sports accomplishments by others, such as coaches or parents, can affect getting on a team, being able to play, and other opportunities for participation in sports. Secondly, as has already been suggested, women's internal cognitions stem from societal standards and attitudes about the suitability of women for sports.

The available research suggests that women are expected to do more poorly than men at numerous tasks.[17] These expectations directly affect the performance of women. Research has indicated that when people are randomly assigned to high and low expectancy groups, the high expectancy group tends to perform better than the group to which low expectancies were assigned.[43] Similar results were obtained by Rosenthal and Jacobson[37] who found that teacher expectations had major effects on student performance even though teacher expectations had been based upon randomly assigned information. Thus a coach who has low expectations for an athlete may convey these expectations to her and thereby affect her performance. This situation is especially debilitating for women athletes when the expectations of the coach are not based on previous performance, but on the sex role standards and stereotypes of society.

Causal attributions for performance also differ according to the sex of the person being evaluated. Deaux and Emswiller[6] asked both male and female college students to evaluate another's performance at finding hidden objects in a complex design. The task was described as either masculine or feminine; males were expected to do better at the masculine task and females at the female task. When given information that the person had succeeded at the task, males' successes on the masculine task tended to be attributed more to ability, while females' successes were more likely to be attributed to luck. There were no differences on the feminine task. Translated to a sports situation these findings would suggest that males would be expected to do better at a "masculine" sport like basketball, while females might be expected to do better at a "feminine" activity like dance. When a male excels at basketball, others would attribute his success to ability, but when a female excels at basketball, her performance is viewed as lucky. However, a successful female dancer is not viewed as having more ability than a successful male dancer.

As has been documented in earlier portions of this chapter, the causal attributions made about a person have important implications not only for the affect and expectancies of that person, but also for the rewards given that person by others. People are constantly being evaluated by others. The kinds of attributions made by the decision makers in any situation have major consequences for those being judged. For example, if a coach thinks that the reason a woman won a meet was that she cheated, the reaction of the coach will be quite different than if he/she felt that the woman had trained hard for the event. Also, an athlete will probably be more motivated to train in an event where she thinks the coach determines starters on the basis of the competence and the effort of the athlete rather than by chance or favoritism. Another example of this process is the reaction of a coach to a poor performance due to external circumstances over which the player has no control (such as being put in a difficult match) or unstable factors which might be expected to change in the near future (the player had been sick and is now better), the coach will be more likely to give that player a second chance. If, however, the coach felt that the poor performance was the result of internal factors such as the player being lazy or generally incompetent, the coach might well ask the person to resign from the team.

A pattern of attributing the achievement successes of men more to their abilities than the successes of women and the failures of women more to their lack of ability has been widely reported.[17] Female achievement successes are also more likely to be attributed to unstable factors such as luck or effort, while male successes are more often attributed to the stable internal factor of ability. Such patterns would imply that even when women do succeed, since their successes are attributed more to unstable factors, they would not be expected to continue to be successful.

Valle and Frieze[45] developed a model relating initial expectations and causal attributions which might have important implications for the evaluation of women. Their model suggests that when making a prediction about the future performance of an individual, the perceiver considers both the individual's most recent performance and the expectations which the perceiver had before that performance.

Predictions about the future depend upon how much importance is given to this recent performance and how much to the initial expectations. Valle and Frieze's model suggests that the amount of importance given to a recent performance is related to the attributed cause of that performance. If the performance was attributed to stable factors (e.g., ability or task), the outcome would be weighted heavily. If, on the other hand, the outcome was attributed to unstable factors (e.g., luck or effort), it should be weighted less heavily. Therefore, the more an outcome is attributed to stable causes, the greater weight which will be given to that outcome, regardless of initial expectancy.

In addition, the type of attribution made about a performance is dependent upon the situation. The type of attribution made is a function of the difference between the outcome and the initial expectancies. The greater the absolute value of this difference, the greater will be the tendency to attribute the outcome to unstable factors such as luck, mood, or effort. The less this absolute difference, the greater will be the tendency to attribute the outcome to stable factors such as the ability of the actor or stable effort.

To summarize, Valle and Frieze's model describes a mechanism whereby changes in expectations are minimized by the types of causal attributions which are made. Unexpected outcomes are attributed to unstable causes and, therefore, have less weight in determining future predictions; expected outcomes are more attributed to stable causes and tend to support and reinforce original expectations. These authors[45] found empirical support for these predictions in a number of studies involving judgments made by MBA students about hypothetical life insurance salespersons.

This model as shown in Figure 7 has important implications for an athlete who is expected to do poorly. If such an athlete performs well, the performance will be attributed to unstable factors, which in turn means that the coach will still expect the person to do poorly in the future. This process would be especially detrimental for a woman who is expected to do poorly because she is a woman. Because of these initial low expectations on the part of coaches, it would be more difficult for women to establish their competence to their coach. This model for expectancy changes is particularly applicable to the situation of women in sports or in any field which is not traditionally considered feminine.

This model suggests then that the major concern of coaches who work with female athletes should be an analysis of their personal biases and sex-role attitudes. Coaches who feel that females are unsuited for a particular sports activity or that female participants are inferior athletes would have debilitating effects on the women with whom they work. Their low expectations for women may limit the individual's capacity to perform to full potential both by affecting the athlete's own cognitions and performance, and by denying them sufficient opportunities to perform.

Rather than limiting the individual's capacity to perform, it is the coach's responsibility to aid female athletes in developing their potential. In her/his efforts to guide the female athlete the coach can attempt to affect the individual's self perceptions and cognitions in addition to supervising physical training. The coach that understands the implications of various attributions can emphasize the importance of particular causal factors when evaluating wins and losses of the individual sportswoman. The selective training of certain attributions would depend on the philosophy of sports accepted by the coach, and the motives of the individual athlete. For example, a coach that accepts the 1973 *Philosophy and Standards for Girl and Women's Sports* might believe that the knowledge that one has given one's best, regardless of the outcome, provides self satisfaction and a sense of achievement. This emphasis on effort attributions has been a major plank in women physical educators' philosophy of sport.[23,29] Training athletes to make effort attributions would increase their pride in success, and also lead to increased effort and training after failure.

Another attributional pattern that coaches may choose to emphasize is that of attributing wins to high ability. This pattern would result in pride in one's success and increased confidence in and expectancies of future success. This pattern, then, would be especially relevant for athletes that lack confidence in their own ability.

It has been suggested by Neal and Tutko[34] that male coaches have encouraged their athletes to make external attributions for failure. This attributional pattern may also be perpetuated by the "win-at-all-costs" philosophy of competition. While external attributions decrease the debilitating effects of failure, they do not theoretically result in increased effort for the individual and may be seen as increasing hostility and frustration.

Encouraging cheating or unfair play may also affect the athlete's attitudes about his/her performance. Winning the game does not result in pride and high expectancies if the individual feels that success was due to cheating.

Thus attribution theory has important implications for coaches and female athletes. As stated earlier, the most functional attribution depends on the situation, the motives of the individual athlete, and the philosophy of sports accepted by the coach and athlete. Applying attribution theory to female sports participation may increase both the performance levels and the self-esteem and confidence of female athletes. Thus, a coach who has considered her goals and those of the athletes may move toward these goals more effectively by helping the athletes to develop "healthy" attributions patterns. While the definition of "healthy" may differ among groups of athletes and coaches, the above discussion indicated the negative effects of viewing female athletes as lacking ability and/or perseverance. For coaches, the necessary first step is to treat female athletes with respect in regards to their ability and desire to succeed in sport situations.

REFERENCES

1. Allen, D. J.: Self concept and the female participant. In D. J. Harris (Ed.), *Women & Sport: A National Research Conference.* University Park, The Pennsylvania State University, 1972.
2. Atkinson, J. W.: *An Introduction to Motivation.* Princeton, New Jersey, Van Nostrand, 1974.
3. Bar-Tal, D. and I. H. Frieze: Achievement motivation and gender as determinants of attributions for success and failure. *Learning Research and Development Center Publications,* 1976.
4. Blake, R. R. and J. S. Mouton: Overevaluation of one's group product in intergroup competition. *J. Abnormal and Social Psychol., 64,* 237, 1962.
5. Carroll, J. and J. W. Payne: Judgement of criminality: An analysis of the parole decision. Paper presented at the American Psychological Association, Chicago, 1975.
6. Deaux, K. and T. Emswiller: Explanations of successful performance on sex linked tasks: What's skill for the male is luck for the female. *J. Personality and Social Psychol., 29,* 80, 1974.
7. Diggory, J.: *Self-Evaluation: Concepts and Studies,* New York, John Wiley & Sons, 1966.
8. Dustin, D.: Member reactions to team performance. *J. Social Psychol., 69,* 237, 1966.
9. Elig, T. and I. H. Frieze: A multi-dimensional scheme for coding and interpreting preceived causality for success and failure events: The C.SPC. *JSAS: J. Selected Documents in Psychology,* 1975.
10. Feather, N. T.: Effects of prior success and failure on expectations of success and subsequent performance. *J. Personality and Social Psychol., 3,* 287, 1966.
11. ————: Attribution of responsibility and valence of success and failure in relation to initial confidence and perceived locus of control. *J. Personality and Social Psychol., 13,* 129, 1969.
12. Feldman-Summers, I. and S. B. Kresler: Those who are number two try harder: The effects of sex on attributions of causality. *J. Personality and Social Psychol., 30,* 846, 1974.
13. Ferguson, C. K. and H. H. Kelley: Significant factors in over-evaluation of own-group's product. *J. Abnormal Social Psychol., 69,* 223, 1964.
14. Fitch, G.: Effects of self esteem, perceived performance and choice on causal attributions. *J. Personality and Social Psychol., 16,* 311, 1970.
15. Frieze, I. H.: Causal attributions and information seeking to explain success and failure. *J. Research in Personality, 10,* 293, 1976.
16. ————: The role of information processing in making causal attributions for success and failure. In J. S. Carroll and J. W. Payne (Eds.), *Eleventh Carnegie Symposium on Cognition.* Potomac, Md., Lawrence Erlbaum Assoc., 1976.
17. Frieze, I. H., J. Fisher, B. Hanusa, M. C. McHugh and V. A. Valle: Attributions of the causes of success and failure as internal and external barriers to achievement in women. In J. Sherman and F. Denmark (Eds.), *Psychology of Women: Future Dimensions of Research.* Psychological Dimensions, in press.

18. Frieze, I. H., M. C. McHugh and M. Duquin: Causal attributions of women and men for sports participation. Paper presented at A.P.A., Washington, D.C., 1976.
19. Frieze, I. H. and B. Weiner: Cue utilization and attributional judgements for success and failure. *J. Personality, 39,* 591, 1971.
20. Genov, F.: The nature of the mobilization readiness of the sportsman and the influence of different factors upon its formation. In A. Craig Fisher (Ed.), *Psychology of Sport.* Palo Alto, California, Mayfield Publ. Co., 1976.
21. Gelbert, B. and N. Williamson: Women in sport: Part 3, Programmed to be losers. *Sports Illustrated,* May 21, 96, 1973.
22. Gerber, E., J. Felshin, P. Berlin and W. Wyrich: *The American Woman in Sport.* Reading, Massachusetts, Addison-Wesley Publishing Co., 1974.
23. Halsey, E.: *Women in Physical Education.* New York, G. P. Putnam's Sons, 1961.
24. Hammer, B.: A brief look at motivation in coaching. In A. Craig Fisher (Ed.), *Psychology of Sport.* Palo Alto, California, Mayfield Publ. Co., 1976.
25. Iso-Ahola, Seppo: A test of the attribution theory of success and failure with Little League baseball players. *Mouvement: Actes du 7 symposium en apprentissage psycho-moteur et psychologie du sport.* October, 1975.
26. Kelley, H. H.: The processes of causal attribution. *American Psychologist, 28,* 107, 1973.
27. Klafs, C. and M. Lyon: *The Female Athlete.* St. Louis, The C. V. Mosby Co., 1973.
28. Kukla, A.: Attributional determinants of achievement-related behavior. *J. Personality and Social Psychol., 31,* 86, 1975.
29. Lockhart, A. and B. Spears (Eds.): *Chronical of American Physical Education 1855–1930.* Dubuque, Iowa, Wm. C. Brown Publishers, 1972.
30. Mann, L.: On being a sore loser: How fans react to their teams' failure. *Austral. J. Psychol., 26,* 37, 1974.
31. McHugh, M. C.: Sex differences in causal attributions: A critical review. Paper presented at E.P.A., New York, 1975.
32. McMahan, I. D.: Relationships between causal attributions and expectancy of success. *J. Personality and Social Psychol., 28,* 108, 1973.
33. McMahan, I. D.: Sex differences in expectancy of success as a function of the task. Paper presented at EPA, 1971.
34. Neal, P. and T. Tutko: *Coaching girls and women: Psychological Perspectives.* Boston, Allyn and Bacon, 1975.
35. Roberts, Glyn C.: Win-loss causal attributions of little league players. *Mouvement. Actes du 7 symposium en apprentissage psycho-moteur et psychologie du sport.* October, 1975.
36. Rosenbaum, R. M.: A dimensional analysis of the perceived causes of success and failure. Unpublished Ph.D. dissertation. University of California at Los Angeles, 1972.
37. Rosenthal, R. and L. R. Jacobson: Teacher expectations of the disadvantaged. *Scientific American, 218,* 19, 1968.
38. Rotter, J. P.: Generalized expectancies for internal versus external control of reinforcement. *Psychological Monographs, 80,* 1, 1966.
39. Shaw, M. E. and G. R. Breed: Effects of attribution of responsibility for negative events of behavior in small groups. *Sociometry, 33,* 382, 1970.
40. Simon, J. G. and N. T. Feather: Causal attributions for success and failure at university examinations. *J. Educational Psychol., 64,* 46, 1973.
41. Smith, C. H.: Influences of athletic success and failure on level of aspiration. *Res. Quart., 20,* 196, 1949.
42. Throop, W. F. and A. P. MacDonald Jr.: Internal-external locus of control: A bibliography. *Psychological Reports,* Monograph Supplement 1, *28,* 1971.
43. Tyler, B. B.: Expectancy for eventual success as a factor in problem solving behavior. *J. Educational Psychol., 49,* 166, 1958.

44. Tyler, S.: Adolescent crisis: Sport participation for the female. In D. Harris (Ed.), *DGWS Research Reports: Women in Sports.* Washington, D. C.: American Association for Health, Physical Education and Recreation, 1973.
45. Valle, V. A. and I. H. Frieze: The stability of causal attributions as a mediator in changing expectations for success. *J. Personality and Social Psychol., 33, 579,* 1976.
46. Wankel, L. M.: A new energy source for sport psychology research: Toward a conversion from D-C (Drive Conceptualization) to A-C (Attributional Cognitions). In D. M. Landers (Ed.), *Psychology of Sport and Motor Behavior.* University Park, The Pennsylvania State University, 1972.
47. Weiner, B.: *Achievement Motivation and Attribution Theory.* New York, General Learning Press, 1974.
48. ————: *Theories of Motivation.* Chicago, Markham Press, 1972.
49. Weiner, B., I. Frieze, A. Kukla, L. Reed, S. Rest and R. M. Rosenbaum: *Perceiving the Causes of Success and Failure.* New York, General Learning Press, 1971.
50. Weiner, B., H. Heckhausen, W. Meyer and R. E. Cook: Causal ascriptions and achievement behavior: Conceptual analysis of effort and reanalysis of locus of control. *J. Personality and Social Psychol., 21, 239, 1972.*
51. Weiner, B. and A. Kukla: An attributional analysis of achievement motivation. *J. Personality and Social Psychol., 15, 1, 1970.*
52. Weiner, B. and P. A. Potepan: Personality correlates and affective reactions toward exams of succeeding and failing college students. *J. Educational Psychol., 61, 144, 1970.*
53. Weigers, R. M.: The cognitive mediation of achievement-related behavior. Unpublished Ph.D. dissertation. University of Pittsburgh, 1975.
54. Zander, A., R. Fuller and W. Armstrong: Attributed pride or shame in group or self. *J. Personality and Social Psychol., 23, 346, 1972.*

Part 2

Women's Sport: Myth, Reality, and Social Change

Wilma Scott Heide is prominently recognized as a political activist and leader of the women's movement. She is only slightly less well known as a behavioral scientist and semanticist. Many may be surprised to read in these pages that she is a former athlete as well. We learn in this essay that Heide attributes a portion of her strength and vision to her experiences in sport.

One recent focus of Wilma Scott Heide's interests has been future study. She has served as a consultant for many organizations as they have turned attention toward the year 2000. Heide performs this future study function for sport administrators and scientists in her formulation of imperatives for change within traditional sport. She challenges us to re-think what we *really* intend when we speak with words which have ceased to have life-enhancing meanings: the opposite sexes; contest; normal training for children; protection for girls and women. She encourages us to devote ourselves to a thorough re-formulation of the meaning and definition of sport.

Heide is joyously anti-androcentric and pro-feminist. (One must not mistake this for an anti-male, pro-female view.) Her stance is uncompromising, but consider her message: we are killing one another! She proposes a more humane world for women and men. She says that you and I are responsible for bringing that world to be and that makes for difficult reading.

C.A.O.

Chapter 10

FEMINISM FOR A SPORTING FUTURE

Wilma Scott Heide

As recently as October, 1975 *Esquire* magazine published a special issue: The Joy of Sports! No question about the joy of sports, real and potential. However, the cover graphics include a "real" boy in dishevelled baseball uniform in the foreground, hands on hips, apparently ready for and experienced in action. In the background, is a "real" girl, hands passively folded in front of her, toes pointed inward as of shy, self-effacing children. The girl, in a frilly dress, looks admiringly at her 'hero'.

But, then, what can one expect of Esquire but androcentricity? Ms Magazine would probably include this in its No comment section. True, it's almost too anachronistically sexist to dignify with comment. Real girls increasingly reject these gender role stereotype characterizations as do real boys. I don't know if the Esquire folks are easily educable, yet it is precisely its readers and their counterparts, educators, broadcasters, writers, politicians, religionists, health personnel, citizens, including parents and all others who participate in socialization, who must become educated to feminist imperatives.

Truly, the emperor has no clothes. Feminists don't even like the idea of emperors, of either sex. In demythologizing 'old husband's tales', we critique and lay bare the nude power games of much male-oriented sports as one more male ball game. Feminists are essentially gestalt futurists. Our visions of the future of sports and society mean girls and women are rejecting the cheerleader syndrome, refusing to be the unilateral emotional jock straps for men and boys. It's part of what I call: feminism for the health of it.

The symbol of justice in the United States is a blindfolded woman. We are removing the blindfolds.[1] Most sports have not provided women a sporting chance. Much sport has been and is essentially a male-defined power phenomenon. The rebirth of feminism means that she is risen to redefine and reassign power in sports, in every other dimension of our lives and the public world. Feminism has been predicted to be the most profound revolution the world has yet known by others as well as myself. It is one of the few (so far) bloodless revolutions of values, institutions, individuals and indeed of what human beings can be and become.

Women and men, girls and boys are not *opposite* sexes and should never be referred to in that language. They are members of different sexes. It reinforces mythologies, stereotypes and polarities. There is one sex and there is an other sex. The differences of individuals within each sex are greater by far than the differences between the sexes in abilities, interests, potentials. It is our common humanity that transcends the so-called "femininity" and "masculinity" of *both* sexes.

If the so-called "feminine" social traits were *natural* for all females and for females only and the so-called "masculine" social traits were *natural* for all males and for males only, then why are girls trained for 'femininity' only and boys for 'masculinity' only so assiduously from the moment of birth? The very existence of such training by exclusion and narrowing superbly demonstrates its unnaturalness. If such traits were truly natural and sex-limited, the training would be neither necessary nor artificially sex-limited. Thus, while such sexism is still normal, it is very unnatural. Normal means average or typical; natural means in the intrinsic nature of the organism. Normal and natural are *not* synonymous. Feminism is not yet normal but it is natural.

One vital part of the feminist revolution is the reality that sports participation can be a joy for girls and boys, for women and men. I write from the perspectives of an athlete, spectator, behavioral scientist and activist who has shared in the generating of the changes in consciousness, laws, practices and socialization. The perspectives are interrelated.

In spite of the sexism and discrimination encountered throughout life, I have functioned as an athlete in several sports and had some gratifying experiences. Remember the "in spite of": for me and most sisters of my generation, we'll never know what heights of joy, self-confidence, exhilaration, thrill, vigor and delight we might have experienced, what boundaries of the human body and spirit we might have challenged and changed, without pervasive sexism. Feminists are committed to the free spirits and bodies of our daughters, sisters and mothers soaring wherever and however we choose.

Nonetheless, my experiences as a sportswoman provided enormous self-confidence and feelings of self empowerment. In countless instances in my decades as a human rights activist, this background has provided the self-confident courage to participate in and lead in necessary demonstrations, confrontations, sit-ins, microphone liberations, conference takeovers, often unpopular decisions and actions reflecting individual and organizational integrity. I've confronted the practices, illegal acts and/or recalcitrance of: U.S. cabinet secretaries, sheriffs, voter registrars, senators, congresspeople and other institutional and organizational officials as well as would-be assassins and other intimidators. There is no doubt that the experiences as a sportswoman (when even more than now sports was considered primarily a male preserve with girls and women as marginal participants and/or cheerleaders) provided the courage of my convictions in spite of criticism, misunderstanding and overt actions to keep me and my sisters "in our place." Someone preparing biographical material about me once suggested that a fruitful area of research might be the relationship between athletic confidence and citizen activism.

There are two particular reasons for mentioning these realities. The first reason is to emphasize one of the values of sports vis à vis self-definition and self-determination, for learning the lesson of "I can" e.g., I can participate, I can develop, I can change my world and the world. The other is to remind readers that Congress and government officials and others finally *responded* to years of educated pressure. It was and is mostly volunteer feminists who generate(d) the unyielding and unequivocal demands for change so that sportswomen, academicians and scholars could do their/our thing.

Others contributing to this book have focused on other vital dimensions of women and sports. I want to share some power implications of feminism for a sporting future, i.e. the political potential using politics in the generic sense. Much of sport has represented a test *with* oneself and/or others. Yet contest is generally defined in typical androcentric dictionaries as a test *against* others. It is here posited that we may need to create, one more time, a new word to fit the concept of testing *with* others rather than *against* for superiority vis à vis oneself or others. The word would be comtest, i.e. com-test, testing *with* another, not a power struggle *against* another to destroy or defeat. Feminists can thus recreate the original Greek concept of sport in the context of justice where people sought their "arete", i.e. their own excellence and update the Greek men by extending the opportunities to both sexes.

In emphasizing the testing with others in mutual growth and self empowerment rather than testing against to overpower, control, defeat, no reader should assume that this feminist is avoiding the sports desexigration and the separate but (allegedly) equal controversy. It is not an either/or issue. Again, that is the male-oriented adversarial dichotomy.

Girls and boys, women and men must participate together in sports with decisions about participation of individuals and groups to be based on current skill, agility, experience, strength, size, weight, interest, speed and/or other relevant criteria, not the irrelevant factor of biological sex. This includes contact and non-contact sports and

I do include wrestling, football, boxing. One may recognize the brutality dimensions of these sports and at the same time recognize the justice of individuals of both sexes deciding for themselves about participation.

To avoid desexigration or integration of the contact sports is to implicitly and/or explicitly perpetuate the mythology that all heterosexual encounters do or must or have engender(ed) or consummate(d) in sexual intercourse and/or sexual responses. For women and girls, especially, it perpetuates our presumed sexual object, sexual nature-only, baggage and limitations. Furthermore, long experience has taught us that separate is inherently unequal, to the disadvantage of women and girls.

Anyone who wants to really "protect" women and girls should remember a few facts: males' externality of reproductive genitals makes them more vulnerable than women's internal and compact design; there is no evidence that blows on the breast cause cancer or that breasts can be less protected than male genitals; indeed, when one considers what women often experience in sex play, nursing babies and wife-beating, contact sports may be a breeze for the conditioned women who choose such activities. It can prepare girls and boys to play, live, and work together in mutual respect in ways that sex-segregated sports and culture never have.

As further reality checks, women and girls need enormous compensatory financial, programmatic, psychosocial supports to value, condition, and control our own bodies. Some girls and women will opt to avoid sports with boys and men temporarily or permanently. The insistence that sports in *any* way financed with public funds must be sex-integrated is not to be equated with forcing individual girls and women to so participate against their will.

Presently, standards of performance excellence in sports were invented by males to magnify those aspects of anatomy and physiology in which males generally (not always) excel. When sports in which female physiology generally excels or the generally differential physiology is of no moment are invented by feminists (as will surely happen), we shall see even more the male presumed "superiority" of self-fulfilling prophesies demythologized.

Mary Daly has succinctly stated the principle in another context: "if God is male, then the male is God."[2] Adapted to sports, therefore, we recognize that if sports is male, then the male standards prevail in sports. God is not male, sport is not male; God is the divine in us all; sport is human.

Not so parenthetically, if the male is sport, then the male can be exploited in sports and often is, the male can be exploited in the extension of much male rivalrous "sport" (i.e. organized violence or war) and indeed has been and is. It is for the feminist future to see if we can indeed redefine sport as fun and self actualizing and power as self empowerment and for life.

Feminism for a sporting future requires some imperatives:

1. Recognize that, in addition to the potential fun, exhilaration and testing of our abilities, that sports participation may also be a political statement of our humanity.

2. Some massive education via feminist consciousness-raising is needed for many would-be educators, sportswriters, sports announcers, broadcasters, coaches, health personnel, parents as well as children, sports fans and athletes. I have two brothers who are sportscasters and I am generally hopeful about the educability of those who have mostly believed that sport is a male rite and right. Male chauvinism can become a no-no, rather than an assumption of some pseudo "virility".

3. Insist that educators at every level obey the civil rights laws and executive orders that apply to those receiving public funds. Obedience to these laws and orders including those applying to sports and athletics must become one basic bona fide occupational qualification to be even employed and receive funds.

4. Withhold funds from any United Funds or agencies thereof which disproportionately give more funds to men's and boys' than to women's and girls' organizations. (Average nationally is twice as much, e.g. YMCA compared to YWCA, Boy Scouts compared to Girl Scouts.) Some of these funds go for sports programs.

5. Refuse to dignify, by discussion, the alleged superiority or inferiority of men or women in sports. Those who try this gambit generally do it on male terms and criteria and already have stereotyped the sexes so may not yet be educable. My own inclination when pressed to say *something* in response to patriarchal assertions is: "I have every reason to believe that you believe everything you have just said; you have my sympathy." Patriarchal assertions can come from men or women and are the result of using the consequences of male dominance to justify their perpetuation as though it were all very "natural".

6. Desexigrate toys so they may be seen and used as aids in the human socialization of all children absent sex-stereotyped expectations about who will be interested in and benefit from them.

7. Given the fact of compulsory education to age 16 and the continuing teaching of girls to be submissive, subordinate and subservient, lawsuits at any such schools on the grounds that such "education" is a violation of the XIIIth amendment pro-

hibiting involuntary servitude would make a dandy educational
project via litigation.

8. Insist that women teach women and girls about sports; men may
be able to teach some skills but women must teach the persons
who are girls and women for the reasons of role modeling and
empathy. The reverse is not true; men and boys need women to
teach the sport perspective of the majority of humanity to balance the traditional male-only perspective.

9. In January of 1974, after speaking at the University of Alabama,
I paid a courtesy call on the then president, David Matthews
(later secretary of Health, Education and Welfare). He con-
gratulated himself that women (about 50 per cent of the student
body) had all of $13,000 for sports programs and that only be-
cause of their own arduous efforts. The men had over $2 million.
I told him he was very deserving—of a lawsuit. Some such
reality checks and massive education of the David Matthews
of this nation are painfully necessary to even qualify them for
such positions.

10. Since the super-bowl, all-male football games are partly subsi-
dized by public funds (in that tickets are bought as tax writeoffs
and as "legitimate" business expenses, partly public funds are
used for stadiums and publicly funded police and other protec-
tions are used) how about a feminist takeover of a super-bowl
game by liberating the various microphones? I once did this at
a public university to educate the assembled crowd. Afterwards,
officials who had threatened me with arrest acknowledged they
would never be the same. I replied: "Promise?" This super-bowl
action could become part of a Transformation Sunday. In the
morning, we could nail feminist declarations to church doors
and exit from patriarchal churches. It could be a beautiful day of
redemption for the nation. Those who consider this "masculine"
behavior are reminded that women are partly "masculine" and
that nothing destructive is included.

11. Insist that all places of public accommodation be open to the
public throughout the time of possible usage whether that be
golf courses, tennis courts, playing fields or wherever and that
public bodies which control public funds for sports (or anything else) have a majority of not more than one of either sex
on commissions, councils, cabinets, boards, et al. Continue to
assume that the National Collegiate Athletic Association and
similar bodies are educable; to remind the men of what busy-
bodies they've been to try to limit, preclude, rip off and/or
control sportswomen and women's sports.

12. Approach the scholarship issue warily. Certainly, women have

been limited by discrimination. It could be a (well) disguised blessing. Scholarships given to guarantee that one college dominates another perpetuates the male conquest and con-test *against* another rather than the com-test concept of testing *with* others and merely prostitutes the humane potential of sports and sportspeople. In truth, as a working civil libertarian, I have some value conflict here. If the phenomena of scholarships exist, justice would dictate desexigration and people being free to make choices. I would resolve the value issues here in favor of educating educators to take leadership in generating scholarship aid for potential poets, writers, artists, sportspeople, dancers, teachers, physicists, sociologists, scholars to develop their interests and aptitudes independent of participation/performance in competitive, commercial events. Some educators are doing this; feminism's validity and growth should enhance this healthy development.

In the context of feminist power, lacking the control or domination of others, participation and excellence in sports can give women, the historical nurturers of others' lives, some primary enjoyment of life. The risks, the challenges, the stresses, the exhilaration of sports provide a growing process wherein women and girls are learning that we *can* act to change our lives and the world we share with men and boys. As we tighten our abdomens, gird our loins, loosen or eliminate our girdles, we free our dynamic and creative energies to be and become.

Protect us from any more male "protectors". As girls and boys, women and men learn and exercise feminist perspectives in sports and elsewhere, I predict that rape, the political act via physical brutality, the true original sin, will disappear. Sex inequality, sexual apartheid, sports as domination and submission will increasingly be seen as barbaric and primitive. Men and boys will finally learn how to become good sports which should strengthen some currently fragile egos.

The current manifestation of much sports is the epitome of the too typical male power game, a primitive exercise of "manhood" which includes ultimately sanctioned violence. Note the quotes of the Pittsburgh Steelers after Superbowls IX and X. Such "manhood" is too often synonymous with notions of nationhood and national "honor", a euphemism for male chauvinism. Much of this is part and parcel of men's often ill-gained power, including making war like physical atomic giants and conditioned behavioral incapacity to conceptualize peace other than as intellectual midgets.

The androcentric concept of sport as contest *against* others to defeat and dominate, rather than a com-test *with* others to grow, have fun, to play, contributes mightily to the learned aggressiveness exemplified in much of the arrogance of male power. Assertiveness to achieve goals is a necessary human trait that need not include aggressiveness *against* others. Feminists can and are making these distinctions with positive implications for the quality of life and humane values. We insist that all of us, as women and men, in sport, in all of life be free to exercise the positive aspects of our femininity and masculinity which are indeed our very humanity.

It is indeed the end of real or feigned innocence, especially for white women in the United States. Minority women have seldom had that dubious luxury. The masks are off; this drama is for real. The world of sports, politics, education, religion, health care leadership, public policy, finance, is not by nature man's world anymore than home and children are by nature woman's world. We share this common world and are committed to ending the pathology of patriarchy. It has been said that where there's the will, there's the way. Equally true is the reality that where there's the way, there's the will. Feminism is the way to develop the will of women, men, and children to create a sporting future.

In putting sex and sexuality in their places, far from extinguishing human love between and among the sexes, we will finally disencumber it of oppression, false poses, and limited options. In seeking an end to the battle of the sexes and a genuine partnership of women and men everywhere we choose, we may create a great renewal of humankind with the realization that women and men are not opposites and are more alike and related than different, except as individuals. Women who have been taught to care are learning to care *enough* to be brave; men who have been taught to be brave must learn to be brave *enough* to care.

Feminism as a values revolution envisions sport as fun, as play, as one vital method to grow and know one's power to be humane. Enough of the myths. Let's celebrate the energizing realities that feminism portends a sporting future, a world where the power of love can exceed the love of power.

REFERENCES

1. Brady, Anne Hazlewood: Justice Has Become a Woman, in Unwritten Testament. Camden Herald Publishing Co., Camden, Maine, 1972, p. 44.
2. Daly, Mary: *Beyond God the Father, Toward a Philosophy of Women's Liberation.* Boston, Beacon Press, 1973, p. 19.

Chapter 11
FEDERAL CIVIL RIGHTS LEGISLATION AND SPORT

Elizabeth R. East

It is an assumption of the authors that many, if not all, the readers of this book will have personal goals for the reform of sport. The following three chapters deal with legal and quasi-legal procedures for accomplishing change in sport. East's chapter succinctly presents information about the use of four federal laws for change purposes: the Equal Pay Act of 1963 as amended by the Education Amendments of 1972; Title VII of the Civil Rights Act of 1964 amended by the Equal Employment Opportunity Act of 1972; Executive Order 11246 as amended by Executive Order 11375; and Title IX of the Education Amendments of 1972.

Rose's chapter creates an intriguing "you are the judge" situation for the reader. After a brief introduction, she presents the brief for the defendant and plaintiff in an hypothetical case involving the ERA. Since many states already have an ERA and since the federal amendment may be ratified by enough states for passage, its use as a sport feminist tool must be studied. As Rose's well-conceived arguments are spun forth, one wishes for wisdom beyond Solomon's.

The book concludes with my presentation of an analysis procedure which may be utilized to identify changes needed in a sport organizational structure and where the system may be strategically challenged in order to accomplish the change purpose.

C.A.O.

Chapter 11
FEDERAL CIVIL RIGHTS LEGISLATION AND SPORT

Elizabeth R. East

"Obvious discrimination persists in the provision of opportunities for women to participate in interscholastic sports programs, in both high school and college."[40] Discrimination is not limited to the provision of athletic opportunities in the high schools. It extends downward to elementary schools and upward to colleges and universities. It is a phenomenon that appears to be universal in education institutions. It is also an area in which the courts appear to be advancing.[40]

Until recently, women have had to depend upon institutions and organizations to be fair and just in offering athletic opportunities to girls and women. Now, women have available a variety of legal remedies to give them clout in their demands to end sex discrimination. A close look at these laws shows that women, including women in sport, have various tools to help them combat sex discrimination. It is not pleasant to think of filing a complaint against your school or employer, but at times it becomes necessary. Often, however, mere knowledge of your rights is sufficient to strengthen your position.[9]

This chapter will consider four federal Civil Rights laws; the Equal Pay Act of 1963 as amended by the Education Amendments of 1972, Title VII of the Civil Rights Act of 1964 as amended by the Equal Employment Opportunity Act of 1972, Executive Order 11246 as amended by Executive Order 11375, and Title IX of the Education Amendments of 1972. In addition to a brief description of the substantive aspects of each law, the author will attempt to explain the procedural aspects of applying the law.

Following this will be a discussion of some of the problems encountered in filing a complaint and a short summary of court cases and complaints filed involving women in sport.

EQUAL PAY ACT OF 1963 AS AMENDED BY THE EDUCATION AMENDMENTS OF 1972[31]

After almost 10 years of unsuccessful attempts to eliminate sex discrimination in pay scales, the Equal Pay Act was finally passed by the 88th Congress on June 10, 1963. It was amended by the Education Amendments of 1972 to extend coverage to executive, professional, and administrative employees and outside sales employees. It now covers virtually all United States employees.

Provisions

The law provides that people "employed in jobs, the performance of which requires equal skill, effort, and responsibility, and which are performed under similar working conditions"[31] will receive equal pay. The only exception is "where such payment is made pursuant to (i) a seniority system; (ii) a merit system; (iii) a system which measures earnings by quantity or quality of production, or (iv) a differential based on any other factor other than sex."[31] An employer cannot reduce the wage rate of any employee in order to comply with the provisions of the Equal Pay Act.

Jobs need not be identical to be covered by the Equal Pay Act. They must require equal skill, effort, and responsibility. Equal skill includes experience, training, education, and ability. Skills which the employee may have but which are not required for the performance of the job are not considered justification for unequal wages.

Effort is the measurement of physical or mental exertion needed for performance on the job. "Two jobs can be considered equal in terms of effort if the sum of mental and physical exertion in each is substantially equal."[16] Tasks required of one sex which involve physical effort may be offset by other tasks performed by the opposite sex which require more mental effort. Minor differences in the degree of responsibility required do not make jobs unequal.

Generally, people working at the same jobs are working under similar working conditions. However, the fact that jobs might be performed in different departments of an institution or organization does not necessarily mean that working conditions are dissimilar. Quite often, jobs in different departments at a University are more similar than those within the same department.

Enforcement

The agency responsible for the administration of the Equal Pay Act is the Wage and Hour Division of the U.S. Department of Labor. The Wage and Hour Division can initiate investigations without a complaint having been filed, but investigations generally occur in response to individual complaints.[4] To file a complaint, an individual can call or write to the nearest Wage and Hour Division Office. The Department of Labor will investigate all complaints received and will not reveal the identity of the complainant. The employer is given the opportunity to voluntarily comply with the law. If the employer does not wish to comply, the Secretary of Labor or the individual complainant may then file suit. At this point, the identities of both parties are made public.

If a violation of the Equal Pay Act is substantiated by the courts, the employer is required to discontinue the discriminatory practices, raise the wages of the workers subjected to discrimination, and restore back pay for up to 2 years. If the violation is determined to be willful, up to 3 years of back pay may be awarded.[27] "In a series of successful cases in Federal courts, including the U.S. Supreme Court, the Department of Labor has won both forceful interpretations of the law and large awards of back wages predominantly for women. This record has strengthened the Government's capacity to win compliance without going to court. In the 3-year period from 1972–1974, $16,816,380 in income was restored to 47,553 people under supervision of the Secretary of Labor."[36] Millions of dollars have been awarded to individuals through private litigation.[36] Over 95% of Equal Pay Act complaints are resolved through voluntary compliance.[1]

"As of 1974, seven cases have been filed against higher education institutions in four different regions, and at least five cases have been filed against school districts involving the pay of teachers and athletic coaches."[26] Since 1974, the number of cases has tremendously increased.

Benefits of Filing A Complaint Under the Equal Pay Act

There are several advantages of filing a complaint under the Equal Pay Act. The process of filing a complaint is simple and informal. Unlike Title VII, which requires a notarized complaint, filing under the Equal Pay Act requires only a letter or a telephone call. No documentation of discrimination practices is required. This information is generally difficult to obtain as it is confidential at many educational institutions.

All complaints are investigated and an individual can file a complaint anonymously. The advantage of filing anonymously cannot be underestimated. Although all four of the federal laws to be discussed have provisions against employer harassment of the complainant, it still occurs, and is difficult to prove. Thus by filing under the Equal Pay Act, an individual can have an entire school or school system investigated without having his/her identity revealed, and thus reduce the possibility of damage to his/her professional career.

Backlog

In filing a complaint under the Equal Pay Act, an individual can expect almost immediate action. The Wage and Hour Division estimates that it takes a maximum of 90 days from receipt of the complaint for them to begin an investigation. Many complaints are resolved before ever reaching the courts, but if it is necessary to take an employer to court, the process can take from 2 to 3 years. It should be noted, however, that there have been complaints filed in which efforts at conciliation have failed and no suit has been filed in the course of 2 years.[25] Although the backlog in equal pay cases is considerably less than the backlog in Title VII and Executive Order 11246 cases, there are continuing problems with enforcement.

TITLE VII OF THE CIVIL RIGHTS ACT OF 1964 AS AMENDED BY EQUAL EMPLOYMENT OPPORTUNITY ACT OF 1972[32]

Provisions

"It shall be an unlawful employment practice for an employer to fail or refuse to hire or to discharge any individual, or otherwise to discriminate against any individual with respect to his compensation, terms, conditions, or privileges or employment, because of such individual's race, color, religion, sex or national origin. . ."[32]

When enacted in July 1964, Title VII did not cover educational institutions. In March 1972, Congress passed the Equal Employment Opportunity Act of 1972,[32] and extended the coverage of Title VII to teachers and administrators in educational institutions as well as to state and local government employees. The law now covers all employers of fifteen employees or more with the exception of Federally owned corporations and Indian tribes. Title VII covers all aspects of employment including recruitment, selection, assignment and transfer, layoff, discharge and recall; opportunities for promotion; in-service training opportunities; wages and salaries; sick leave time and pay; vacation time and pay; overtime work and pay; medical, hospital, life and accident insurance; retirement plans and benefits.[29]

Title VII provides that jobs may be restricted to one sex "in those certain instances where religion, sex, or national origin is a bona fide occupational qualification reasonably necessary to the normal operation of that particular business or enterprise."[29] The Equal Employment Opportunity Commission has interpreted the BFOQ exception provision very narrowly. It may only apply where necessary for the purposes of authenticity or genuineness (e.g. an actor or an actress) but does not include discrimination based on stereotyped characterizations of men and women, assumptions about employment characterizations of men and women, or the lack of separate facilities for a person of the other sex.[29] The only other exception is employers with less than fifteen employees. The Courts have upheld the Equal Employment Opportunity Commission interpretations generally.

Title VII's coverage of pay is broader in scope than the Equal Pay

Act. Title VII covers the situation where women only are employed in a job classification and the wage rate is depressed because it is traditionally a woman's job. Under Title VII, rates paid men doing comparable work in the company or institution involved or men doing the same work at other plants in the industry or at other institutions could be used as evidence of violation of Title VII, but not as evidence of violation of the Equal Pay Act.[39]

Enforcement

A complaint may be filed with The Equal Employment Opportunity Commission by any person or group of persons who believe they have been subjected to discrimination prohibited by Title VII. An organization may file on behalf of persons but must attach a notarized form from specific individuals who believe themselves to be aggrieved.

The individual or pattern complaints must be filed within 180 days of the alleged discrimination. Complaints may be filed with The Equal Employment Opportunity Commission: 2401 E Street, N.W., Washington, D.C. 20506 or with the regional office in the complainant's area.

Title VII requires that if a state or community has a fair employment law that meets federal standards, that office must have an opportunity to resolve complaints before the Federal agency takes jurisdiction. The State agencies normally have 60 days in which to process the complaint. If it is not processed within 60 days, the charge is filed in the District office of the Federal Equal Employment Opportunity Commission. The employer charged is sent a Notice of Charge of Employment Discrimination. An investigation begins with interviews with the complainant and the employer in an attempt to gather necessary information.

If the investigator finds discriminatory practices, the case is assigned to a conciliator who works with the complainant and the employer to try to develop a conciliatory agreement. If the conciliator is not able to work out a voluntary agreement, The Equal Employment Opportunity Commission has authority to sue the employer except as noted below. However, suits are brought in only a small percentage of the cases in which discrimination is found but not corrected by conciliation efforts. Complainants in such cases are given a right to sue letter and may sue on their own.

If the complainant is successful in showing discrimination and the court finds the employer in violation of Title VII, it may order the discontinuance of discriminatory practices, the awarding of back pay, the reinstatement of employees and the payment of the complainant's attorney fees.[20]

The identity of the complainant is revealed when the employer is notified of the complaint. Charges are not made public unless court action becomes necessary.

The Equal Employment Opportunity Commission cannot sue State, County, or City governments but must refer such cases in which it is not able to conciliate to the Justice Department for suit.

Backlog

Originally, The Equal Employment Opportunity Commission focused solely on the individual filing a complaint in seeking relief from discriminatory practices. "By 1968, the Commission felt that correcting systemic forms of discrimination would result in more effective compliance, and shifted conciliation to include not only relief to the complainant, but removal of discriminatory practices within the institution."[26] This has resulted in benefits to many others not involved in the original complaint, but has prolonged the investigations and increased the backlog of unresolved complaints. As of January 1974, 2,100 charges had been filed in higher education alone. It is estimated that one-half of the charges are by professionals. The total backlog of unresolved complaints was over 100,000 in 1975.[26]

A number of organizations have made proposals for improving the efficiency of The Equal Employment Opportunity Commission, including the U.S. Civil Rights Commission and the National Commission for the Observance of International Women's Year. Single copies of the reports are usually available free by writing the agency.[33]

EXECUTIVE ORDER 11246 AS AMENDED BY EXECUTIVE ORDER 11375[11]

Executive Order 11246 as amended was the first legal tool to combat sex discrimination in education. The Executive Order is a series of rules and regulations that Federal Contractors must comply with in order to receive or maintain Federal contracts of $10,000 and over.

Provisions

It states in part,

"The (Federal) contractor will not discriminate against any employee or applicant for employment because of race, color, religion, sex, or national origin. The contractor will take affirmative action to ensure that applicants are employed, and that employees are treated during employment without regard to their race, color, religion, sex or national origin."[11]

Although few elementary and secondary schools have Federal contracts, many colleges and universities do, and are thus covered by Executive Order 11246. Institutions covered by Executive Order 11246 must not discriminate in any aspect of employment, including hiring, discharge, promotion, wages, benefits, and training.

Not only does Executive Order 11246 cover discrimination in employment, but it requires institutions with a Federal Contract of $50,000 or more and more than 50 employees to have on file a written affirmative action plan with goals and timetables.

The requirement of an affirmative action plan by Executive Order 11246 is unique among the civil rights laws affecting employment. The employer must have an affirmative action plan regardless of whether a complaint has been filed or discrimination has been found. Even though the Federal contract may be with only one small department within an institution, the affirmative action plan covers the entire work force of the institution. For example, if the chemistry department at a large university has a Federal contract to do research on heart disease, the university must have an affirmative action plan that covers the entire university. A set of regulations known as Revised Order No. 4[12] describes this affirmative action plan as a "set of specific and result-oriented procedures to which a contractor commits himself to apply every good faith and effort."[6]

Enforcement

The Office of Federal Contract Compliance Programs (OFCCP) of the United States Department of Labor, which is the agency responsible for the enforcement of Executive Order 11246 as amended, has designated the Higher Education Division of the Department of Health, Education and Welfare's Office of Civil Rights as the agency responsible for enforcing the regulation as it applies to education institutions. The Department of Health, Education and Welfare investigates only complaints of discrimination against a class of individuals and refers all individual complaints to the Equal Employment Opportunity Commission for investigation under Title VII.

After a complaint is filed, an investigation begins. If the institution is found to have either no affirmative action plan or an inadequate one, the compliance agency (in this case, the Department of Health, Education and Welfare) must issue a notice to the contractor giving him/her thirty days to show good cause why enforcement proceedings should not be commenced. After attempts at informal conciliation, the compliance agency head (e.g. Secretary of HEW) makes a final decision. If the decision goes against the employer, the Federal Government may force compliance with the regulation by delaying new contracts, revoking current contracts, and disqualifying the institution from eligibility for future contracts. Back pay can be awarded to employees not covered by other laws allowing back pay.[11]

Backlog

While the Executive Order 11246 is potentially a powerful weapon for eliminating discrimination, women's organizations and individual educators have been very dissatisfied with the lack of zeal in enforcement.[25]

TITLE IX OF THE EDUCATION AMENDMENTS OF 1972[24]

Provisions

Title IX of the Education Amendments of 1972 is the first comprehensive legislation to protect students from sex discrimination.[25] In general, the law states that,

> "No person in the U.S. shall, on the basis of sex, be excluded from participation in, be denied the benefits of, or be subjected to discrimination under any education program or activity receiving Federal Financial assistance. . ."[24]

Title IX has been law since 1972, but the long awaited official regulations[13] describing the implementation did not become effective until July 21, 1975. The purpose of Title IX is to eliminate discrimination on the basis of sex in any education program or activity receiving Federal financial assistance. Title IX covers virtually all aspects of all education programs or activities of a school district, institution of higher education, or other entity which receives Federal funds for any of those educational programs. Approximately 16,000 public school systems and 2,700 post-secondary institutions are covered.[26] Included in the coverage are admission of students, treatment of students, and employment.

With respect to admissions, Title IX is limited to: vocational, professional and graduate schools, and to institutions of public undergraduate education (except those few public undergraduate schools which have been traditionally and continually single sex).

Although there are some exceptions under the section on admissions, once students of both sexes are admitted to an institution, they must be treated nondiscriminantly. Coverage includes:

1. access to and participation in courses, extracurricular activities, including campus organizations and competitive athletics;
2. eligibility for and receipt or enjoyment of benefits, services, and financial aid;
3. use of facilities and comparability of, availability of, and rules concerning housing (except that single sex housing is permissible).[13]

Included in the provision for "Treatment of Students" and of major interest here are the sections on Physical Education[14] and Athletics[15] of the guidelines issued by the Department of Health, Education and Welfare.

The guidelines interpret Title IX as requiring that all Physical Education classes be fully integrated (co-educational) except classes in contact sports and sex education. Students may be grouped according to ability levels if the ability levels are determined objectively without regard to sex. Skill or progress or both must be evaluated by standards that do not adversely affect members of one sex. For example, if a measure of performance is the number of push ups an individual can do, males will generally score higher because of the average strength difference. A more appropriate standard might be an individual progress chart.[34]

Elementary schools must be in compliance with Title IX within one year of the effective date of the regulation, and secondary and post-secondary schools have three years. During the three year grace period, separate classes must be comparable for members of each sex. The institution must be able to demonstrate that it is moving as quickly as possible toward eliminating separate classes.[35]

Department of Health, Education and Welfare guidelines require that schools provide equal opportunity for both sexes to participate in interscholastic, intercollegiate, intramural, and club athletic programs. If separate teams are offered, an institution may not discriminate on the basis of sex in the provision of necessary equipment or supplies, or in any other way, but equal aggregate expenditures are not required. In determining whether equal opportunities are available, the following factors, although not inclusive, will be considered:

a. provision of supplies and equipment;
b. game and practice schedules;
c. travel and per diem allowances;
d. coaching and academic tutoring opportunities and the assignment and pay of coaches and tutors;
e. locker rooms, practice and competitive facilities;
f. medical and training services;
g. housing and dining facilities and services;
h. publicity.[36]

An institution may offer separate teams for members of each sex where selection for such teams is based upon competitive skill or the activity involved is a contact sport. Where a team in a non-contact sport is offered for members of one sex and not for members of the other sex, and athletic opportunities for the sex for whom no team is available have previously been limited, individuals of that sex must be allowed to compete for the team offered. For example, if swimming is offered for males and not females, and a female wishes to swim on the swimming team, and if opportunities for female athletes have previously been limited, that female may try out for a position on the swimming team.

All employees, both full and part time, in all institutions are covered, except employees of military schools, and religious schools, to the extent compliance would be inconsistent with the controlling religious tenets.[13] The regulation covers: unemployment criteria, recruitment, compensation, job classification and structure, fringe benefits, marital or parental status, effect of state or local law or other requirements, advertising, pre-employment inquiries, and sex as a bona fide occupational qualification.[13]

Elementary schools have one year from the effective date of the regulation (July 21, 1975) to be in full compliance with Title IX, while secondary and institutions of higher education have 3 years.

Although colleges and universities have 3 years to be in full compliance with Title IX, they are required to perform a self-evaluation within one year to determine if their policies comply and if not, to modify them to comply with the law as expressed by the regulation.[13] Self-evaluations were to be completed by July 21, 1976.

Enforcement

Title IX is enforced by both the Higher Education and Secondary Education Divisions in the Office of Civil Rights, Department of Health, Education and Welfare. Both divisions have headquarters in Washington, D.C.

The final regulation requires that institutions set up a grievance procedure to be available for the resolution of student and employee complaints. There is no requirement that a complainant must first go through the grievance procedure at his/her institution. A complaint may be filed directly with the Department of Health, Education and Welfare's Office of Civil Rights.

Complaints of discrimination can be filed by or on behalf of an individual or a group of individuals. Complaints must be filed within 180 days of the date of discrimination. The Office of Civil Rights may also initiate investigations on its own. Once a complaint has been filed, and the complaint is determined to be valid, the institution is notified that a complaint has been made and which part of Title IX applies to it. The Department of Health, Education and Welfare will then attempt to gain voluntary compliance by the institution. If this fails, administrative hearings may begin that can lead to the termination of Federal financial assistance.

Backlog

During fiscal year 1973, there were 161 complaints received and 111 resolved. In 1974, 203 complaints were received, 103 resolved; and up to March 1975, 52 complaints were received and 12 resolved.[25] A total of 226 complaints resolved out of 416 received suggests that the enforcement of Title IX has not been undertaken with much enthusiasm. This could be due in part to the delay in issuing the final regulations as they were not issued until three years after the law was passed. Secondary and post-secondary institutions have until July 1978 to be in full compliance with the sections on Physical Education and Athletics, leaving enforcement in these areas in the near future looking problematic.

The decision to take action: Some problems and some success stories

The process of filing a complaint under the preceding laws can appear very simple. The actual filing procedures are clear cut, but the preliminary work that must be done is often very time consuming and can be expensive. Filing a complaint will take an incredible amount of time and undoubtedly exact a heavy emotional toll. Although the laws[4,14,25,30] have provisions prohibiting any form of harassment, it goes on in a variety of ways. It can come from co-workers who are afraid to cause trouble, from one's employer, and from student/athletes who do not understand that you may be trying to help them in the long run. The harassment can involve anything from tapping phones to being followed. It is very difficult to prove harassment, but in rare circumstances it has been done.[23] In expectation of harassment, the complainant will find the experience more endurable if she/he has support from friends and family. The emotional support from a group of close friends should not be underestimated.

It is important that the complainant know all available facts of his/her situation. For example, in filing an employment complaint, one should have information concerning numbers of employees (male and female), salaries, numbers of employees (male and female) in various positions within the institution/organization, fringe benefits and as much more as is possible. The more the complainant knows about the employer, the better chance of exposing the inequities.

When filing an equal opportunity (Title IX, Executive Order 11246) complaint, the facts necessary to prove the inequities increase. Not only does one need to have facts and figures concerning employment (numbers of teachers/coaches, males and females, salaries) as they affect the quality of the physical education and athletic programs, but one must have at his/her fingertips budget information concerning travel, equipment, medical care; numbers of classes/sports offered; training facilities; and publicity. This information is generally considered to be public, but it is usually very difficult to obtain. It is generally a good idea to consult with a lawyer, preferably one with civil rights experience, before beginning the process.

It can be seen that the laws previously discussed cover sex discrimination in virtually all types of employment (Equal Pay Act, Title VII, Executive Order 11246), virtually all educational programs (Title IX), and in institutions/organizations that have contracts of over $10,000 with the Federal Government (Executive Order 11246).

Many education institutions are federal contractors; athletic programs are part of the overall educational program; and coaches, officials and teachers are employees of organizations/institutions covered by Federal Civil Rights laws. It is a short step to apply these Federal laws to women in sport.

A court suit filed under the Equal Pay Act of 1963 was just recently completed (July 16, 1974) in the State of Delaware involving a differential in pay between a high school girl's softball coach and a high school boy's baseball coach. In Brennan v. Woodbridge School District,[5] it was determined that the softball coach had similar qualifications; their seasons and schedules were of approximately the same length; their rosters had approximately the same number of players; and their practice times were equivalent in number of hours spent. The judge ruled that the jobs were substantially equal in skill, the requirement of effort, and responsibility. An injunction against future violation was awarded and the court stated, "the plaintiff is entitled to interest on the amounts of the back wages found due employees from the median date of the violation to the date of the judgment of this court at the rate of 6% per annum."[5]

A complaint filed recently by the Twin Cities Student Assembly against the University of Minnesota Board of Regents[30] alleges discrimination under Title IX of the Education Amendments of 1972, The Civil Rights of 1964, and Executive Order 11246 as amended by Executive Order 11375, et al. The complaint alleges "a large scale pattern of invidious discrimination exists against women students at the University of Minnesota throughout the University's various athletic programs. Such discrimination permeates the allotment of funding, equipment, facilities, space, time, recruitment, scholarships, financial aid, and staff for the respective male and female athletic programs."[30]

The complaint shows the large disparities in the budgets for men's and women's athletic programs. The budget for men's sports in 1973–1974 was $2,253,470 and the women's budget was $34,970. The complaint proposes an Affirmative Action plan to eliminate discrimination in the provision of athletic programs to men and women.

The Twin Cities Student Assembly held public hearings on campus in May of 1976 for women students to testify as to the effects of exclusion from athletic opportunities at the University of Minnesota. Officials at the University refused to participate, citing gains in the budget in recent years. The Office of Civil Rights in the Department of Health, Education and Welfare sent only an observer to the hearings.[19] The complaint is still pending.

In a complaint filed on May 10, 1976 with the U.S. Department of Health, Education and Welfare, the Project on Equal Education Rights has charged forty states and the District of Columbia with "violating federal requirements for ending sex bias in education under Title IX of the Education Amendments of 1972."[21] The complaint charges that "state education agencies failed to take one or more of five basic steps to end sex bias in their own operations."[21] State education agencies receive a major part of Federal aid to education and redistribute it to local school districts. Thus, if state education agencies are "breaking the law requiring equal opportunity for both sexes, it can affect students and employees in every school district."[21]

There is no doubt that in the last few years women have made, and continue to make progress toward equity in their athletic programs. However, women students are not receiving the scholarship aid they should be; women's athletic budgets are still not adequate; and with the merger of men's and women's physical education departments, many competent, qualified women are being passed over for positions as Department Head. The legal tools to help combat sex discrimination are available, and women in sport have a responsibility to use these tools when necessary to gain equal opportunity for themselves or their students.

REFERENCES

1. Association of American Colleges Project on Status and Education of Women and Women's Faculty Action League (1972). "Federal Laws and Regulations Concerning Sex Discrimination in Educational Institutions."
2. Association of American Colleges Project on the Status and Education of Women (1975). "On Campus With Women." Newsletter no. 11, May, pp. 11–12.
3. Association of American Colleges Project on Status and Education of Women (1975). "What Constitutes Equality For Women in Sport?" September.
4. Boelhoefer, Sandra, Wage and Hour Analyst, Wage and Hour Division, Dept. of Labor, June 1976, personal interview.
5. Brennan v. Woodbridge School District, Employment Practice Decisions, Commerce Clearing House, Inc., Sept. 19, 1974, 9T 9640.
6. 41 CFR 60–2.10.
7. Department of Health, Education and Welfare Office for Civil Rights (1975). "Final Title IX Regulation Implementing Education Amendments of 1972: Prohibiting Sex Discrimination in Education," U.S. Government Publications, July 21, 1975.
8. Department of Health, Education and Welfare Office for Civil Rights (1975). Memorandum, Subject: "Elimination of Sex Discrimination in Athletic Programs," Sept., U.S. Government Publication.

9. Dunkle, Margaret C. (1974). "The Law is On Your Side." *WomenSports*, September, pp. 44–45.
10. East, Catherine S. (1973). "Move Before You're Shoved." Remarks before Association of California School Administrators, San Francisco, April.
11. E.O. 11246 of Sept. 24, 1965, as amended by E.O. 11375 of Oct. 13, 1967, 3/CFR compilation.
12. 41 F.R. Part 60.
13. 45 CFR Part 86
14. 45 CFR Part 86, Section 34.
15. 45 CFR Part 86, Section 41.
16. Hodgson v. Daisy Manufacturing Co., 317 F. Supp. 538 (W.D. Ark. 1970), 445 F. 2nd 823 (8th Cir 1971).
17. Hogan, Candace Lyle (1976). "Shedding Light on Title IX." *WomenSports*, February, pp. 44–48.
18. Knox, Holly. (1974). "Women in Educational Policy-Making: Aspects of Federal Law." Unpublished paper, copies can be obtained by writing Project on Equal Education Rights, 1522 Conn. Ave., N.W. Washington, D.C. 20036.
19. Leventhal, Larry B., A. Hovney, Sept. 23, 1976, personal communication, Minneapolis, Minn.
20. National Education Association (1973). "Combating Discrimination in the Schools: Legal Remedies and Guidelines." National Education Association Publication, Washington, D.C.
21. National Organization for Women Legal Defense and Education Fund Project on Equal Education Rights (1976). "Peer Perspective," Newsletter, Vol. 2, No. 2, July, p. 1.
22. National Organization for Women Legal Defense and Education Fund Project on Equal Education Rights, "Summary of the Regulation for Title IX of the Education Amendments of 1972." Washington, D.C.
23. Pettway v. American Cast Iron Pipe Company, 411 Fed. Register, 2d 998 (5th Cir 1969).
24. P.L. 92–318, 20 USC Section 1681 (1972).
25. Pullen, Dale, Dept. of Health, Education and Welfare, personal communication.
26. Raffel, Norma K. (1975), "The Enforcement of Federal Laws and Regulations Prohibiting Sex Discrimination in Education." Report and Recommendations for the U.S. National Commission on the Observance of International Women's Year. Washington, D.C.
27. Secretary of Labor's Interpretative Bulletin, 29 CFR Section 800, 148 (1971).
28. Skidmore, Patricia (1975), for Women's Equity Action League, a WEAL Fund Kit: "Women in Sports," Copies can be obtained by writing WEAL, National Press Building, Washington, D.C. 20045.
29. Title 29 Code of Federal Regulations, Labor, Chapter XIV—Equal Employment Opportunity Commission, Part 1604—Guidelines on Discrimination Because of Sex.
30. Twin Cities Student Assembly v. University of Minnesota Board of Regents, Complaint filed with the Office of Civil Rights, U.S. Dept. of Health, Education and Welfare, Attorney Larry B. Levenhtal, Minneapolis, Mn. 55401.
31. 29 USC 8 206(d)
32. 78 Stat. 253, 42 USC 2000(e).
32a. 86 Stat. 103, 42 USC 2000(e).
33. U.S. Commission on Civil Rights, *The Federal Civil Rights Enforcement Efforts 1974*, Washington, D.C. 20425 and National Commission for Observance of International Women's Year, ". . . To Form a More Perfect Union. . .," Room 1004 State Department, Washington, D.C. 20520.
34. U.S. Dept. of HEW Fact Sheet (1975) "Title IX—Civil Rights." Distributed with Title IX Guidelines.

35. U.S. Dept. of HEW, Office for Civil Rights (1975). Memorandum, Subject: Elimination of Sex Discrimination in Athletic Programs, September, Wash, D.C.
36. U.S. Department of Labor Employment Standards Administration (1975). *1975 Handbook on Women Workers,* Bulletin 297, pp. 285–295.
37. U.S. Department of Labor (1974). *Equal Pay.* WH Publication 1320, June.
38. Weinberger, Caspar, Secretary of Health, Education and Welfare, Statement on Release of Final Title IX Regulations, June 3, 1975, p. 2.
39. Women's Rights Law Reporter (1973). "The Equal Pay Act," Vol. 1, no. 4, pp. 71–80.
40. Women's Rights Law Reporter (1975). Vol. 2, No. 3, p. 27–28.

Chapter 12
THE ERA AND WOMEN'S SPORT: AN HYPOTHETICAL TRIAL CASE

Carol L. Rose

THE EQUAL RIGHTS AMENDMENT

Proposed Amendment XXVII of the U.S. Constitution

Section 1. Equality of rights under the law shall not be denied or abridged by the United States or by any State on account of sex.

Section 2. The Congress shall have the power to enforce, by appropriate legislation, the provisions of this article.

Section 3. This amendment shall take effect two years after the date of ratification.

[Proposed by Congress on March 22, 1972]

"Lawsuits challenging the male domination of sports may be the best illustration of female impatience with women's place."[1]* A myriad of issues have been dealt with in recent sports litigation. Some of these issues are: the sociological and physiological forces behind segregating or integrating male and female participants, what is equality in sports, cultural questions, whether non-contact and contact sports should be distinguished, the cost of maintaining segregated teams.

The number of cases reaching the courts has been rapidly increasing. Because most athletics are school related, state action in violation of constitutional guarantees generally provides a basis for challenging unequal treatment of the female athlete. Typically, a high school girl wants to compete in a sport that is only offered to boys or she is made to compete on the unsupported girls' team. As some of the following cases show, the decisions rest on whether the sport is contact or non-contact and on whether a separate team is available.

One of the highest courts to rule on the issue of integrating high school teams on the basis of sex is the U.S. Court of Appeals for the Sixth Circuit. Using a rational relation test the court in *Morris v. Michigan State Board of Education*[2] invalidated a rule prohibiting

---

*All footnotes are listed at the end of the Chapter.

girls from non-contact sports when all or part of the team was male. As a result of that case, the Michigan legislature enacted a law guaranteeing all girls the right to play on the boys' team in non-contact sports, even if a girls' team exists.[3]

Suits in other states have involved swimming,[4] golf,[5] tennis,[6] and cross-country.[7] The common factors in each of these cases should be noted: the Plaintiff was involved in a non-contact sport; in all but *Bucha v. Illinois High School Association* the school had no girls' teams; the cases all involve an athlete of proven ability; the Plaintiff complained that although she was an athlete of equal ability, she was prohibited from competing with males solely on the basis of sex and was thereby denied equal protection under the law.

At least two cases have been decided under constitutional provisions comparable to the federal ERA. *Commonwealth v. Pennsylvania Interscholastic Athletic Association*[8] and *Darin v. Gould*.[9] In both cases contact sports were in issue. The former involved softball and the latter, football.

Because the ERA is close to being ratified, feminists interested in athletics should be concerned with the effect of the ERA of the U.S. Constitution on interscholastic athletics. One can look at the cases decided under the state ERAs and analogize, but these decisions are few and the court limited the decision to the specific fact situation in each case.

The purpose of this chapter is to present the opposing arguments that can be expected to be brought before the first court to hear a case involving sex discrimination in interscholastic athletics. Therefore, for the purpose of the trial case which follows, it must be assumed that the ERA has been ratified and is now the 27th Amendment to the U.S. Constitution. In the opposing legal arguments which follow, the reader is left to judge the merits of each argument and to decide the outcome of this case.

An hypothetical case was created involving a typical high school in a typical town. The Plaintiff brought the action in a trial court to enjoin the operation of a rule of the local interscholastic athletic association prohibiting mixed competition between girls and boys. Since this hypothetical case is one of first impression (that is, it is the first case involving the application of the ERA to sports), the arguments are only used for persuasion and cannot be used to argue that precedent should prevail.

At the trial level, the Plaintiff lost and the rule prohibiting mixed competition was upheld. The Plaintiff[10] now brings this action on appeal. When a case is appealed to a higher court, the Plaintiff and Defendant submit legal arguments (briefs). The final disposition will be made on the basis of the following briefs.

Since the case deals with a contact sport (basketball) all the standard arguments concerning the physiological differences between the sexes are employed. A commingling of the physiological with the constitutional aspects of this case creates more than the standard arguments that: (1) girls *are* different and should be treated as such; or on the other hand, that (2) for true equality, girls must be allowed to play with boys.

HISTORY OF THE CASE

On October 10, 1975, the Metropolia Board of Education filed an Application for Preliminary Injunction against the Metropolia Interscholastic Athletic Association ("MIAA"), seeking injunctive relief against the enforcement of By-law 7 of the MIAA By-Laws. The matter is now before Your Honorable Court.

The MIAA is an unincorporated association of public high schools in the city and surrounding suburbs of Metropolia. The membership consists of 23 high schools in that area.

The goals of the MIAA are to develop a variety of athletic programs and to set standards to be followed in competition.

The specific purposes of the MIAA are set forth in Article I of its Constitution:

> To organize, develop, and direct an interscholastic athletic program which will promote, protect and conserve the health and physical welfare of all participants.
> To formulate and maintain policies that will safeguard the educational values of interscholastic athletics and cultivate high ideals of good sportsmanship.
> To promote uniformity of standards in all interscholastic athletic competition.[11]

Plaintiff, a 15-year-old sophomore at City High School, is seeking injunctive relief of MIAA By-law 7. The relevant By-laws of the MIAA are:

By-law 7: There will be two divisions of the championship tournament, one for boys and one for girls.
By-law 10: No team will be permitted to compete in the city tournament unless it followed the tournament rules throughout the season.

Article II of the MIAA By-laws declares that an athletic program for girls should provide opportunities for participation to all girls desiring athletic experience; that athletics for girls should be recognized on a basis equitable to that given boys; that therefore facilities for girls' athletics should provide suitable playing fields, gymnastics, and equipment, and that for interscholastic athletic competition all provisions of the MIAA By-laws shall apply equally to girls' and boys' athletics.

Plaintiff seeks the opportunity to compete on the all-male basketball team sponsored by the high school. An all-girl team was created after the ERA was adopted. It is Plaintiff's contention that she will increase her opportunity for exposure to college recruiters competing on the all-male team. City High School, represented by the Metropolia Board of Education, supports Plaintiff's position.

Upon the passing of the ERA, the MIAA Executive Council presented it with the option of either opening previously all-boys' teams to girls, or of creating counterpart teams for girls. The decision to increase the availability and quality of counterpart girls' teams, rather than opening previously all-boys' teams to participation by girls, was made by the member schools for the following reasons:

1. Certain physiological differences between males and females prevent the great majority of females from competing on an equal level with the great majority of males.

2. The vast majority of girls are and would be unable to compete successfully with boys for team positions.

3. The number of girls who can participate in interscholastic athletic competition will be negligible if they must compete with boys for membership on a single school team, but will be equal if they are able to participate on separate girls' teams. Similarly for boys.

4. Certain sports, by virtue of physical contact, are not suitable for joint participation by boys and girls. Such sports include football, wrestling, basketball, soccer, field hockey, and lacrosse.[12]

Once separate teams were created in each sport, certain regulations were invoked. The relevant regulations are procedural. At each event (except male football and its female counterpart field hockey), both male and female teams play. They alternate with respect to which team plays first. The scores are totaled to determine which school has won the event. Furthermore, scouts and recruiters are encouraged to observe both teams perform. Media are encouraged to cover both teams. In effect, then, both teams represent the school.

It is to be noted that this case involves particularly high school interscholastic competition in contact sports. It does not purport to make any argument involving intramural competition, non-contact sport competition on any level, or the physiology of pre-pubescence. The following studies do not apply particularly to ages prior to 14 because at such ages, girls and boys are evenly matched in weight, strength, and reaction time.

QUESTIONS FOR THE COURT

A. Does the MIAA By-law prohibiting girls from competing on boys' athletic teams violate the ERA of the United States Constitution?

B. What standard should be applied to interpret the ERA with respect to interscholastic athletic competition?

INDEX TO BRIEF FOR DEFENDANT

Introduction

Argument for Defendant

Introduction to the Brief for Defendant

There can be little doubt that females are not at the same stage of athletic development as males. Whether this is a result of physiological differences or limited training, if single-sexed interscholastic teams were offered in each sport, females would generally be excluded from participation because they could not perform competitively with males.

For these reasons the MIAA is not alone in its belief that the growth of girls' interscholastic athletics depends upon the By-law prohibiting competition between the sexes. In addition to the NEA and the AIAW submitting proposals supporting separate teams, women coaches and experts in sports studies along with the AMA have concluded that "separate teams for male and female athletes are necessary in order to have a broad-based and meaningful girls' sports program."[13]

The courts have recognized that males possess a higher degree of athletic ability in the traditional sports offered by most schools.[14] The physiological differences between males and females, the determinative factor in athletic ability, has also been recognized by the courts:

There are, of course, substantial physiological differences between males and females. . . . Men are taller than women, stronger than women by reason of a greater muscle mass; have larger hearts than women and a deeper breathing capacity, enabling them to utilize oxygen more efficiently than women, run faster, based upon the construction of the pelvic area, which, when women reach puberty, widens, causing the femur to bend outward, rendering the female incapable of running as efficiently as a male. These physiological differences may, on the average prevent a great majority of women from competing on a level equal with the great majority of males. The differences may form a basis for defining class competition on the basis of sex, for the purpose of encouraging girls to compete in their own class consisting of boys involved in interscholastic athletic competition.[15]

Furthermore, it has been recognized that allowing females on all-male teams is nothing more than a form of tokenism:

It needs to be clearly stated and understood that having women on men's teams does *not* offer equality of opportunity. It offers tokenism for a few top female athletes. We are not interested in a few girls or women becoming token members of boys' or men's teams. This encourages and leads to the possibility (and a reality throughout New York State) of athletic departments in high schools and colleges justifying not providing varsity teams for women by insisting they are providing equal opportunity for women by permitting them to try out for men's teams.[16] (Emphasis in original)

It is with these thoughts in mind that the Defendant contends that equal opportunity in athletics is best achieved by enforcing the MIAA By-law which prohibits mixed competition.

Argument for Defendant

I. *Equality of Rights has not been abridged or denied since equality of rights means having equal opportunity to compete.*

To understand why the status quo does not deny or abridge equality of rights, it is necessary to define "equality of rights" with respect to athletic competition. Equality of rights is encompassed within equality with respect to: facilities and equipment; provision of medical and training facilities and services; scheduling of games and practice times; availability of funds for travel and athletic scholarships; recruiting athletes; media coverage of sport.[17]

In interscholastic competition, equality of rights means having equality of opportunity to compete. Only the team that represents the school will have the opportunity to even consider the facilities and services, scheduling, funds, etc. Any secondary teams have no opportunity for travel, scholarships, and media coverage. If the school's representative team is composed solely of males (with possibly one or two females who could "make the team"), did females *effectively* have the opportunity to compete for that team? Physiological differences which effectively eliminate the vast majority of females from the opportunity Plaintiff is seeking will be proven below. Although Plaintiff may be an exceptional athlete and would succeed on the all-male team, she will have to be sacrificed for the good of the vast majority of female athletes. As the court found in *Darin v. Gould*:[18]

> The approach being followed will provide equality to girls in the sense of an equal emphasis on girls' interscholastic programs. . . For this court to now mandate that girls be permitted to play contact football, involving a corresponding right of boys to join all girls' teams, would not only be destructive to the programs being developed but make it extremely difficult, if not impossible, to develop balanced and equal sports programs. . . The rights of the Darin girls must be balanced against the collective rights of all high school girls to have the best and most balanced programs developed and available to most of them.

It is Defendant's contention that having an equal opportunity to compete creates equality of rights. In high school interscholastic competition this is best achieved by enforcing separate teams. It is important "to look to the results and effects of policies, as well as the policies themselves, to determine if there is equal athletic opportunity for women."[19]

A. *In order to apply the law, the court must determine which structure, single-sexed or mixed teams, will provide equal opportunity in interscholastic competition.*

In evaluating the two structures, one must keep in mind that the impact of a policy or practice must fall equally on both sexes. That is, does the policy have a disproportionate effect on one sex over the other?

If a team were to be completely coeducational, this appears to be the simplest and least discriminatory solution. However, because membership on teams is competitively determined, physiological and training differences, would in effect, eliminate opportunities for females to play in competitive athletics. Only a few exceptionally talented females would make the team. The great majority of the females would be at a disadvantage since they would not receive the benefits of interscholastic competition.

Separate teams are supported by the leading athletic and educational associations.

In November, 1974, AIAW, in interpreting the guidelines of Title IX, feared schools might open all teams to both sexes. This, they said, would in reality provide only the exceptional athlete an opportunity to compete and would inhibit development of sports programs. They made the following resolution:

Whereas a single team for male and female would discriminate against females due to sex-determined physiological disadvantages in strength and speed. BE IT RESOLVED: There shall be separate teams for female and male. No male may compete on a female team and no female may compete on a male team.[20]

At the 1974 NEA (National Education Association) annual meeting in Chicago, delegates to the Representative Assembly passed the following resolution: "The NEA believes that, at all educational levels, female and male students must have equal opportunity to participate in athletic programs."[21]

In a legal opinion submitted to the NCAA (National Collegiate Athletic Association), classifications on the basis of sex are supported when there is

> a substantial and legitimate purpose, such as the minimization of physical injury, or as in *Schlesinger*,[22] to the provision of equal opportunity in fact. . . We thus believe, for example, that the NCAA might constitutionally exclude females from participating in intercollegiate football or wrestling programs involving integrated contact with males.

The different treatment for members of one sex can be constitutionally justified, "if the purpose of the difference is to achieve equality between the sexes in fact or effect."

The opinion goes on to note that for females to have equal opportunity, championships must be limited to the female student-athlete.[23]

The "equal opportunity" the AIAW, NEA and NCAA are seeking will be defeated by the effect of a mixed team.

In *Darin v. Gould*,[24] the Washington Interscholastic Athletic Association had a ruling forbidding girls from playing contact football on boys' teams. In upholding this ruling the court found on the evidence that the vast majority of girls are simply unable to compete with boys in contact football and that the potential risk of injury is great. In discussing the doctrine of "separate but equal" that the schools are following, the judge notes that

> the approach being followed will provide equality to girls in the sense of an equal emphasis on girls' interscholastic programs. Discrimination by sex will occur only where the inability to compete or risk of injury require it. For this court to now mandate that girls be permitted to play contact football, involving a corresponding right of boys to join the all girls' teams, would not only be destructive to the programs being developed but make it extremely difficult, if not impossible, to develop balanced and *equal* sports programs. (Emphasis added)

1) *Inherent differences.*

The question as to whether girls can successfully compete on the same team with boys depends upon two issues: Are there inherent and unchangeable differences between the sexes which make the competition unequal? Are any of the differences that are presently noted cultural, and can they be eliminated by proper training? A discussion of the first follows.

"In spite of improved training methods and mental psyche, the average 5'5", 120 lb. male will be stronger and more powerful than the average 5'5", 120 lb. female. . . Conversely females are superior in feats involving balance and flexibility."[25] Physical fitness is made up of strength, speed, muscular endurance, cardiovascular endurance, balance, flexibility, neuromuscular coordination, reaction and movement time. Strength is associated with power, muscular endurance, speed and movement time. Males have a definite advantage but females can compete equally with males in sports involving coordination, agility, or reaction time. However, society has chosen to value sports involving strength, a predominantly male characteristic.

Dr. Thomas Shaffer, pediatric professor at Ohio State University,[26] indicates that adult men are at least 30 per cent stronger than women. The reason lies predominantly in the male hormone androgen. Androgen produces denser bones and stimulates the growth of muscle tissue. The result is that men are not only larger and heavier than women in general, but a normal man of any given size will have more muscle mass (lean body mass) than a woman of similar build. The muscle mass protects bones. With females having less protection for the bones, great risk is invoked if girls collide with boys.[27]

Furthermore, from infancy males have less fat tissue. At adolescence the amount of difference sharpens. "Apparently no amount of conditioning can make a woman as lean, proportionately, as a man. College-age men in the United States, for example, average 15 per cent body fat; women some 25 per cent."[28] There are exceptions of Olympic athletes who have a smaller difference (some less than 10 per cent). "Despite the exceptions, even most women athletes are like racehorses with a heavier handicap; that extra load of fat they have to carry around has a direct and negative effect on their work capacity and stamina."[29]

Since girls are at a distinct disadvantage to boys in sports because of their lesser muscle-mass per unit of body weight and bone density, it is advisable that they do not participate in vigorous contact sports together. Corbitt states, "If competitors are matched according to weight, girls are still exposed to greater injury, since the ratio of adipose tissue to lean body weight varies considerably between the two sexes, to the disadvantage of girls."[30] He goes on to say that because the injury risk to the female athlete outweighs the benefits of mixed competition, the AMA Committee is opposed to contact sports for girls on boys' teams.

9

Women's stamina, that is, their ability to perform at maximum capacity over an extended period, may be genetically less because of aerobic capacity. The significance of a high degree of oxygen consumption may be explained in two ways:

1. The more oxygen an athlete can supply to working muscles, the greater capacity for efficient energy formation to make muscles work. If the body weight is taken into account the difference in aerobic capacity between males and females is 25 to 30 per cent.[31]

2. Some physical educators believe the main reason for the difference in aerobic capacity to be the hemoglobin and red blood cells, the level of which is lower in females. Men have approximately 15 per cent more hemoglobin and 6 per cent more red blood cells indicating a greater oxygen carrying capacity.[32]

The volume of the heart muscle in females is 85 to 90 per cent that of males so the volume of blood ejected from the heart is less. The total blood in females is proportionately less than in males. The heart is pumping harder in males to circulate blood to the body. This all leads to a higher endurance level of the male.[33]

2) *Proper training will not bring the great majority of females on a competitive level with the great majority of males.*

Sportswoman polled champion women athletes on two questions: Are women lazy athletes? Do they train less than men? The women polled agreed on one question—that women athletes are culturally conditioned to consider their athletic prowess inferior to men's. Two thirds of the women polled agreed that women cannot become as proficient in sports and cited male superior strength.[34]

Dr. Al Thomas, Kutztown State College, Pennsylvania, said women's performance in strength sports is limited by improper training and lack of encouragement.[35] Since "the most striking thing about research on women athletes is the lack of it in the U.S.,"[36] it would be ill-advised to predict that with proper training and encouragement women can achieve what men have attained.

Atty. Brenda Feigen Fasteau in "Sporting Change,"[37] an article in *Ms.* magazine, does not think that any amount of training will bring women on a competitive basis with men in high level competition. "Unfortunately, no American woman would have made the Olympics if the team had been integrated and if the same criteria for selection were applied to both sexes. The very best men—the ones who enter the Olympic tryouts—are still better than the very best women. . . . It is debatable whether Billie Jean King would even make the top 10 if male and female professional tennis players competed against each other."[38] It is unlikely that any Olympic athlete or professional athlete on a level equivalent to Billie Jean King has not been training since early childhood, yet many researchers find males superior by at least 10 per cent in the traditional athletic abilities such as strength, endurance, speed, etc.

II. Equality of opportunity would best be achieved by operating parallel male and female single-sex teams.

It is the Plaintiff's contention, as the court held in *Brown v. Board of Education* that "in the field of public education the doctrine of 'separate but equal' has no place. Separate educational facilities are inherently unequal."[39] Plaintiff's emphasis is misplaced. In *Brown*, it is equality which is sought and equality which is mandated. In the context of racial classification, the court found as a matter of fact that separate could never be equal. Therefore separation of races was prohibited. The court discredited the notion of "separate but equal" not because the concept was unconstitutional per se, but because, in the context of race, separate can never be equal. Here we too argue for equality, but in a quite different context. Where some sex classifications are concerned the possibility of separate but equal remains viable. In fact, in order to guarantee equal treatment of the sexes in areas where their physical differences are controlling, separate treatment is required.

Too often people equate race discrimination with sex discrimination. The only analogy between them is that "both classifications create large, natural classes, membership in which is beyond the individual's control; both are highly visible characteristics on which legislators have found it easy to draw gross, stereotypical distinctions."[40]

However, physiological differences cannot be denied. Women are physiologically different from men, in more ways than having biologically distinct organs, (e.g. muscle mass, fatty tissue, aerobic capacity). Generally, women and men cannot do the same physical tasks. Because of the undeniable differences between the sexes contrary to no differences between the races, *Brown* cannot apply other than to hold that when discrimination occurs, equality is sought.

As noted previously, equality of rights means equality of opportunity. To reach the standard required by the ERA, male and female must be given the same opportunities. Having a single team only eliminates the opportunity of the great majority of females for two reasons: (1) if superior females "moved up" to the male team, female teams would be undercut by losing their best athletes. (2) Only a very few exceptional women would be physically able to achieve the status of the representative team in interscholastic athletics. With separate teams (1) female teams would not be undercut and (2) as many females as males would represent the school (see below). Thus, "separate," in interscholastic athletics, reaches the standard of the ERA, equality between the sexes.

The advantages of having parallel teams result in a fast and effective way to rectify the current imbalance in resource allocation and spectator interest. The use of combined scoring (girls' and boys' scores totaled to be the school's score) and alternating team playing order (the second game is generally the main attraction) places more emphasis on the female team; equality of importance and performance will result, and girls' sports will be taken seriously. The school and community would have a stake in the success of the girl athlete. There are further advantages to having teams playing at the same event. For example, traveling expenses are minimized when the teams travel together, the college talent scout would be exposed to the girl as well as to the boy athlete, and media coverage would be equalized.

Plaintiff argues that in reality, girls' sports are not taken seriously. She argues that there is little community enthusiasm and support for the girls' games maintaining the concept of the inferiority of the female athlete. The result is lack of interest and motivation on the part of the players themselves.

The passing of the ERA and the resultant MIAA By-Laws are recent phenomena. It is too soon to realize any significant change in the attitudes which have permeated society since the creation of this country. Although it has taken many years to see some result in the thinking of people with respect to race, the struggle is not abandoned. It will take time for community support of female teams to be on a par with the present support for all-male teams. After all, it was the boys' team which represented the high school and received support accordingly. Now, both the girls' and boys' teams represent the school. The efforts of the girls directly affect the result of the event. This will soon be realized and appreciated by the community and the girls themselves.

The By-laws and regulations of the MIAA are followed by every public high school in Metropolia which competes on an interscholastic level. These By-laws are designed to promote a separate, yet fully supported, girls' team in every sport. The By-laws are monitored closely and any violation is taken seriously and can result in disqualification from the city-wide tournament or even disqualification from the Association.

III. *If the court finds equality of rights has been abridged or denied, sex is to be interpreted under the ERA under a suspect classification test or an absolute test.*

Classifications on the basis of sex now specifically controlled by a constitutional amendment will require strict scrutiny under a suspect classification test or an absolute test.

Under the ERA, sex is at least suspect. Four members of the Supreme Court in *Frontiero v. Richardson*,[41] in the concurring opinion, found sex to be suspect: "Therefore, although it appears that classifications on the basis of sex may be suspect, this cannot be said without hesitancy. It must be noted that should the Equal Rights Amendment be ratified, classifications on the basis of sex will immediately become 'suspect'."

If the court chooses to follow a suspect classification test, all that would be necessary to allow the sex-based discrimination would be a compelling state interest. Protection of the general welfare of the population is of vital concern to the government. Congress enacted the President's Council on Physical Fitness in its concern for the general welfare, evidencing the state's interest in physical education. In *Brown v. Board of Education,* the Supreme Court emphasized the state's interest in education.

> Today, education is perhaps the most important function of state and local governments. . . . Today, it is a principal instrument in awakening the child to cultural values, in preparing him for later professional training, and in helping him to adjust normally to his environment. In these days, it is doubtful that any child may reasonably be expected to succeed in life if he is denied the opportunity of an education. Such an opportunity, where the state has undertaken to provide it, is a right which must be made available to all on an equal basis.[42]

The institution of mixed teams will place the *physical* education of half of the population at a distinct disadvantage. Since the females will have less opportunity to compete, they will have less incentive and less motivation and thus less interest in training and physical development. The result: less active and healthy females than males. The good health and physical education of America's youth is undeniably a compelling state interest.

If the court chooses to follow an even stricter standard, an absolute standard, the words of the amendment would be taken literally and no rights could be abridged or denied. Not even a compelling state interest could justify a classification on the basis of sex. Two aspects of an absolute standard should be considered.

First, as has been discussed, equality of rights means equality of opportunity in interscholastic competition. Separate teams causing equality of opportunity necessarily imply that the ERA has been upheld. Taken absolutely, no rights have been abridged.

Secondly, if one argues that equality of rights means identity of rights, it must be noted that completely identical treatment could not be expected when such treatment relates directly to the physiological differences between the sexes such as:

(1) cohabitation and sexual activity between unmarrieds[43]
(2) protection of fundamental right of privacy[44]
(3) characteristics unique to one sex

Certainly competition in contact sports between male and female athletes falls within the area in which it is expected that differential treatment should apply.

Therefore, whether the court chooses to use a suspect classification test or an absolute test, equality of rights is best achieved in interscholastic contact sports competition by single-sexed teams.

IV. Conclusion

At first glance the challenged By-law appears to be clearly discriminatory against girl athletes. Why then do such women's associations as the AIAW support the challenged By-law? Why do they fear that the great leaps in the advancing female programs will be destroyed by mixed team competition?

The MIAA, through its By-law, has begun to harness the increased interest in quality girls' sports, and has channeled it in the direction of establishing a strong girls' program.

The challenged By-law not only does not discriminate, but seeks to further the development and training of females. It offers an equal opportunity for this development which has long been afforded to male athletes. As girls' programs develop on a par with boys', the physiological differences between the sexes will still justify separate competition in contact sports on the interscholastic level. Even with intensive and concentrated training, it will be many years before mixed teams in contact sports should be considered, if at all.

Defendant respectfully submits that equality of opportunity be maintaned by the court refusing to enjoin enforcement of the challenged By-law, " in the interest of enabling an ever-greater number of girls to participate in a more well-developed sports program"[45] in Metropolia.

INDEX TO BRIEF FOR PLAINTIFF

Introduction

Argument for Plaintiff

I. Equality of rights has been denied by "separate but equal" teams.
   A. Only mixed competition can provide equal treatment under the law.
   B. Sexual stereotypes eliminated, females can compete successfully with males.
      1. Physiological capabilities.
      2. Proper training will bring females to a competitive level with males.
      3. Stereotypic myths rebutted.

II. The ERA should be interpreted by an Absolute Standard thereby requiring mixed interscholastic athletics.

III. Conclusion.

Introduction to the Brief for Plaintiff

> Sports are a vital, cultural expression of America. They are as expressive of the American way of life as are freedom of speech, the right to vote, schools and choice of church. . . Sports portray the true character of America and they are filled with vitality, with ideals and opportunities. . . They are fundamental to the purposes of education and democracy.[46]

The Minnesota Supreme Court has stated that "Interscholastic activities are recognized as an integral facet of the educational process."[47] The National Federation of State High School Associations contends that "Emphasis shall be upon teaching 'through' athletics in addition to teaching the 'skills' of athletics."[48]

There are many intangible benefits to be derived from participation in interscholastic athletics. The chance to compete comes at a particularly formative stage of life and can never be recovered. Therefore, it is especially important that all student-athletes be given the opportunity to compete on an equal basis. Ability should be the only determinative factor for those competing to "make the team". Yet the Metropolia Interscholastic Athletic Association By-law which bars females from competing on male teams is using sex as a basis of disallowing the opportunity to compete. This sex-based discrimination cannot stand.

> "There may be worse (more socially serious) forms of prejudice in the United States, but there is no sharper example of discrimination today than that which operates against girls and women who take part in competitive sports, wish to take part, or might wish to if society did not scorn such endeavors. . . There is a publicly announced, publicly supported notion that sports are good for people, that they develop better citizens, build vigorous minds and bodies and promote a better society. . . Sports may be good for people, but they are considered a lot gooder for male people than for female people."[49]

The stereotypical female does not have the ability to compete with males in any activity depending on strength. However, the courts have held that such an overbroad generalization cannot be used to prohibit women from attempting to compete. If the activity requires strength, then those who can participate must be selected on the basis of strength, not sex. And the selections must be made individually. . . Each woman must be given the opportunity to prove that regardless of stereotypes, she is qualified. In a case challenging a rule that women could not be employed in any position in which the employee would have to lift over 30 pounds, the court found the 30-pound limit unrealistic and rigid:

Rather, they would have us 'assume', on the basis of a 'stereotyped characterization' that few or no women can safely lift 30 pounds, while all men are treated as if they can. While one might accept, arguendo, that men are stronger on the average than women, it is not clear that any conclusions about relative lifting ability would follow. . . Technique is as important as strength.[50]

The same is true in athletics. Many factors compensate for a lack of speed or strength. Some of them are: "mind-body coordination, mental determination, sensory perception, courage, intelligence, willingness to practice and experience".[51]

From the above arguments and the ones that follow, it will be obvious that a rule barring girls from competition with boys in interscholastic basketball competition is based on an impermissible presumption that females are physiologically unable to compete with males. This over-inclusive classification based on sex is a denial of equality of rights violating the ERA.

I. Equality of rights has been denied by "separate but equal" teams.

In interscholastic athletic competition, equality of rights is equivalent to equality of opportunity. With equal opportunity for both sexes to compete, equality of rights follows.

Judge DeBruler in his discussion of separate but equal competition supports mixed competition:

Whether such a dual system would deny to male or female athletes, as well as the entire student body, substantial educational benefits which should flow to them from interscholastic athletic competitions is a much broader issue. . . Anyone who would seek to support the rationality of the separatist principle served by such dual systems would have a difficult burden indeed. . . The defender of such a system in court, surely could not be successful merely by presenting evidence that high school track and field records of men are better than those of women, as was done by appellee in the case before us. No trial court investigation into the relative athletic abilities of men and women could be complete merely upon a demonstration that male track and field champions have historically bettered their female counterparts in the record books. Such evidence cannot support a conclusion that the male sex is athletically superior. An objective observer could not determine which of two opposing armies is superior merely by examining the strongest and bravest soldier in each. For constitutional purposes, such an investigation would necessarily focus on the causes of any differential in the relative performances of male and female athletes.[52]

In assessing which situation, single-sex or mixed teams, creates true equality, the court must look to both tangible and intangible factors. In *Kirstein v. Rector and Visitors of University of Virginia*,[53] the court held that even though there were other coeducational universities in existence the female plaintiffs had been denied equal protection of the laws by their exclusion on the basis of sex from the University of

Virginia at Charlottesville. The court considered intangible factors such as prestige.

Furthermore, in a legal opinion submitted to the NCAA, the NCAA was advised on the basis of decisions such as *Kirstein v. Rector and Visitors of University of Virginia*,[54] and *Sweatt v. Painter*:[55] "and in the light of the Supreme Court's total abandonment of the 'separate but equal' standard in racial cases, beginning with *Brown v. Board of Education*,[56] we believe that any 'state' organization would be ill-advised to rely upon a 'separate but equal' approach to the administration or operations of programs designed to benefit both males and females."[57]

A. *Only mixed competition can provide equal treatment under the law.*

A survey of recent cases in the area of sex discrimination in high school athletics will demonstrate the lack of advancement in girls' athletics when "separate but equal" programs are instituted.[58]

Gunnar Myrdal in *An American Dilemma*[59] says the basic problem with the so-called "separate but equal" teams is that they are not equal. He parallels this problem to the plight of Blacks. He notes the same psychological, educational and social harm, appearing in separate teams as appears in the separate classrooms in *Brown v. Board of Education*.[60] The psychological harm: feeling of inferiority (the boys do not want to play with the sissy girls). The educational harm: lack of motivation that results from the separation perpetuating the achievement orientation of males as opposed to females. The social harm: perpetuation of the social barriers which leads to a blockage of communication and interaction between the groups. This reinforces stereotypes and perpetuates negative attitudes such as "girls are weaker and don't know how to play properly." Myrdal says, "Togetherness breeds equality and is carried over to the rest of education."[61]

On the other hand, a look at an actual experience of mixed competition is in order. After New York regulations preventing girls from playing on boys' teams were challenged in 1969, a study was conducted to determine the effects of girls' participation on boys' teams.[62] Results found no evidence of physical, psychological or social harm to the female participants or their male teammates. The study revealed that the boys put forth equal or greater effort with girls on their teams. Furthermore, the majority of boys felt no difference between playing with or without girls. Ninety-nine per cent of the girls liked being on the boys' team, citing reasons such as more challenging, more skill.[63]

Furthermore, a study panel of the Connecticut Board of Education recently recommended that girls be allowed to play contact sports such as football on the same school teams with boys. The group that studied the proposal found that girls are less vulnerable than boys to contact-sport injuries.[64]

In order to be assured of equal treatment, identical treatment is necessary. Girls and boys should be treated, not as two separate groups competing in interscholastic athletics, but as students competing based on their individual abilities. With the opportunity to "make the team", the girls' enthusiasm to become as involved in training and development as boys have been in the past, will facilitate the equality for which physical educators strive. As will be shown, there are girls today physically ready to "make the team". The effect of these girls competing will be the incentive necessary to effect more girls competing and a healthier population. With boys and girls striving together in competition, the stereotypic myths perpetuated through the athletic institution as it is today will soon die and the reality of the female's physical potential will take over.

B. *Sexual stereotypes eliminated, females can compete successfully with males.*

"Because athletics reflect cultural norms, they have tended to perpetuate sex stereotypes and myths about what is 'right' for men and what is 'right' for women. Men are 'supposed to be' strong and aggressive, both physically and emotionally, while women are 'supposed to be' weak and passive."[65] Women have been discouraged from participating in sport so that they may develop the qualities acceptable to society:

> The present generation of our younger male population has not become so decadent that boys will experience a thrill in defeating girls. . . Athletic competition builds character in our boys. We do not need that kind of character in our girls, the women of tomorrow.[66]

Only an understanding of (1) the physiological capabilities of women, (2) the effect of proper training, and (3) a response to the myths concerning women competing alongside men, will work to dispel these attitudes and show that females can compete successfully with males.

1) *Physiological capabilities.*

In sport as it is defined today, strength and endurance govern who will compete and at what level. The gap between male and female with respect to strength and endurance has narrowed considerably in the last few years. In fact, the differences of strength within each sex are far greater than between the sexes.

Dr. Jack H. Wilmore, Professor of Physical Education at University of California at Davis, has written that the superiority of males over females in strength and endurance may be more of an "artifact of social or cultural restriction imposed on the female . . . than a result of true biological difference in performance potential between the sexes."[67] Dr. Wilmore feels that the physically inferior are those who do not develop their physical capabilities, both females *and* males included.

> Nowhere is the narrowing gap between young men and women so well demonstrated as in the record books of international competitions. Twenty-five years ago the women's outdoor world record for the 100-meter dash was 11.5 seconds, compared with a men's record of 10.2.[68]

Today, men have shaved .3 seconds off their score, but women have shaved .7.

In swimming, women have also been rapidly approaching men's scores. In the 1924 Olympics, in the 400-meter freestyle, men were 16 per cent faster than women. In 1948, this was reduced to 11 per cent and in 1972, to only 7.3 per cent.[69]

Although these scores are achieved by high level competition, their mention is of value in proving that women do have the capability to compete with men given the same opportunities men have in training, coaching, facilities, and psychological and social support.

Strength does not dominate sport alone, endurance is of vital importance. In a study "Physiological Differences Between Females and Males Relative to Athletic Performance" by Robert C. Serfass and John F. Alexander (Department of Physical Education at University of Minnesota), it was found that females have a higher endurance level relative to peak strength.[70] Also, females' endurance levels are much higher proportionally to body weight than males'. Therefore, it is not surprising that although sprints are best run by males, some physical educators feel long distance running is soon to be overtaken by females. In the well-known Boston Marathon, women have performed competitively in this 26 mile, 385 yard race.

As Serfass and Alexander observe, "(a) some females are stronger than some males; (b) some women have a higher aerobic capacity than some men and; (c) there are undoubtedly greater differences between the 3rd and the 97th percentile in each sex than there are differences between the average female and the average male in terms of physical performance".[71]

2) *Proper training will bring females to a competitive level with males.*

Some of the physiological changes that occur with proper training are: (1) more economical ventilation rate (2) greater breathing capacity (3) greater efficiency in relation to oxygen utilization (4) greater pulse rate recovery after exercise.[72] Depending on the subject, age, initial level of fitness, and type and extent of training, the extent of cardiovascular improvement ranges from zero to an excess of 35 per cent.[73] Through identical training, females consistently increased their performance significantly more than males. All areas of training were studied. The authors concluded with "Training for girls should parallel that of men (sic) based on their physical, psychological and emotional capacities."[74]

Although skeletal growth is determined by heredity, nutrition, vascular conditions and functional stresses, it can be strengthened by vigorous activity. This activity would maximize blood circulation within the bones, which in turn, develops stronger bones. Therefore the female body is not necessarily inferior, but has adjusted to disuse.

Dr. Jack H. Wilmore, thinks "females can beat males"– it is all in the training. A recent study of two groups of non-athletic people, one male, one female, was conducted in California consisting of 10 weeks of slinging weights around. Females had improved how much weight they could lift by 30 per cent, males improved too, but not proportionally as much. When strengths were expressed relative to the estimated weight of the muscle itself, females came out 5.8 per cent stronger, strength that Wilmore suggests may be buried under cultural prohibitions.[75]

The above studies, including the statistics on the past Olympics previously noted, indicate that through proper training, females can improve with such success as to "catch up" to males. With females training alongside males, they will be assured of the best advantages in all the factors that determine success (coaching, equipment, encouragement and support, etc.).

3) *Stereotypical myths rebutted.*

"Although some societies have encouraged women in sport more than others, there have always been vigorous women. The great bull-leaping acrobats of the Minoan culture were women. Etruscan and Spartan women and men trained together. Egyptian and Greek legends credit women with the invention of ball games. Henry VIII complained of the expense of keeping Anne Boleyn in archery equipment."[76]

The encouragement that women get with respect to sport is based on the prevailing attitudes. Today, many myths exist which influence the opportunities available to women. The following myths have been disproven:

MYTH: Vulnerable reproductive organs make females more injury prone than males.

FACT: Vigorous activity is believed by gynecologists to improve muscular support in the pelvic area. The uterus is positioned so as to be shock absorbent and much less vulnerable than the male genitalia.[77]

MYTH: Athletic activity causes menstrual problems and impedes menstrual regularity. Women cannot reach peak performance during menstruation.

FACT: It appears that physical activity reduces many problems. Furthermore, over one-third of all female Olympic winners achieved their medals during menstruation. Several studies show that a female performs at a consistent level throughout the menstrual cycle.[78]

MYTH: Females should not play with males since females are more likely to get hurt. Their bones are more fragile.

FACT: The injury rate for females is lower than males in all sports. The bones are not more fragile, just smaller.

MYTH: Females will damage their breasts bumping against males.

FACT: All the protection any woman needs in rough sports is the female version of the jock strap. Breast protectors have already been designed for women.[79]

MYTH: After puberty the male becomes much stronger and a more physiologically proficient athlete than the female. The differences between the male and female increase in magnitude with time.

FACT: "Recent evidence . . . indicates that these differences may be more of an artifact of social or cultural restrictions imposed on the female either at or just prior to the outset of menarche, than a result of true biological differences in performance potential between the sexes.[80]

MYTH: By their nature, girls are not interested in sport, so why place them in the same arena as boys.

FACT: If girls are encouraged on any level that boys are, they show great interest in sports.[81]

The elimination of these myths leaves little argument as to why girls should not compete with boys. From the previous sections, it is clear that while noting the physiological distinctions between girls and boys, with proper training and encouragement, there is no medical reason to separate the sexes in sport. A 5'2", 120 lb. male can play on a competitive level with a 5'2", 120 lb. female given the same training opportunities. These opportunities will not be the same unless females are permitted to not only play with, but train with, their male counterparts.

II. *The ERA should be interpreted by an Absolute Standard thereby requiring mixed interscholastic athletics.*

The relationship of the MIAA to the public school system qualifies the MIAA as state action. See: *Brenden v. Independent School District*,[82] and cases cited therein. Therefore, the ERA is applicable to the By-laws of the MIAA.

As set forth in its legislative history, the purpose of the ERA is:

> . . . to insure that the Federal government, the State governments, and local governments treat each person, male and female, on the basis of his or her individual abilities and characteristics—and not on the basis of arbitrary sexual stereotypes as is now all too often the case. The principle on which we should all be able to agree: a person's sex should not be a factor in determining one's rights under the law.[83]

To fulfill that purpose, it is the Plaintiff's contention that an absolute standard must be applied. The intention of the authors of the ERA is shown by the rejection of the Wiggins Resolution by the House Committee on the Judiciary. The issue with respect to the Wiggins Resolution was to clarify the ambiguous language, that is, whether "equality of rights under the law" requires identical treatment for each sex or still permits a rational classification (hence different treatment) based on sex. The Judiciary Committee considered the former standard too rigid and therefore submitted the Wiggins Resolution, allowing Congress to exempt women from the military and allowing Congress and the state legislatures to formulate laws which provide different treatment according to sex for the promotion of health and safety. The rejection of that Resolution demonstrates the intention of Congress that complete and absolute equality be established.

Further support for this conclusion is found in the interpretations of Professors Emerson and Freund, and Senator Ervin. Professor Emerson states that the language "equality of rights . . . shall not be denied or abridged" constitutes an unqualified prohibition. The "differentiation on account of sex is totally precluded, regardless of whether a legislature or administrative agency may consider such a classification to be 'reasonable', to be beneficial rather than 'invidious', or to be justified by 'compelling reasons'. Furthermore, . . . the clause would not sanction 'separate but equal' treatment."[84] This suggests the effect of the ERA on athletic programs requires mixed and not separate but equal.

Professor Freund, in coming to the same conclusion, suggests that the ERA would make girls eligible for the same athletic teams as boys in the public schools.[85]

Senator Ervin testified that equality of rights "would imply rigid absolute equality."[86] Proponents of the Wiggins Resolution as well as Senator Ervin said the ERA would compel mixed participation. To assure compliance, the violator would lose federal funds and a private right of action would accrue for two reasons:

1—Plaintiffs in *Brenden, Reed* and *Haas* were able to assert a private action under the 14th Amendment, thus Plaintiff can do so under the ERA.

2–42 USC Section 1938 provides an injured party with an action at law for deprivation of constitutional rights by someone acting under color of state law.

III. Conclusion.

By-law 7 of the MIAA seeks to establish exactly what the ERA seeks to eliminate—classifications on the basis of sex. No justification can be allowed for the unequal treatment of the female athlete. It is only through identity of athletic programs that girls are able to reach the level of athletic ability that boys have attained.

Cases such as *Brown v. Board of Education* demonstrate that the intangibles as well as the tangibles must be considered when striving for full equality. The intangible factors relating to sport are especially significant. Such factors as incentive, encouragement, and community support, play a major role in successful competition. Separate teams do little to change society's attitudes—because these intangibles will go toward the support of the boys' team and leave the girls at a disadvantage once more. Only through mixed competition will society begin to view the female athlete as significant. Only through mixed competition will the male athlete begin to give his female teammate or opponent the respect and support she needs and deserves.

Once the purpose of the ERA is fulfilled and girls with the ability to "make the team" will be competing with and against boys of the same ability, equality of rights will be upheld in interscholastic athletic competition.

The significance of sex discrimination in athletics cases extends beyond the immediate changes which they will cause in high school athletic programs. A basic tenet of equality is that people should be treated as individuals and not on the basis of commonly-held stereotypes. One such stereotype posits that women cannot perform physical tasks as well as men because of their physiological disabilities. A sound and well-reasoned holding that such assumptions are sufficient to justify differences in treatment without an individualized determination would be a step forward in the area of women's rights.[87]

FOOTNOTES

[1]Barbara Babcock, Ann Freedman, Eleanor Norton, Susan Ross, *Sex Discrimination and the Law, Causes and Remedies* (Boston, Little, Brown & Co., 1975), p. 1020.

[2]472 F.2d 1207 (6th Cir. 1973).

[3]Brenda Feigen Fasteau, "Sporting Change," *Ms.*, July, 1973, p. 56.

[4]*Bucha v. Illinois High School Ass'n.*, 351 F.Supp. 69 (N.D. Ill. 1972).

[5]*Reed v. Nebraska School Activities Ass'n.*, 341 F.Supp. 258 (D.Neb. 1972); *Haas v. South Bend Community School Corp.*, 289 N.E.2d 495 (Ind. 1972).

[6]*Harris v. Illinois High School Ass'n.*, Civ. No. S. Civ. 72–25 (S.D. Ill., Mar. 21, 1972); *Gregorio v. Board of Education of Asbury Park*, No. A–12770–70 (Super. Ct. of N.J., App. Div., Apr. 5, 1971).

[7]*Hollander v. Connecticut Interscholastic Athletic Conference, Inc.*, No. 12497 (Super. Ct. Conn.. New Haven Cty, Mar. 29, 1971).

[8]334 A.2d 839 (Pa. Commonwealth 1975).

[9]Slip opinion 43276, Sept. 25, 1975 (Wash. Sup. Ct.).

[10]To follow the case clearly, the Appellant will be referred to as Plaintiff.

[11]Pa. Interscholastic Athletic Ass'n. Const. art II. Pennsylvania has an ERA parallel to the proposed ERA of the US Constitution.

[12]Brief for Defendant, *Commonwealth v. Pa. Interscholastic Athletic Ass'n.*, pp. 7–8.

[13]*Ibid.*, p. 13.

[14]Joan Hult, "Separate But Equal Athletics for Women," *JOHPER* 44, No. 6 (June, 1973), 57–8.

[15]*Haas, supra,* at 499.

[16]*Brenden v. Independent School District 742*, 342 F.Supp. 1224, 1233 (D. Minn. 1972), aff'd 477 F.2d 1292 (8th Cir. 1973).

[17]Project on the Status and Education of Women, *What Constitutes Equality for Women in Sport.* (Association of American Colleges), p. 1.

[18]Darin v. Gould, *supra,* n. 9.

[19]Project, p. 12.

[20]Mary Slaughter, "Should Women Athletes Be Allowed to Play on Men's Teams?" *The Physical Educator*, 32, No. 1 (Mr. 1975), 10.

[21]Blaufarb, "Equal Opportunity for Girls in Athletics," *Today's Education*, 63 (Nov. 1974), 55.

[22]*Schlesinger v. Ballard*, 419 U.S. 498 (1975).

[23]Opinion from Cox, Langford & Brown, 21 DuPont Circle, N.W., Wash., D.C. 20036, pp. 18–19.

[24]*Darin v. Gould, supra.*

[25]Gilchrist, "The Truth About Our Anatomy," *The Sportswoman*, 3, No. 1 (Jan/Feb 1975), 45.

[26]Dr. Thomas E. Shaffer, "Physiological Considerations of the Female Participant," *Women and Sport: A National Research Conference.*

[27]Kathleen M. Engle, "The Greening of Girls Sports," *Nations Schools,* 92, No. 3 (Sept. 1973), 30.

[28]Fasteau, p. 56.

[29]*Ibid.*

[30]Richard Corbitt, "Female Athletics," *JAMA*, 28, No. 10 (June 3, 1974).

[31]John F. Alexander, Robert C. Serfass, "Physiological Considerations About Conditioning and the Female," *The Pa'thlete*, 34, No. 6 (Feb./Mar, 1974), 12.

[32]*Ibid.*

[33]*Ibid.*

[34]Roche, "Do Females Achieve Their Athletic Potential?" *The Sportswoman*, 1, No. 3 (Sept/Oct. 1973), 18.

[35]*Ibid.*

[36]A. S. Espenschade, "Women and Competitive Sports," *Proceedings of the First Institute on Girls Sports,* (1963).

[37]Fasteau, p. 56.

[38]*Ibid.*, p. 58.

[39]347 U.S. 483, 495 (1954).

[40]"Sex Discrimination and Equal Protection: Do We Need a Constitutional Amendment," 84 *Harv. L. Rev.* 1499, 1507–8 (1971).

[41]411 U.S. 677, 691 (1973).

[42]*Brown, supra* n. 39, p. 493.

[43]USCC & AN 841 (1972).

[44]*Griswold v. Connecticut*, 381 U.S. 479 (1965).

[45]*Brief for Defendant, Commonwealth v. Pa. Interscholastic Athletic Ass'n.*, p. 63.

[46]"Sex Discrimination in High School Athletics," 57 *Minn. L. Rev.* 339, 360, from Minn. State High School League undated pamphlet entitled *An Introduction to Interscholastic Activities*, p. 1.

[47]Babcock, *et al.*, p. 1022.

[48]*Ibid.*, p. 1023.

[49]Bil Gilbert, Nancy Williamson, "Sport is Unfair to Women," *Sports Illustrated*, May 28, 1973, pp. 88–9.

[50]*Weeks v. Southern Bell Telephone Co.*, 408 F.2d 228, 236–6 (5th Cir. 1969).

[51]"Sex Discrimination in High School Athletics," 57 *Minn. L. Rev.* 339, 363.

[52]*Haas, supra*, at 502–3.

[53]309 F.Supp. 184 (E.D. Va. 1970).

[54]*Ibid.*

[55]339 U.S. 629 (1950). The court held that equality of opportunity had not been granted a Black student by establishing a separate law school for Blacks, and upheld his entrance into Univ. of Texas Law School.

[56]*Brown, supra*, which held that separate educational facilities are inherently unequal.

[57]Opinion from Cox, et al., p. 16.

[58]A typical example: *Minnesota v. Independent School District*, (male program provides statewide competition and female does not).

[59]p. 1073 (Twentieth Anniv. ed. 1962).

[60]*Brown, supra*.

[61]Slaughter, p. 10.

[62]Report on Experiment: *Girls on Boys' Interscholastic Athletic Teams*, (Univ. of N.Y., State Educ. Dept., Div. of Health, Physical Education & Recreation, Mar. 1969–June 1970).

[63]"Sex Discrimination in Interscholastic Athletics," 25 *Syracuse L. Rev.* 551, 552 (1974).

[64]"Girls Win Support for Boys' Teams," *N.Y. Times*, Sept. 19, 1975, p. 37.

[65]Project, p. 2.

[66]*Hollander v. The Connecticut Interscholastic Athletic Conference, Inc.*, No. 12–49–27 (Conn. Supp. Ct. 1971).

[67]Ann Crittendon Scott, "Closing the Muscle Gap," *Ms.*, Sept. 1974, p. 49.

[68]*Ibid.*

[69]*Ibid.*

[70]Unpublished, p. 3.

[71]*Ibid.*

[72]E. Metheny, L. Brouha, R. Johnson, W. Forbes: Some Physiological Responses of Women and Men to Moderate and Strenuous Exercise: A Comparative Study, *Amer. J. Physiol.*, 137, 318, 1942.

[73]Alexander, p. 2.

[74]*Ibid.*, p. 12.

[75]Gurney E. Williams, III, "Superbowl Time in the Battle of the Sexes," *Sci. Digest*, 77, 10, 1975.

[76]Project, p. 3, from Majorie Loggia, "On the Playing Fields of History, *Ms.*, July, 1973, p. 63.

[77]Bil Gilbert, Nancy Williamson, "Are You Being Two-Faced.?" *Sports Illustrated*, July 4, 1973, p. 45.

[78]Doolittle, Engebretsen, "Performance Variations During the Menstrual Cycle," *J. Sports Med. and Physical Fitness*, 12, 54, 1972.

[79]Bayne, "Pro + Tec Protective Bra," *J. Sports Med. and Physical Fitness*, 8, 34, 1968.

[80]Project, p. 6.

[81]Gilbert, "Are You Being Two-Faced?" p. 46.

[82]*Supra*.

[83]118 Cong. Rec. No. 41, S4135; Senate Report No. 92–689, 92nd Cong., 2nd Sess.

[84]Thomas I. Emerson, "In Support of the Equal Rights Amendments," 6 *Harv. Civ. Rights–Civ. Lib. L. Rev.* 225, 231 (1971).

[85]Paul Freund, "The ERA is Not the Way," 6 *Harv. Civ. Rights–Civ. Lib. L. Rev.* 234, 238 (1971).

[86]Hearings on H. J. Res. 208 before Subcommittee No. 4 on the House Comm. on the Judiciary, 92nd Cong., 1st Sess., ser. 2, at 72 (1971).

[87]"Sex Discrimination in High School Athletics," 57 *Minn. L. Rev.* 339, 371.

Chapter 13

WOMEN AND THE SPORT GOVERNANCE SYSTEM

Carole A. Oglesby

The primary objective of this chapter is to enable readers to analyze the structure of the international sport governance system. Because it appears that national, regional, and local sport organizations replicate many elements of this structure, the chapter is also intended as a tool by which analysis can be completed on sport social systems in which readers have direct membership.

In preparing this chapter, a half-remembered Disneyland experience provided the tonal setting. The Monsanto Company exhibit at Disneyland, Anaheim took the customer "into the world of chemicals." As each was seated in a comfortable chamber an ethereal voice informed passengers that he/she was to be transformed to atomic size and would enter, and travel through, a drop of water. In this chapter, we shall enter and travel through the international sport governance system. We shall contemplate the intricacies of Olympic Games, Pan-American Games, World University Games, World Games in all the individual sports; decisions of who shall pay and who shall play. These elite athletic events are nothing but examples of human play (as the Monsanto exhibit concerned nothing but a drop of water) made momentous, however, by the transforming power of public attention. To enter into the governance system responsible for these events, for *analysis* purposes only, is an interesting and psychologically safe activity. To enter that system as participant and change agent is, however, both perilous and corrupting and not to be faced (as the frivolous Disneyland journey) with relish. To propose that the sport organization system is corrupting is not to judge it harshly by comparison to other large social institutions. The international sport system is probably not more corrupting than international politics, nor international business. It is a corrupt system, however, when measured by the absolute standards of its own stated purposes. . . . its own essence. International sport, indeed big time American sport, is not promulgated for all human beings whether male or female, white or black; is not guided by decisions made in representative assemblies as often as it is by those agreed to within closed door cliques.

When it is proposed that newly emerging sport and athletic programs should aspire to the "heights" attained by traditional elite (big time) programs, there is cause for alarm. In this country and others, great "heights" have been achieved in budget and costs. Great success has been achieved in persuading people that the expense for a tiny elite percentage is justified. This seems, in reality, a limited accomplishment and sport humanists/feminists have resolved to enter the sport organizational system and change it. All who seek to create change within the system must continually perceive a certain personal space from the system itself. Unless the perception of the need for alternative methods of sport is maintained as a personal buffer zone, the system can easily corrupt the participant to accept its own traditional form. When an individual perceives keenly the need for alternative sport models, a protective space between change agent and the system is provided. A thorough knowledge of the present model is necessary, however, to the conception of those alternatives. The remainder of the chapter attempts to increase knowledge and understanding of the system which creates and maintains international elite sport.

THE STRUCTURE OF THF SPORT ORGANIZATION SYSTEM

In Figure 8, the five major sets of actors in the international sport governance system are identified. (Oglesby, 1974)

The first actors to be considered are the international, multi-sport bodies. For reasons which will later become clear, the best known and most powerful of these bodies is the International Olympic Committee. Another example of international, multi-sport bodies is the International Federation for University Sport (FISU) which semi-annually sponsors Universiades open only to university student-athletes. International, multi-sport bodies are composed of organizations responsible for selected sport programs in specific geographical regions (usually countries). The responsible organization within each country is (theoretically) recognized by, but not directly under the control of, the national government.

The international, multi-sport bodies perform at least six functions:

1. Stage premier events—Olympic and World University Games.
2. Identify sites and organizing committees for such events.
3. Determine eligibility regulations for its own events.
4. Determine criteria for membership in the organization.
5. Recognize eligible organizations as members.
6. Allocate income from own events and program.

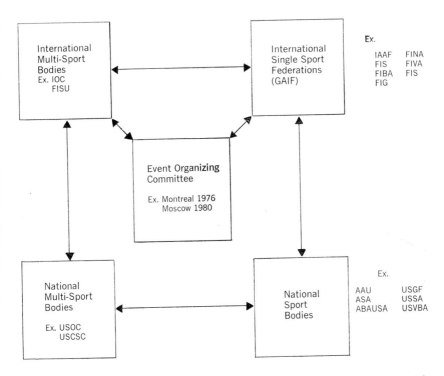

Fig. 8. Amateur Sport Governance System

The next actors to be considered are the international, single sport federations. In general, every sport conducted at the international level is "ruled" by a federation of national member organizations. The international federation often has a secretariat located by convenience and tradition in Europe. In the examples of these federations seen in Figure 8 are the following: International Amateur Athletic Federation (IAAF); International Ski Federation (FIS); International Amateur Basketball Federation (FIBA); International Gymnastic Federation (FIG); International Amateur Natation (Swimming and Diving) Federation (FINA); International Amateur Volleyball Federation (FIVA); International Softball Federation (FIS). Approximately 60 of these international sport federations have banded together, for specific and limited purposes, in an organization called the General Assembly of International Federations (GAIF). In many respects the GAIF is able to negotiate better with the IOC and the national Olympic committees than is any one of the federations alone.

The international federations perform at least five important functions:

1. Hold world championships and identify champions.
2. Determine criteria for entry into own events.
3. Determine rules of play for own events.
4. Determine criteria for eligibility of organizations as national members (official national sport governing body).
5. Recognize national members. (Ed. note. Before a national Olympic committee will receive IOC recognition it must be affiliated with at least 5 of the international federations.)

The third actors to be identified are the national, multi-sport bodies. National Olympic committees, like the United States Olympic Committee, would be classic examples of national, multi-sport bodies. Within the United States, however, there are many such organizations. Each administers (or is responsible for) a nation-wide program in many sports. Examples of other such bodies are the United States Collegiate Sports Council (affiliated with FISU), the various collegiate sport organizations (AIAW, NAIA, NCAA, NJCAA), and the Amateur Athletic Union.

The functions of these national, multi-sport bodies reflect those expected in the conduct of an athletic program. In addition, when the national body is affiliated with an international organization, the national body is charged with maintaining the international policies within the country. Examples of general functions of the USOC are listed below:

*1. To comply with and enforce all rules of the IOC;
*2. To exercise exclusive jurisdiction over all matters pertaining to participation of the U.S. in the Olympic and Pan American Games;
*3. To identify team and staff participating in Olympic and Pan American Games;
*4. To provide funding for team and staff to Olympic events.

It is common for U.S. multi-sport organizations to be structured for governance in stratas which have unequal power. The basis for the stratification will be presented later. In order to better visualize this common structural arrangement Table 14 presents categories of membership and voting power for the USOC and the USCSC.

The fourth actors to be described are the national sport governing bodies. These are the organizations, recognized by the international federations, which are regarded to offer the most expertise in the sport within the country. Each organization offers a national program of training and competition within the sport, usually culminating in a

---

*Constitutions—see bibliography.

Table 14. National, multi-sport bodies: USOC and USCSC

USOC*	% of total votes	USCSC*	% of total votes
Category A members—National sport governing bodies (1200 votes	55%	*Active members*—National collegiate sport organizations offering national championships or involved in physical education and athletic administration	60%
Category B members—National sport bodies having provided champions for Olympic or Pan American teams and offering national championships (324 votes)	15%	*Associate members*—National coaching associations	30%
Category C members—National sport bodies having championships but not A or B (260 votes)	12%	*Affiliate members*—Other organizations intimately involved with national collegiate athletics	10%
Category D members—State Olympic committees (82 votes)	3%		
Category E members—Organizations, not national, but offering programs in Olympic or Pan American sports (262 votes)	12%		
Category F members—National organizations with programs in non-Olympic/Pan American sports (33 votes)	2%		

*Constitutions—see bibliography.

national championship. Among the functions shared by the national sport governing bodies are two of particular importance:

1. Approve athletes representing the country in international competition;
2. Take primary responsibility in selection of team and staff for international competition.

In Table 15 examples of U.S. sport governing bodies are listed, along with the international federation which recognized them.

The fifth actors to be identified are those members of the event organizing committees. These are the local, on-site people who actually stage the elite spectacles like the Munich or Montreal Olympic

Table 15.   International federations and U.S. sport governing bodies

U.S. governing body		International federation
AAU	(track and field)	International Amateur Athletic Federation
AAU	(swimming, diving, water polo)	Federation Internationale de Natation Amateur
ASA	(softball)	International Softball Federation
USGF	(gymnastics)	Federation Internationale de Gymnastique
ABAUSA	(basketball)	Federation Internationale de Basketball Amateur

Games. These actors, perhaps slightly more than the other participants in the governance system, are concerned with "selling tickets" to the event. These actors, perhaps slightly more than anyone else, are concerned that "big name" countries and "big name" athletic stars are in attendance and competing in the event. Because of this concern with gate receipts, the event organizing committee is a group upon which an athlete (if he or she can be considered an "attraction") may exert leverage for desired treatment. This kind of individual consideration (while unhealthy in many respects) seems inevitably to be sought by athletes, for ordinarily the sport governance system functions without any representation from them. In the United States, steps have been recently taken to insure athlete representation on governance boards of USOC members.

Through the identification and descriptions of the five sets of actors shown in Figure 8, a system has been outlined which is composed of innumerable separate organizations. These organizations have similar, sometimes discrete yet sometimes overlapping functions, membership and jurisdictional boundaries. How do decisions evolve? How does the system function? While many would answer that the amateur sport system, especially in the United States, does not function well (President's Commission on Olympic Sport, 1977), it does function. In another publication, it has been proposed that the decisions in the sport governance system are reached, and conflict control is achieved, by unequal distribution of power among organizations.[2] It was proposed that this unequal distribution was rationalized and agreed upon by virtue of an acknowledgement that certain organizations deserve more power because of the scope and eliteness of their sport program. The sport governance system functions without complete stalemate because extra decision-making authority is vested in organizations which sponsor programs (1) in many sports; (2) across extensive geographic areas; (3) producing superb athletes and coaches. This latter quality (production of elite champions) is related to the availability of expert personnel for training and coaching, revenue, and access to top competitions.

Is this a "good and fair" system? Does it function as efficiently as possible to serve its human purpose? While we can be confident that no human social system is perfect, would change of this particular system lead to more benefit than harm?

There is no simple answer to these questions but sport feminists have asserted that the sport governance system is, at the very least, unfair to women, unfair to athletes, and thus in need of change.[3]

STRUCTURE ANALYSIS PROCESS

In the belief that the various organizations of the sport governance system can be persuaded and/or negotiated into necessary change when the needed changes are clearly identified, a process for structure analysis of any sport organization(s) has been devised. The following process is an adaptation of that presented by John Loy in Singer's *Physical Education: An Interdisciplinary Approach.*[1]

Table 16.   Structure Analysis

Step 1—Identify the organization's stated purposes/goals

Step 2—Identify the norms expected within the organization
  A. Formal norms
    1. Prescribed—behavior demanded for all
    2. Proscribed—behavior denied to all
    Formal norms exist in tangible form such as written documents which are officially adopted by the organization and promulgated.
  B. Informal norms
    1. Preferred behavior
    2. Tolerated behavior
    Informal norms do not exist in a tangible form but are introduced and reinforced usually through interpersonal exchange.

Step 3—Identify the sanctions within the organization
  A. Formal (tangible)
    1. Positive—rewards
    2. Negative—punishments
  B. Informal (intangible)
    1. Positive
    2. Negative

Step 4—Diagram the structure of the organization. Show membership boundaries and linkages with other organizations.

Step 5—Identify funding sources.

Step 6—How are decisions made and where (in the structure diagram) are they made?

When one has completed such an analysis, an improved understanding of the structure and function of the organization has been obtained. A further step remains. A basic morality underlies organizations in our society. In part this morality is enunciated by federal, state, and local laws. It is also enunciated in the avowed purposes of the organization. The structure analysis is not complete until we reach a decision about whether the structure and functioning of the organization is consistent with the imperatives of the law and the organization's own goals.

The stated goals of sport organizations speak much of the promotion of ethical conduct, fair play, and the achievement of human betterment through sport. If the eradication of sexism is viewed as fair play and human betterment, then we must conclude that virtually all sport organizations fall short of their avowed purposes and require change. Utilizing information gained through analysis of the organizations, the change agent can present the needed changes to the appropriate body of the organization and begin the process.

The political process of change creation is often difficult, often passed unfinished from person to person. It is worth the struggle. The other difficult element in the process which has been described is the devising of the "needed changes." This is the crux of the problem of creating the alternative model to replace (or at least temper) big time, show biz, SportsWorld. These needed changes within each organization will differ from group to group and from time period to time period. To identify the needed changes will require individuals with knowledge and understanding of the organization involved and a deep commitment to the human purposes which the organization is unsuccessfully attempting to serve. Such individuals exist in great numbers and their time has now come.

REFERENCES

1. Loy, John W. Jr.: Sociological inquiry. *In* Physical Education: An Interdisciplinary Approach edited by R. N. Singer et al. New York, Macmillan, 1972.
2. Oglesby, Carole: Social conflict theory and the sport organization system. *Quest, 22*, 63–73, 1974.
3. ————: Unpublished testimony before President's Commission on Olympic Sport, Washington, D.C., 1976.
4. United States Collegiate Sports Council. *Constitution and Bylaws*, USCSC Executive Offices, Suite 102, 7250 State Ave., Kansas City, Kansas, 1976.
5. United States Olympic Committee. *Constitution, By-Laws, and General Rules,* Olympic House, 57 Park Avenue, New York, 10016, 1974.

EPILOGUE: THE REALITY

Each author hopes that knowledge of the reality of women and sport has been advanced by this book. It is intended as another step forward on the path recently marked out by Dorothy Harris' Penn State Conference on Women and Sport and Gerber, Berlin, Felshin and Spirduso in *The American Women and Sport*. Some chapters are dispassionate and theoretical. Some are utilitarian and frankly intended to move readers to action and commitment. As editor I have been concerned that the work might be dismissed because it begins openly from a feminist perspective rather than being safely value-free. There is great doubt, however, concerning whether social psychological research can be value-free. These authors suggest that unconscious sexism has pervaded that which appeared to be value-free. What sort of women are these authors who make such assertions? Only Wilma Heide stands as a self-and-other-proclaimed radical in the traditional meaning of that word. All share, however, a common quality: they perceive the world of sport and sport science in an uncommon way.

I want to conclude with three comments which form an addendum to the book.

It seems that athletics can never again be dominated by champions appearing without the support of an expensive, institutionalized system. Just as we cannot locate individuals able to sing difficult arias without training, we will not be able to *find* great athletes who, by their own resources alone, have developed to world class.

The school/college community provides an expensive, institutionalized system for the production of champions for boys who participate in the "major" sports. Girls are excluded from this system on a massive scale, as are boys participating in minor sports. If we, in the United States, are going to achieve diverse goals such as equal opportunity for all, increased participation by the masses, increased quality of performance in international competition, several steps should be taken.

1. On a systematic basis, present funds for educational sport and athletics should be equitably divided across a wide variety of sports and present boys' and girls' programs. Resultantly, the

vast resources expended on boys' basketball and football will have to be reduced.

2. The local and state political entities should unite with the federal government in order to offer sport and recreational opportunities which supplement those within the educational community.

3. Innovative methods should be devised to encourage and allow the private sector to subsidize the development of quality sport performers both within the educational system and recreation systems which focus on post school individuals.

Secondly, there appears to be, within the sport society, an obsessive focus on the superstar; the end, the product, the Other. This focus should be markedly modified so that at least equal emphasis is given to age group programs; the training; the process; and, most importantly, the *potential* which is in Everywoman (and Everyman). Just as there is a little bit of failure in every champion, so there is a little bit of champion in each of us, no matter how undistinguished our present performance level may be. It is (at least partially) a redeemable, trainable, improvable bit. Its quantity and quality could be enhanced in our children if they start a little earlier and move into sports which suit them, rather than having to fit themselves into the demands of narrowly defined "sport types."

Finally, we should attempt to create a sport environment wherein the values which have been associated with the "feminine principle" are recognized and honored in balance with the celebrated values of achievement, assertiveness, and dominance. As Roszak[44,Ch.4] has stated so eloquently, if the effect of the women's movement is to make everyone—men and women alike—hard, then the current revolution will not be the last.